RESILIENCE

Turning Your **Setback** into a **Comeback**

To

From

I wish for you a life of wealth, health, and happiness; a life in which you give to yourself the gift of patience, the virtue of reason, the value of knowledge, and the influence of faith in your own ability to dream about and to achieve worthy rewards.

– Jim Rohn

Published by
Lessons From Network
www.LessonsFromNetwork.com

Distributed by
Lessons From Network
P.O. Box 93927
Southlake, TX 76092 817-379-2300
www.LessonsFromNetwork.com/books

ISBN-13: 978-0-9983125-7-6

Printed in the United States of America.

Dedication

To the late Jim Rohn, Zig Ziglar, Charlie "Tremendous" Jones, Paul J Meyer, Og Mandino, Warren and Marge Wilson and other mentors that have shaped so many of us through their example and philosophy!

Acknowledgments

To Takara Sights, our editor and project manager extraordinaire, for your endless hours of work and passion in this book! Despite the complexities involved with a project like this you keep this a pleasure and always provide a first class result. A thousand praises! You are a rockstar! #millennialsrule

To Brian Tracy, Jeffrey Gitomer, Robert Helms, Tom Ziglar, and all the amazing mentors and world class thought leaders who took the time to read this manuscript and give us their endorsements.

Additional Resources

Order in Quantity and SAVE
Mix and Match
Order online KyleWilson.com/Books

Introduction

by Kyle Wilson

In April of 2018, I was at The Real Estate Guys Investor Summit at Sea and was asked to be on a panel. On stage, the event's founder and host and my 20-year good friend, Robert Helms, made a comment about the need to always be resilient. And then, shortly after, he said the words "resilience, turning your setback into a comeback." I knew that was it.

Takara Sights, my awesome editor and book project manager, and I had been circling around this powerful topic of resilience. After Robert's words, I knew resilience was the direction I wanted to go.

The stories and lessons in this book are so powerful and in many cases will be the story behind the story, shared publicly for the first time. I know that is the case with my story.

2x US Memory Champion Ron White shares the period of time when he lost everything and was homeless living in his car. Through resilience he turned his setback into a comeback and now is able to impact veterans all over the country through The Afghanistan Memory Wall.

Nathan Ogden shares how a horrifying accident left him quadriplegic. Through resilience he wrote an entire book using the knuckle of his pinky finger, and now he is helping tens of thousands of others through his speaking, writing, and non-profit work.

PGA Golf Mentor Nick Bradley shares his experience of being at the top of the professional coaching world, then how losing his dad to suicide turned his life upside down. Through resilience he is now able to use that experience of overcoming his own form of PTSD to help others.

This book is loaded with powerful stories, lessons, and insights that will inspire, encourage, and in some cases challenge you to look past your current difficulties to see the possibilities of change and, further, how you can use those difficulties to make a difference.

As the publisher and a coauthor of this book, I'm beyond proud and honored to share these amazing stories from my fellow coauthors with you.

May your setback become your comeback!

Kyle Wilson, Founder Jim Rohn Int, Your Success Store, Lessons From Network, and KyleWilson.com

DISCLAIMER

The information in this book is not meant to replace the advice of a certified professional. Please consult a licensed advisor in matters relating to your personal and professional well-being including your mental, emotional and physical health, finances, business, legal matters, family planning, education, and spiritual practices. The views and opinions expressed throughout this book are those of the authors and do not necessarily reflect the views or opinions of all the authors or position of any other agency, organization, employer, publisher, or company. Since we are critically-thinking human beings, the views of each of the authors are always subject to change or revision at any time. Please do not hold them or the publisher to them in perpetuity. Any references to past performance may not be indicative of future results. No warranties or guarantees are expressed or implied by the publisher's choice to include any of the content in this volume.

If you choose to attempt any of the methods mentioned in this book, the authors and publisher advise you to take full responsibility for your safety and know your limits. The authors and publisher are not liable for any damages or negative consequences from any treatment, action, application, or preparation to any person reading or following the information in this book.

This book is a personal collaboration between a number of authors and their experiences, beliefs, opinions, and advice. The authors and publisher make no representations as to accuracy, completeness, correctness, suitability, or validity of any information in the book, and neither the publisher nor the individual authors shall be liable for any physical, psychological, emotional, financial, or commercial damages, including, but not limited to, special, incidental, consequential, or other damages to the readers of this book.

Foreword

by Newy Scruggs

I n my 25 plus years of being a sportscaster, I have been blessed to witness some incredible performances by individuals in sports that have made me marvel, made me tear up, and just left me stunned.

I've had a front row seat to watch what resilience is in sports arenas at the highest levels.

In watching others, I have sometimes found an inspiration to find that within myself.

I, like many of us, have shortcomings I wish I could improve upon.

My career has allowed me to see that many of the people we deem successful have areas in their personal lives we don't see in which they fall short. Some ignore, self-medicate, or just plain run away from issues they should address.

How can we find the resilience in ourselves to improve, win, and succeed in our own lives? How do you keep punching when you have nothing left?

This is where the magic of Kyle Wilson and his Inner Circle came into play in my own life.

I have battled weight problems basically my entire life. I have a love of sugar that is dangerous. We all have our own bad habits. Mine is sugar. Call me a sugar fiend. My habit was to the point that I became a Type II diabetic in my mid-20s. It's a family trait that I spent most of the last 20 years trying to ignore, wish away, and suppress.

At the first Inner Circle Mastermind of 2018, I finally found my way to fight back and take control of this disease. I finally did.

After trying and failing and failing and failing... an amazing group of friends at the Inner Circle introduced me to choosing a "word of the year." The exercise was to find a powerful word that would inspire us to do small things that would make an incredible difference in our 2018 life.

Habit was the word I came up with.

I needed to develop a habit of exercising on a regular basis to lose weight. I needed to develop a habit of making healthier food choices because working long, stressful hours in newsrooms and on location at stadiums provided some of the worst food choices a person can make. I'm just being honest.

Kyle spent decades with his partner, the late, great business philosopher Jim Rohn, who famously said, "We must all suffer from one of two pains: the pain of discipline or the pain of regret. The difference is discipline weighs ounces while regret weighs tons."

Kyle's Inner Circle gave me the strength to bounce back from my anger with myself and my shame of being overweight and becoming a Type II diabetic by developing that one word, *habit*. I put that word on my desk at work and on my mirror that I look at each day. I started winning my fight with obesity. Habit is part of discipline.

After finding my word for 2018, the next Inner Circle Mastermind in September 2018 took me to unexpected health success. Another Inner Circle member connected me to successful entrepreneur in the group who introduced me to their nutrition company. The products they had addressed everything I was trying to fix on my journey to better health. I was using my word *habit* but not as consistently as I wanted to. They helped me find that next gear I needed to achieve optimal results.

I took control of my blood sugar levels, an important key all diabetics must manage to live right. I lost weight. I became a regular at the gym. I finally liked to exercise. Finally! After giving up, after all the stopping and starting, the fat guy on TV was taking control of a disease that kills many Americans.

It happened because of my friendship with Kyle who, for over 15 years, has been my mentor, champion, and a super mensch to me. He has constantly connected me to THE best people, materials, and resources that truly have improved my life.

This book is another Kyle Wilson project that can change your life if you dig into these incredible stories. These are authors who have recovered from difficulties and developed toughness to push through life's challenges to come out on the sunny side of life.

I tear up as I write this because I cherish my friendship with Kyle and our Inner Circle. I know at least one story in this book will help change your life or someone in your life.

Stay resilient, my friends.

Newy Scruggs
7x Emmy-Winning Sportscaster, @newyscruggs

Table of Contents

"Rock bottom became the solid foundation
on which I rebuilt my life."
– J.K. Rowling

CHAPTER 1

Setbacks and Comebacks
The Inside Story of My 18 Years With Jim Rohn

by Kyle Wilson

In 1989, I had the serendipitous good fortune to get a job in the seminar business. I experienced a huge learning curve. I had to make 50 to 100 cold calls a day to book myself to speak at companies two or three times a day. Then, after speaking I would offer the audience an opportunity to buy tickets for an upcoming seminar featuring whoever we were promoting. Little did I know, that job would lead me to Jim Rohn.

Within a couple of years, I went out on my own and started doing my own events. I, along with my wife and a partner and his wife, traveled all over the country. We would go into Chicago, Washington DC, Atlanta, Houston, Kansas City, etc. and put on an all-day event. We would always promote two speakers, usually a combo of Jim Rohn and Brian Tracy or Jim Rohn and Og Mandino.

After a couple of years, we had become really good at it. We were having a lot of success. Then, in 1993, I was able to make Jim Rohn an offer he couldn't refuse, and I started Jim Rohn International.

Although we said we were partners, it wasn't actually a partnership. We agreed it would be my company, I would pay for everything, and I would pay Jim a high percentage of everything I booked for him to speak in addition to a royalty on the products that I would exclusively have the rights to market as well as new products I would create.

That first year, I took Jim from 20 public speaking dates at $4,000 each to over a 100 dates at $10,000 each and eventually $25,000. We were on fire.

I also started creating new products. The first was *The Treasury of Quotes* by Jim Rohn hardbound book with 365 Jim Rohn quotes along with the little leatherette quote booklet, *Excerpts From The Treasury of Quotes* by Jim Rohn with 110 Jim Rohn quotes. Keep in mind, this was way before

Google and there were no list of Jim Rohn quotes laying around. It was a solid 10 months of me finding and gathering over 365 Jim Rohnisms from Jim's seminars and the conversations we had. I created *The Treasury of Quotes* based on Jim's secret sauce, a thing I talk about in conjunction with The Wheel.

The Wheel is a business model I've used to create many businesses and something I always use when coaching and consulting for clients.

The Wheel has spokes, and each spoke is your current products and services. The goal is, once you get prospects and customers on The Wheel, you want to take them around to other spokes (your products and services) on The Wheel. Now, the other big part of the wheel is figuring out how to get more people on the wheel!

Based on Jim's secret sauce of being a phenomenal wordsmith and such a profound philosopher, and the fact that people loved him and wanted to be his advocate, I thought creating the Jim Rohn quote booklet would be very strategic as a new spoke on the wheel to get more people on it.

I guessed right. People bought 10, 100, 1000 quote booklets at a time and gave them away. It had a special To and From page you could personalize plus a special quote by Jim at the opening and 110 more amazing quotes by the master.

Over time, we sold and gave away over six million booklets. For us, they were a viral marketing tool that became a fantastic lead generator and introduction to Jim Rohn. I also created similar booklets for Brian Tracy, Mark Victor Hansen, Denis Waitley, and Zig Ziglar through my other company I started Your Success Store.

After just a few short years, business was booming. I felt amazing.

Then I got the phone call. It was late 1995, and Jim said, "Hey Kyle, I have some tough news."

Herbalife, a company that Jim had been with for many years as a spokesman and that Jim had been with before he and I started Jim Rohn International in 1993, wanted Jim to go full time with them.

They were having some major challenges with Jim out speaking for me so much, sometimes for their competitors, and so they said, "Hey Jim, you've been with us all these years, and we want to control your schedule. So we're prepared to offer you up to four times what we've been paying you, but you're going to limit Kyle promoting you to our competitors."

It was a tough phone conversation, but the reality was that Jim was with Herbalife before he was with me, and they needed him. They had some major things going on publically, and they wanted Jim to be the solution.

It did leave me in a pinch! Fortunately, I was still able to market and sell Jim's products. I just wasn't able to book him to speak.

At the time, I had 20 employees, and I had a sales team that would go into cities and sell tickets to fill up my seminar rooms for Jim's two day weekends. How would I come up with enough work for my workforce? This was a big challenge.

The first thing I did was call my good friend Brian Tracy. We came up with a two day program called The Success Mastery Academy, which later we turned into one of Brian's all time best programs. That gave my sales team alternative events to sell into. But, I still was losing all those other speaking dates.

One of the biggest lessons I had to learn was that I couldn't keep all 20 employees. It took me 11 months before I learned the lesson. I didn't want to lay anyone off, and the idea was one of the hardest things I've ever faced. But I almost went bankrupt. Eventually, I had to get small. I went from 20 employees down to three. And I started paying closer attention to all the details. I became customer centric again.

Within two years, I got Jim back. Jim was able to renegotiate with Herbalife, and we were rolling again. I had now raised his fee to $25,000 and had him booked up solid. Things were amazing.

But a few more years went by, and it happened again. But this time Herbalife was fine letting me and Jim do 20 or so public seminars as long as we didn't do corporate or network marketing dates (which unfortunately was where Jim's biggest revenue came from when I booked him). Plus I still had the exclusive rights to market and sell Jim's products.

Still, I wasn't offended because I knew Jim and Herbalife had worked together way before Jim and I had. Jim and I were not only business partners, we were great friends, and I was always happy for him to do what was in his best interest, as was he with me. We were both free agents.

The unintended BENEFITS were HUGE! These limitations forced me to start figuring out how I could build a company around Jim not having to show up for more than 20 dates. Figuring out how to do this had a cascade of positive consequences:

- I found the internet and online marketing faster than any of my competitors.

- I was able to focus and go build a million plus email list.

- I created products and sold like we had never before.

- I launched YourSuccessStore.com, which became a huge revenue source! (Once someone discovered Jim Rohn, fell in love with him, and bought everything he had, then they wanted other related products from other personal development powerhouses. Through YourSuccessStore, I was able to bring those people and products to them.)

- I became the agent for multiple other speakers including Denis Waitley, Chris Widener and Ron White.

- I started a Speakers Bureau where I booked Les Brown, Brian Tracy, Mark Victor Hansen and many others for multiple dates a year.

- I started online publications including Messages from the Masters, Quotes from the Masters, Denis Waitley Newsletter, Chris Widener Newsletter, The Ron White Newsletter, and The Slightedge Newsletter in which I would feature content from Zig Ziglar, Brian Tracy, Jeffrey Gitomer, Les Brown, Denis Waitley, John Maxwell, etc. and would sell their products.

- Finally, I was able to create, market, and put on some of our biggest events like the 2001 Dallas 3-Day Event with Jim Rohn, Zig Ziglar, Jeffrey Gitomer, and Charlie Tremendous Jones and the 2004 LA 3-Day Event with Jim Rohn, Brian Tracy, Dennis Waitley, Chris Widener, Robert Helms, and Vic Johnson. I had Hollywood film crews film the entire event, and those became some of my biggest selling products.

My setback, losing the opportunity to book Jim Rohn for a few years twice to Herbalife (even though I could still create and sell programs), was the very thing that allowed me to start YourSuccessStore, start multiple other publications, and get a massive head start with online marketing. Because while everyone else was focused on speaking gigs, I was focused on building an online audience for whom Jim didn't have to show up a 100 times a year.

And the beauty of Herbalife was many of their people later became my subscribers and my customers once I launched online.

At the 2004 LA 3-Day Event I put on, Vic Johnson shared that the very things that he failed at 10 years previously were now the things that he made all his money from. I found that to be the case for me too. My challenges and failures became my opportunities.

One of the challenges so often for us all is that we expect and want instant gratification.

But the reality is, some of the things we want we are not even ready for. Often we haven't learned the lessons we need to learn yet.

I know I had to learn some lessons the first time I lost Jim. I had 20 employees, and I kept them way too long. I wasn't revenue centered. I also was taking on too many opportunities without the bandwidth. My sales teams were costing me, not making me money, so I had to get small. I started checking my numbers daily, and by doing the small stuff well, I was able to go build a company five times bigger than the company I had before I lost Jim the first time.

The 18 years I had with Jim were like any relationship. We had ups and downs. But we gave each other the freedom to do what was best for ourselves. Ultimately, that helped us have our most profitable and rewarding personal and business relationship the last eight years we were together. Our friendship grew and we got closer the longer we worked together.

In late 2007, based on some family decisions, I decided to sell all my companies. The company that bought me was also buying SUCCESS Magazine.

I stayed on with them for 18 months.

In 2008, unfortunately, Jim Rohn was diagnosed with pulmonary fibrosis. I, with the help of the new owner of SUCCESS and Jim Rohn International Stuart Johnson along with Reed Bilbray, organized a powerful tribute video that included Jim Rohn's closest friends, colleagues, and peers sharing their appreciation and love for Jim and the impact he had in their lives. I secured interviews with everyone from John Maxwell to Denis Waitley, Brian Tracy, Zig Ziglar, and close personal friends including me.

It was my great honor to deliver that video to Jim a month before he passed away. We sat down and watched it together. He was blown away. He was able to hear the appreciation and love from over 50 people in his life. It is something I will never forget!

Jim passed in December 2009. In February 2010, SUCCESS put on an amazing public tribute for Jim. I was honored to speak along with Tony Robbins, Les Brown, Darren Hardy, and many others. People that were there still share with me how special it was for them to attend it and how much Jim Rohn had impacted them.

After Jim's passing, I still had three years left of my five year non-compete. I used that time as a Mr. Mom at home with my wife and two teenagers. It was a priceless time.

In 2014, I got the itch again, and I started a few new companies.

It's a whole new phase of my life, and I am so excited as I embrace it. Now I'm hosting my Kyle Wilson Inner Circle Mastermind which meets multiple times a year and has members who fly in from all over the US and internationally. It is one of the most favorite things I do. I also offer coaching for high-caliber clients and have started publishing books again (like this one) that are made up of amazing contributors and stories that will encourage and help others on their entrepreneurial journeys.

And, as always, I'm still spreading the message of the great Jim Rohn, my 18-year business partner, mentor, and friend.

Jim's wisdom, mentorship, lessons, and friendship have been a huge, undeniable part of my success.

Thank you, Jim, one more time!

TWEETABLE

One of the challenges so often for us all is that we expect and want instant gratification. But the reality is, some of the things we want we are not ready for.

Kyle Wilson is a strategist, marketer, and entrepreneur. Go to KyleWilson.com to download Free his 52 Lessons I Learned from Jim Rohn and Other Great Legends I Promoted! *plus other valuable resources.*

Kyle is founder of Jim Rohn International, and KyleWilson.com. He leads the Kyle Wilson Inner Circle Mastermind. Kyle has filled big event rooms and produced 100s of programs including titles by Jim Rohn, Brian Tracy, Zig Ziglar, Denis Waitley, and recently the books Purpose, Passion & Profit *and* The One Thing That Changed Everything.

CHAPTER 2

Broken Days to Triumphant Ways

An NFL Take on Resilience

by Keith Elias

Wen I first sat down to write this, I couldn't think of one time when I had a true setback. Sure, like everyone else, I've had challenges and my fair share of adventures (or misadventures—depending on your point of view). But a setback?

Maybe it's just semantics. I don't believe in the Kobayashi Maru, *Star Trek*'s no-win scenario. Maybe I just believe everything that happens is part of life's great adventure, and it will all work out in the end. If it hasn't worked out yet, it isn't the end.

Just so you don't think I'm glib, I'll share the five worst things that have ever happened to me, and then I'll share the five best.

One. In 1995, going into my second year as a running back for the NY Giants, we spent a first round pick on a back named Tyrone Wheatley, and we picked up legendary Herschel Walker in free agency; not to mention, we still had starter Rodney Hampton, Charles Way, and a host of others for just five roster spots. Needless to say, in a preseason article about our position, the writer never even mentioned me. To make matters worse, my father was languishing in his last death struggle against cancer.

So, I was using every last bit of time working on the game, knowing my father could die during my last rep of sprints. And then he did die, two weeks before camp started. I reported to camp feeling bitter, angry, depressed, overwhelmed, and racked with guilt. There was no way I could compete and earn a roster spot.

That was a bad day.

Two. I spent my third season in the NFL on injured reserve, and then, after a coaching change, I found myself without a team. I spent the entire off-season on the phone with my agent begging him to get me into a camp. My career couldn't be over yet. It just couldn't.

No one called.

I spent the season watching the games from my couch, dying a little bit inside every week because once you are out of the game for a year, you simply do not get back in. It doesn't happen. They have 400 new bodies coming from college, so they aren't looking for the undersized running back who just came off knee surgery and didn't play last year.

Bad day.

Three. When I left the NFL behind, or rather, when it left me behind, I felt abandoned, drifting in a vast ocean of uncertainty. My body was beaten; I was super-stressed about my finances since I knew it would be difficult to make the same amount of money, and I hadn't met my financial goals. I had no clue what I wanted to do, and worst of all, my "I do" became my "I don't."

For the first time in my life, I felt like a complete failure. I had never failed at anything in my life, and now I failed at the most important thing in life: marriage. Forget drifting. I was shipwrecked! Where was my mansion? Where was my Ferrari? Where was my happily ever after? Nowhere.

Bad day.

Four. I think you get to a place in life where you begin to realize what's truly important. Call it perspective. I may have been married before, but I never truly had a wife until Christa. We couldn't wait to start our lives and a family together. But, we couldn't. We languished for eight long years of bad doctor reports, broken dreams, and "huddled on the floor in tears" moments. Then, when we were going to jump on a plane to Russia to be matched with an orphaned boy, Vladimir Putin made it illegal for Americans to adopt Russian children. We felt like, what good is life if you have no one to pass it on to? It was hopeless.

Bad day? The worst yet.

Five. The final bad day is alive and well today. All my life, besides playing in the NFL, all my brothers and I have wanted to do is become amazing writers. We would stay up all night telling each other stories and offering how such and such movie should really have ended. On team flights on the way back from games, I'd tell the guys ideas for movies or novels. To date, I have written a middle-grade adventure novel, a young adult fantasy novel, and eight screenplays with my brother. I remember telling my father on his deathbed that I love playing football, but being a storyteller is my true calling.

If that's true, then why haven't I achieved success as a storyteller?

Every day I wake up with a pit in my stomach feeling unfulfilled, like I haven't yet reached my full purpose. It gnaws at me, and there is no end in sight. What's worse is there is no guarantee it will ever happen. So what do you do?

Interestingly, you may recognize the five best times of my life.

One. The first was in 1995, entering my second camp with the Giants. You know, the one where my father had just passed and I wasn't mentioned in the article about our backfield. As it turns out, I found myself supported by my teammates to an amazing degree. Especially John Booty, who taught me how to find peace no matter my circumstances through Philippians 4.

I played that preseason with a "peace that surpasses understanding," and I not only made the team, but by the end of the season, I was named the NYG's Unsung Hero of the Year by the NFLPA.

That was a good day.

Two. After missing the entire season in 1997, Bill Polian became the general manager of the Colts, remembered me as a hard worker, and decided to give me a shot to try out for the Colts just as they were turning it around with rookie quarterback Peyton Manning. I made the team, led the Colts in kick-off returns in 1998, won the AFC East title in 1999, and fell in love with Indianapolis and its people.

Very good day.

Three. With my NFL experience and a very short-lived marriage in my rearview, I felt like a ship without a rudder. Frank Vuono, Anthony DiTommaso, and Rusty Warren, alums from my university, took me under their wings, got me working, and got me on my feet again. My supportive family and church gave me purpose. Bob Nash, Preston Centuolo, and Harry Flaherty fanned a gift of speaking in my life, and I found deeper meaning in awakening the truth in others.

Oh, and then I met Christa. I spent seven years after my divorce walking alone, learning how I contributed to my marriage's demise, and preparing for what God would have for me. It turns out, it was Christa.

I don't mind telling you, that was a very good day indeed.

Four. Hope deferred makes the heart sick. It's true. But it is also true, that hope fulfilled is magic in the soul. In the summer of 2018, our wonderful, delightful daughter turned one.

God is good, and that was the best day.

Five. This one hasn't happened yet. My novels aren't published and our screenplays have yet to be produced. And that's okay. The future celebration is fuel for the hard work today.

If you've noticed a pattern, so have I. Sometimes the darkest times turn into the brightest moments. I'm writing this as my daughter babbles in my ear for my attention. She has it because the wait has made the fulfillment even sweeter and almost impossible to take for granted. In fact, one night while walking downstairs in the dark, I split my big toe on my daughter's walker. My normal reaction would have been anger and cursing. Instead, I just laughed, so thankful that the walker was there because it meant we had a daughter.

I am also reminded sharply that none of these glorious moments and memories would have occurred if I jumped ship, gave up, or threw in the towel.

Setbacks are just part of God's great adventure. For how can you boast of great victory if you don't overcome the mightiest dragon? That's why, after countless rejections and seeing the bottom drop out of so many opportunities, my brother and I still write. There is no guarantee of victory, but if there was, it wouldn't be called a battle. And by the way, we are all warriors in our own way.

When I mentor former NFL players during their transitions, I often tell them about one of my family's core values, adventure. My wife and I have created a culture where we've decided to look at challenges and disappointments through the lens of adventure. Life in all its wonderful ups and downs is the greatest adventure.

So, as for me, I've never felt like I made a comeback because I've never felt like I've been knocked out.

It all works out in the end. If it hasn't worked out, it isn't the end.

TWEETABLE

Life's disappointments and challenges are really just adventures in disguise. Remember, it all works out in the end. If it hasn't worked out yet, it isn't the end.

After playing football at Princeton, Keith Elias left with 21 school and 4 NCAA records. He played six years in the NFL with the Giants and Colts and became an international speaker. He now works for the NFL in Player Engagement, mentoring players through transition into and out of the game, coaching them in their purpose off the field. He is a mentor, speaker, and team builder who inspires and empowers others to find vision and purpose for their lives or companies. He truly believes, "When you become YOU, you are unstoppable." To contact for speaking, coaching, weekly email, or just to connect, email keithelias@verizon.net.

RESILIENCE

CHAPTER 3

How Death & Dyslexia Taught Me The Strategies of Success

by Carla Lee Martinez

remember being six. I remember being Daddy's little girl, loving pink, *The Little Mermaid*, and my baby brother. I remember being curious and making friends everywhere I went. For a six-year-old in the early 90s, life couldn't be more magical.

I have another vivid memory from when I was six. I remember being in a car, pulling up to a building, and walking in. To this day, I still get the same feeling when I drive by it. I don't remember who I was with walking in, but I do remember what I saw. I saw a lot of people sitting in pews. And as I walked down the aisle, I saw my idol, one of my older cousins, who, in my six-year-old eyes, was the coolest person in the world. I wanted to be just like her. But she was crying, and I had never seen her cry. I thought to myself, "Why is she so sad?" and kept walking, being tugged along. As I continued down the aisle, I saw people grouped together at the front of the room. Then, the next memory I have is sitting next to my aunt, when I heard a shriek! I turned to the front left, and I saw my grandmother wailing and family members catching her and carrying her back to a pew. "Why is Grandma so upset?" When everyone cleared, I saw someone that appeared to be sleeping, but not moving, in a box.

I don't remember much after that until I heard my aunt's voice telling me to go up and say goodbye. It was time to tell my dad I love him and give him a kiss. She walked me to the casket, picked me up, and I saw my dad, sleeping, but not breathing. I also saw lots of stuff around him, things that he loved. There was a hot air balloon shirt, flowers, and other items. I heard my aunt whisper, "It's okay to touch him. Give him a kiss because he is in heaven now." And even though I didn't understand what heaven was, I did understand that this was going to be the last time I ever saw my dad.

The final thing I remember is hearing my mother's voice at the cemetery saying, "She, (meaning me), wants to wait until the casket is in the ground." At six years old, I knew that was that going to be my last physical connection to him. That day, I realized that nothing is forever. I understood the difference between life and death. I learned that I could not rely on anyone to be there for me, except for me. I became a lone wolf cub (something some adults don't ever have to learn to be).

Losing a parent is hard for everyone, but it can have a significant impact on children that lose a parent before the age of 10. Studies have shown that a child that loses a parent is more susceptible to emotional and psychological problems such as depression, anxiety, distrust, and relationship problems. They often will show more problems in school and have poor grades compared to their peers who did not lose a parent in those crucial formative years. I was no different. I had trouble making friends from a fear of being abandoned. Having a parent that has passed had a stigma in school. When asked, I'd say that I didn't want to talk about it, even though I wanted to burst into tears. I also suffered from dyslexia which added to my isolation. I was called "stupid" and bullied. I further withdrew from others. My parents were told that I'd be lucky to graduate high school and that I would not form any lasting relationships.

Fortunately, I have an amazing mother, who through all of that, and through grieving herself, taught me what real resilience is. She never gave on up me. She worked two jobs to send me to counseling and tutoring, and it helped. She eventually got remarried to the man I call my father. He raised my brother and me, taking us in like his own. He taught me the value of teamwork and that we can accomplish more than we think in one day. He sacrificed to raise us, a second set of children. Through him, we got a second chance to grow up with both parents.

My parents did all they could to help me, but I still continued to struggle in school. In seventh grade, I still did not read as well as my peers, and one day a teacher pulled me to the side and said that I was going to go to a new English class. When I walked into my new class, I realized I was in the special education class. In this special education class, other students had some serious conditions like Down Syndrome. At the time, I was mortified. When my mom found out they had placed me in this class, she came rushing in like a momma bear to protect her young! She told the school that I did not need to be in special education. She then had a very candid conversation with me later that evening. She said, "Carla Lee, you have a choice to make. You can stay in this class, or you can go back to your regular classes. It's not going to be easy, and all that I ask is that you give it 100%. I don't care if you get an F, as long as it was your best. There is no such thing as failure, only feedback. You got it?!" I agreed and took on the challenge—and boy, was it hard. I had to get up earlier and stay up later to do my homework. I was still ridiculed and called "stupid" by my peers. While my brother and friends got to play outside, I was inside studying. I didn't get to hang out after school or on weekends as much. I would get off the bus, and immediately go to the library to get started on my homework.

I started keeping a detailed planner with all of my school work and activities. I also kept a journal to express my thoughts and emotions. This helped me channel the pain, the anger, and solve problems my own way. Doing school work immediately after school when I wanted to be outside taught me discipline and creativity. I wasn't like everyone else. I had to work harder and invent new ways of learning and coping.

Along with this, I learned to manage my emotional state. I didn't know what "state management" was at the time, but later I learned that managing one's own state is being aware of one's own emotions and thoughts, and choosing how to respond, rather than reacting. Every day I started making conscious decisions about how I was going to show up at school, and I wouldn't let the bullies get to me. I even convinced myself that they were just jealous because they couldn't break me, and the more they tried, the more I prevailed. I was ambitiously managing my state every day with determination.

Because I spent a lot of time alone, I quietly observed. I observed how the popular girls reacted to boys and how the boys reacted to them. I watched how the bullies would try to trip me up. I watched how the teachers responded to me versus the other kids. Soon enough, I became hyper-aware of myself and others around me. I remained quiet, listening and watching. I started to see patterns in people's behavior and could predict someone's move before it happened. I became proficient in saying less but getting more done. Out of necessity, I had to find my own path to survive.

Soon, innovation became my norm. My creativity and ability to learn skyrocketed. I started earning A's and reading books non-stop, and I went on to get my MBA. It turns out that discipline, creativity, state management, and keen observation of people is an excellent skill set for sales and entrepreneurship. And since I never really fit into anyone's box, I've created my own sandbox.

Today, I'm a real estate investor and have a successful sales training company. My mission is to lead others, using my own strategies combined with neuroscience and neuro-linguistic programming, to become more effective in their sales and communication. My experiences helped me go from a lone wolf cub to leading the pack, teaching others to tap into their own talents and abilities. Within a few weeks of going through my program, clients are able to get more done in less time, become top producers, and take their careers to the next level.

In his 2013 book, *David and Goliath: Underdogs, Misfits, and the Art of Battling Giants*, Malcolm Gladwell talks about how psychologist Marvin Eisenstadt found that from a survey of 573 famous or high-achieving individuals, 25% had parents who passed away before they were 10. I would never wish on anyone the pain that I went through growing up, but losing a parent at six years old taught me that I can get through anything. My dyslexia taught me that anyone can learn to do to anything. To become who I am today, I had to go through those lonely experiences, so I could realize the power within. The day of my biological father's funeral changed the trajectory of my life. That day, I learned that life is short, and every day we get to make a choice. We choose to be a victim of our circumstances or to use those setbacks to empower us to make the most out of our lives, take chances, say what we have to say, and live an unconventional life. Life is a gift and should be filled with love, joy, family, and friends. Our time here is finite, and it is up to us to take full advantage of our past to propel us into a wonderful future.

TWEETABLE

Learn to embrace what's different about you. It's an untapped gift waiting to be expressed.

Carla Lee Martinez is a sales trainer, real estate investor, and speaker from Albuquerque, NM. Carla Lee specializes in helping sales professionals and consultants grow their businesses by teaching them the modern art and science of selling that shortens the sales cycle and closes more deals.

She is laser-focused on using what she has learned through her experience to help businesses, entrepreneurs, consultants, and salespeople to Say Less, and Close More™ through a proven sales training program. Are you ready to take your business to the next level? Schedule a free strategy session with Carla Lee at CarlaLee@MarcovConsulting.com or visit www.MarcovConsulting.com

CHAPTER 4

Two Neck Breaks And Still Kick'n

How Paralysis Has Given Me a Platform to Help Others

by Nathan Ogden

I was a driven 26-year-old man who felt my life was right where it should be. I had a college degree, a beautiful wife, our first home, two very young children, and a great career. Life was perfect. Three days before Christmas in 2001, we traveled to Bend, Oregon, to celebrate the holiday with my wife Heather's family. Having grown up snow skiing and wanting some extra excitement, my younger brother-in-law and I drove to Mt. Bachelor to have some fun on the slopes. On our last run, following an amazing day, I decided to go off one more jump I had never hit before.

"It's my turn—am I ready for this?" I think to myself as I slide my skis into position, standing sideways in the snow, 40 yards uphill from the jump.

"Hurry up! Let's see what you've got," someone yells from behind me.

I bend my knees and then spring into the air while pivoting both legs downhill, directing my newly waxed skis straight down the steep slope. Digging my poles in the snow, I thrust myself forward toward my target.

I slow down as fear creeps into my mind, commanding my full attention. The fear of messing up, the fear of getting hurt, but most of all, the fear of looking foolish. Then the adrenaline kicks in and I move swiftly past confident to cocky.

"I've got this! I'm going to go bigger and better than anyone else here, and they will all be in awe."

I pull my skis tightly together for the last 15 yards, now hurling down the hill and aiming directly at the middle of a giant drift of packed snow.

As the back of my skis leave the top of the intimidating jump launching me skyward, I hear faint gasps from those gathered to watch. I instantly know something is wrong. I'm off balance as my body keeps climbing higher in the thin mountain air. Not 10, not 20, but 30 feet above the snow-packed slope, I reach the pinnacle of my flight as my body rotates backward.

Looking to my right, I see skiers watching me take flight through the slightly scratched lenses of my goggles. Suddenly, gravity grabs ahold of me and I am quickly thrown back to Earth. "This is really going to hurt."

The force of the impact feels as though I have been dropped from an airplane holding nothing but a cocktail umbrella to slow me down. I slam head first into the frozen mountain with the full weight of my 180-pound body crushing my neck like an accordion. I violently tumble down the hill, rolling out of control until sliding to a stop, facing downhill on my right side in the fetal position. My skis, poles, and gloves are scattered far from my limp body.

I slowly open my eyes to get a visual of the scene around me. My first thoughts are not concern for my well-being, but rather others' perception of me. I immediately think, "I look stupid and need to get up. I've really embarrassed myself in front of everyone watching. What an idiot."

I try to sit up, but only my left elbow raises, moving slowly into the air and then immediately falling back to the packed snow. "That's okay, no big deal. I just knocked the wind out of myself. Just wait a few moments and I'll be back to normal," I assure myself.

An intense burning pain resonates throughout my whole body as if I were laying on an open fire pit, burning alive. My breaths shorten, and I realize I'm struggling to breathe! An immense pressure is squeezing the life out of my lungs. I glance down at my legs stacked one on top of the other. Thoughts begin racing through my mind. "Why aren't they moving? What has happened to me? What about my wife and kids? How can I fix this?"

My future forever changed when I launched myself off that fateful ski-jump three days before Christmas. I suffered an incomplete cervical spine fracture and spinal cord injury at the level of C7. What does that mean? I severely broke my neck and am classified as a quadriplegic. How do you go from being invincible one moment to laying lifeless on a hospital gurney hooked up to a ventilator keeping you alive?

I spent the next year fighting to survive a number of serious health complications and striving to become as strong as possible. You're told in the hospital after a spinal cord injury, "If you regain any physical movement it will most likely happen during a two-year window. The majority of your return, however, will take place in the first few months to a year."

Progress Is the Key to Success

Why is progress so important? The act of moving forward, or progressing, builds faith and confidence. Without progress in life, we feel insignificant, unimportant—almost invisible. We lose hope. It's not as important how fast you are progressing towards your goals as it is that you are moving forward, even if it's just a little bit each day. Initially, they couldn't even sit me up in a bed for 10 seconds without me passing out. Start with smaller realistic goals so you can build up to the big ones. My big goal was to live. My first goal was to have three doctors and nurses hold me in a sitting position for one minute without blacking out. Now that's taking it back to the basics. The results you desire may not be immediate, but they will come as you exercise discipline and patience.

"If there is no struggle, there is no progress." – Frederick Douglass

I worked painstakingly hard each day, experiencing difficult physical therapy with excruciating pain. With any idea or cutting-edge therapy that was available, I gave it my all—*anything* to increase the possibility of walking again. During the first year of my recovery from the neck break, I regained full use of my shoulders, arms, most of my hands, and a tiny bit in my legs. Even though only small movement came from my lower extremities, they were moving. I knew as long as I kept progressing, I would walk again!

With a truck equipped with hand controls, I could now drive and go back to work, starting to provide for my family again like a good husband and father should. Though a little different, our young family was getting back to a new normal because we never stopped expecting our dreams and goals to come true.

Due to the paralysis, my lungs and diaphragm were compromised, leaving me more exposed to certain illnesses, and I contracted a severe case of pneumonia 13 months after my neck break. My blood-to-oxygen level dropped too low one night, and I went unconscious in my sleep. Heather was unable to wake me early that morning and desperately called an ambulance. While in the ER and still completely unconscious, I fell off the X-ray table and broke my neck—*again*. This break was higher up at the C6 level. I instantly lost the use of my hands, triceps, and any movement in my legs I had recovered over the past year. Are you kidding me! This can't be real.

A few weeks into this new battle, a frustrating realization became crystal clear to me, but I didn't want to see it. All of the movement and abilities I had lost falling from the X-ray table were not coming back. I was stuck and unable to move. I couldn't accept this halt in my progress. What about my dreams? There was far too much left for me to accomplish that I needed my legs and hands for. So many adventures I wanted to feel and experience from a standing position. I need to work harder or pray with greater faith. Surely, that would be my breakthrough giving me momentum again.

As much as I've tried over the years, the sought-after physical movement I lost on that fateful early morning in the emergency room still hasn't returned to me.

Life can be hard! It can be paralyzing and make you feel powerless! I fought extremely hard to progress that far in my recovery only to have it ripped out from under me. After the second neck break, I was not only suffering from another physical impairment but was mentally agonizing about my future as well.

I asked myself, *"Am I strong enough to keep pushing forward? What do I do now? How do I keep the hope and faith that everything will be alright? I still want to walk again!"*

My progress came to a halt, and I started manipulating people's feelings and emotions to get what I wanted or felt I deserved. I was more paralyzed mentally than my arms and legs combined, and that changed me. The active, go get em, capable man my wife had grown to love and trust was fading away. Something was seriously wrong, and I either need to fix it or find an excuse.

No Excuses

When we do something wrong, we usually know it's wrong and are already making up an excuse in our heads. In our minds, we don't want others to think poorly of us. It doesn't matter if we have to blame others as long as we don't look bad. By mentioning an excuse, we are hoping, and sometimes expecting, others to overlook or forgive the results of our actions. If you remember, the very first thought that came into my head after I crashed on the ski hill was focused on what others may have thought of me. I wanted so badly to come up with a believable excuse I could tell to explain why I broke my neck, especially to my wife. I wanted something, anything, so it wasn't my fault our lives got turned upside down.

Why do we do this to ourselves? Why don't we just choose what's best for us each time so we don't have to keep going through this? It all comes down to one word—fear. Fear of the unknown. This fear keeps us in our comfort zones when extraordinary opportunities are dangling right in front of our faces. Instead of grabbing on tightly to incredible success, we fold our arms waiting, wondering, if there will be another chance.

All of us are scared to some degree—it's human nature. We are afraid of pain, embarrassment, retribution, responsibility, failure, and even success. In addition to all these fears, we are brutally attacked with guilt, disappointment, and regret. These three words carry a heavy weight. Regret of "what could have been" and "opportunities lost" is not easily dismissed or forgiven. So we attach blame and start pointing fingers at others.

Most of the time the problem is ourselves. We are the ones holding us back from reaching our full potential. Not your boss, family, teacher, coach, or even your health. Here are some examples of different excuses that you may have heard, or maybe even used before:

- I'm too busy for that.
- This is just who I am, I can't change.
- I'm not as qualified as them, so I'd never get that position.
- I'm a single parent, you don't understand.
- It's too hard.
- I'm not worthy.

I had to learn that even though I have an amazing excuse as a quadriplegic to not do hard things, using paralysis as my crutch was keeping me in my comfort zone. My excuse was not allowing me to achieve all I'm capable of. It was stopping me from becoming who I was meant to be and keeping me from helping others in a magnificent way. You must figure out what your excuses are and start getting rid of them, they're only holding you back.

"If you really want to do something, you will find a way. If you don't, you'll find an excuse." – **Jim Rohn**

Never Give Up Hope
Something extremely difficult for others to understand, and nearly impossible to fully explain, is the dark abyss of feeling alone and worthless in this world. You could be stranded on a small deserted island in the South Pacific for months and be completely alone. However, if you believe a ship is on its way, a rescue plane is just over the horizon, or even if an old volleyball named Wilson is your new best friend, you still possess something so extremely powerful that it can't be stopped. Hope! You may be so scared

you're afraid to move, making you mentally paralyzed. Still, no matter how dark your surroundings get, it's undeniable that hope is stronger than fear. You never stop believing someone is thinking of you and wants to save you. In the end, you know everything will be okay.

Hope is what gets us up in the morning, to propose to the women we love, to take that terrifying risk and start a new company, to leave an abusive situation, to have another child, to quit drinking and save your family, and to stand back up after being knocked down. Hope ignites the fire within, allowing a clearer vision into the future. Never give up hope that what you're fighting for will come to pass. NEVER.

"Hope is being able to see that there is light despite all of the darkness." – Desmond Tutu

Because I learned to live these three principles since first breaking my neck 17 years ago, my life today is totally unrecognizable. My wife and I have been blessed with two more girls bringing our family to six. Through a lot of hard work and sacrifice, I've become an international keynote speaker and trainer—something I never dreamed would happen. I mean, who would ever pay to listen to me? With my right pinky knuckle, I wrote the book *UNFROZEN Superior Systems to Move from Paralysis to Progress*. As a quadriplegic, I have been snow skiing again, water skiing, rafting, skydiving, rappelling off a 150-foot cliff, and I have completed a half triathlon.

In 2017, my wife and I started a movement that gives tremendous purpose to all the pain and trials we have had to endure. I say WE have endured because I fully believe we don't do anything in his life without others helping and supporting in some way. If we suffer, they suffer too. We created a nonprofit called Chair The Hope which helps provide wheelchairs and other devices to those in desperate need throughout the world. I want everyone to have the independence and mobility to choose how they want to live their life. Because I know exactly what it feels like to be stuck, to feel frozen and not a part of society. Millions of amazing children and adults struggle each day to go to school, to worship in church, to provide for their families, to play at the park, or to live the life they desperately desire. It's a lonely, frustrating experience. In the first year, we raised over $100,000 and have personally delivered over 400 wheelchairs throughout southern Mexico. This is only the beginning.

If you keep progressing, quit using excuses, and never give up hope, I know you will achieve everything you want. It may not happen the way you plan, but it will happen. Zig Ziglar put it best when he said, *"When obstacles arise, you change your direction to reach your goal, you do not change your decision to get there."* There is no doubt in my mind that I have, and will, achieve more in this life by learning resilience through extraordinary setbacks. Throughout my life, I have never stood taller than I do **pushing forward** in my chair.

TWEETABLE

The act of moving forward, or progressing, builds faith and confidence. Without progress in life, we feel insignificant, unimportant—almost invisible. We lose hope. It's not as important how fast you are progressing towards your goals as it is that you are moving forward each day.

Nathan Ogden has taught thousands how to conquer their fears and move from paralysis to progress through eliminating excuses in their lives. He is an international keynote speaker with Nathan Ogden Presentations, co-creator of Chair The Hope, author of the book Unfrozen, *and a wheelchair athlete. As a Quadriplegic, he uses his powerful life-changing experiences to inspire, teach and mentor leaders throughout the world. Book Nathan at NathanOgden.com or join his extraordinary charity at ChairTheHope.org*

CHAPTER 5

Surviving the City to Owning the City

by Justin Brooks

N o matter what path you're on, you're going to have obstacles. The only way to get where you want is to overcome.

I grew up in your typical blue-collar home with two brothers. Life started out great. I had a loving family, a home, and food on the table; that was until, one day, it all ended. Fourth grade year, I witnessed the last argument between my soon-to-be divorced parents. That was the day my life changed. The divorce didn't bother me as much as the poverty that ensued. We had many days when I would come home to our utilities being cut off and a mother struggling to make ends meet, fighting the grips of poverty with three young boys in the house.

My only escape was in my dreams, dreams of being free from poverty, dreams of being wealthy. One of the seeds planted in me at an early age was entrepreneurship. I loved learning about businesses. I found myself wanting to own a business more than anything else. At age seven I was exposed to cooking. Cooking was my outlet, a way to take my mind off the divorce. Cooking wasn't enough though…. I had to have a better plan to ensure my success, so I started thinking ownership. I wanted a business!

I'd spend hours lying awake at night staring at the ceiling, trying to figure out how I would own a business. I was heavily influenced by Bill Gates as a child, the richest man in the world at the time. It helped that I loved his games. I heard a story about Bill Gates and his alleged software monopoly. I asked my mom what a monopoly was, and she said, "It is someone that controls all of a business and no one else can get in." Now obviously, it is more complicated than that, but at seven years old, it was all I needed to hear to decide I wanted to own a monopoly too, just like my hero Bill Gates. I created my first business plan to own a cooking business. The goal was to own the restaurant AND control the companies contributing all the ingredients from every dish in my restaurant. From the cheese to the noodles to the flour to the cow itself and the land the cows grazed on. I wanted to be the supplier, the producer, the manufacturer—I wanted it all.

I was vertically integrating a business at seven years old and didn't even know it.

When I had the opportunity to attend a stock market camp put on for inner city youth by a gentleman wanting to give back, I found my other major influence. This camp taught the basics of investing, the seed that would grow to fuel my passion. I couldn't get enough as a kid. If it had to do with business, money, or success, I learned about it, because in my mind, that was the answer to not being poor. I absorbed everything I could about business. Then I learned about money.

I spent most of my time alone or with my brothers. Honestly, I wasn't very popular growing up and was made fun of often, which I believe put a bit of a chip on my shoulder. The only friend I had was on the fence about being my friend because he risked being made fun of also. I acted out in class, which got me the label of class clown. I wanted to be funny, that way kids would like me and not make fun of me. Underneath all the ridicule and humiliation I faced, truth be told, I didn't like myself and was desperate for attention.

The pain of ridicule and humiliation transferred over to church. Mom kept us in church because she didn't want us to be exposed to "the streets." We would go to church four to five times a week, just so we could volunteer, help, and have a positive outlet. The problem was, I was not safe from the humiliation of being made fun of at church either. From the preacher's kids all the way down, I was laughed at, teased, and humiliated, and it created an anger in me that I would have to later learn to control. I've forgiven those people, but until recently, I never realized how much it affected me. I always knew I had a chip on my shoulder, but I could never point out the reason why.

I wanted to prove all those kids that laughed at me wrong. I wanted to prove that I was somebody. I wanted to prove to all the adults that looked at me as the charity case kid, I was worth respecting.

It wasn't until I finally decided to live life on my own terms that I got free. I was a grown man before I discovered all the hurt that I was holding. That led to clarity. I stopped caring about what other people thought of me. I stopped caring about the people I grew up with and how they teased and bullied me. I stopped caring about the kids that laughed at me and called me names. I was living life for me.

In 2005, I joined the US Navy. I would go on to serve for five years onboard two aircraft carriers, the USS Kitty Hawk and the USS John C. Stennis as an Air Traffic Controller. In 2008, I married, and we had our first daughter. It was at that moment I got the jolt I needed to wake up and start planning for what her life would be like. I vowed to myself that she would never endure the pain I went through as a child. I got out the Navy in 2010 and set out on my path to discover what civilian life was all about. We moved to Daytona Beach where I planned to go to school until I got hired as an air traffic controller. I spent two semesters in college working toward a degree in air traffic control (to make me marketable) before being told my five years' experience in the military would not count and so I would not qualify to be a civilian air traffic controller. That was a pivotal point in my life. It was one of those fork in the road moments. It left me feeling like I had made a mistake getting out of the Navy. I decided it was time I took control and just went for it....

So, I dropped out of Embry-Riddle University with a 4.0 GPA, and became a Realtor® in Daytona Beach, Florida because I wanted to learn how to become a real estate investor. My goal from the beginning, was to use my air traffic control money to fuel my investing. Since my career path took a detour, I believed being a realtor would help me become a better investor. It did, but it didn't help me run a business. I went full time as a realtor and was completely broke in six months. I had no formal business experience and wasn't prepared for business ownership yet.

I remember, things got so bad, I would go to networking events paid for by the real estate company and take leftovers home so that my family could eat. One of my biggest fears at the time was being so destitute that my wife and kid would be homeless and living out of our 1993 Pontiac Bonneville. This resurrected all those feelings of uncertainty that were all too familiar as I reflect back on being trapped in poverty (except this time I had a wife and kid). There were many days as a Realtor® when I would go to events just to make sure I ate that day, and while I was there I would try to make connections.

A miracle needed to happen or we would soon be on the streets. I had to get a job to take care of my family. I gained employment after we were down to our last $500. We ended up having to move in with our parents until I gained employment, but ultimately, I was back in control. We moved back to where it all began, Kansas City, where I would have to face my past, except this time, I was ready. I started investing in real estate immediately and learning all I could. Those next several years would take us on a roller coaster ride of emotions. We nearly went broke three times over the course of the next few years. We had to sell off all our real estate, then bought it back, only to sell it off again. I felt like for the longest time I was spinning my wheels. Amazingly, the whole time I was gaining clarity, even when I didn't know it. Thankfully, I had the will to persist.

I spent several years persisting through the hard times. I read and studied like my life depended on it, because it did! I worked on my mind. I knew that without the investment in my mind, I wasn't going to be able to live out the life of my dreams. And for a kid like myself from "the inner city," that was like death to me and meant failure in my mind.

I remembered something I was taught, and it's been mentioned several times by successful people like Tony Robbins and the late Jim Rohn: successful people invest in themselves AND they invest in their education. So, I knew that no matter how bad it got, no matter how little money or resources I had, I needed to invest in my mind, because that's what successful people do. I doubled down and invested even more in my personal development.

And I'm glad I did, because here's how things have changed.

My life took off. My partners and I have created a multi-million dollar real estate business. My wife and I run a successful real estate fund. We also run a successful podcast called *Real Life Real Equity* where we talk about business, life, and money from the perspective of a couple with the responsibility of a family. The world needs more real and less acting, so we give the reality behind being successful.

I wished I could have seen successful couples and families, people with kids and a job and a spouse and the responsibilities of life, killing the game and winning big back when I was getting started. We want to be the example and inspiration other people need to succeed and grow. We also acknowledge the REAL "equity" in life—family, time spent with friends, and investment in your mind, body, soul.

I never could have imagined a kid like myself being around so many successful people as I am today. Because of my friendship with people like Robert Helms and Russell Gray of The Real Estate Guys, I am able to attend private parties with Robert Kiyosaki in the president's suite in New Orleans, or have drinks and dinner with Ken McElroy and the guys. My syndication club has raised hundreds of millions of dollars, and it was relationship that created this possibility.

When I look at my four girls, I remember that life is more than just money or business. It is about those real equities. I am not opposed to wealth creation, but I find that the free things in life, the things money can't buy, are much more valuable. I have read over 700 books on money, business, finance, success, and personal development. I have taken dozens of courses. I have acted on my knowledge and created millions of dollars in project developments and real estate ownership. However, the real equity I have accrued can't be bought with a price tag and can never be taken away from me.

You now know a part of my story that most people never learn, and because of that, we have started our relationship. You have access to me, and you just learned the company I keep. Thank you for reading my story. My goal is to help others live in a better place because we have found out how to live in our better place.

TWEETABLE
No matter what path you're on, you're going to have obstacles. The only way to get where you want is to overcome.

Justin Brooks is a US Navy veteran, father, and husband. He has taken the disciplines learned in the Navy to grow into a professional real estate investor, entrepreneur, and podcaster. As a real estate fund manager, Justin's funds specialize in developing and operating assisted living homes.

He also helps listeners grow through his podcast Real Life Real Equity, *cofounded by his wife Keisha Brooks. Through his podcast he founded* The Real Equity Club, *to help listeners learn more about investing in alternative assets like real estate.*

Email me: justin@realliferealequity.com or visit our website at realliferealequity.com

CHAPTER 6

The Two Hundred Million Dollar Fax

by Carl Wehmeyer

t was December 23rd, the last working day before a long-deserved Christmas break. I was the last salesman in the office. Our company at the time was made up of about eight people. The sales office consisted of old elementary school desks that were lined up single file. I had just finished making my calls for the day, all 150 of them, and no one was biting. It was 2003, and the impacts of 9/11 on the economy were taking a toll on the business. People weren't traveling, budgets were cut, and we were way under quota. At the time, I remember thinking, if this keeps up we could be finished. The dream would be over and I would have to skulk back to college with my tail between my legs.

A year earlier, I had defiantly claimed to my father that "business was my calling" and "college is for those who haven't found their purpose yet." I dropped out and started working full-time. To say he was less than amused was an understatement. He was sure I was going to fail, and I was about to prove him right. But I wasn't ready to give up. Back then it was a gut feeling. It was this driving force within me that said, "I can and will win," and the funny thing is, he was the one who instilled it in me.

Now I realize that this gut feeling is actually the fundamental key that separates those who are successful from those who are not. Those moments, when things are looking the grimmest, are usually the points of breakthrough. I know it sounds like a catchy Instagram quote, but it's proven to be true for me time and time again. This moment was no exception. As I headed out of the office to call it a day, I noticed a fax sitting on the old fax machine. Normally these faxes just get discarded. Email was taking hold, and most people didn't use fax. The only faxes that came through were from the "HR department" announcing that we'd won a free cruise and to call now! Total spam. But I wasn't going to take a chance. Something within me told me to grab that fax.

On Christmas Eve, the party was in full effect. I had flown from New Jersey to Texas to visit my family for the holidays. Everyone had come to Mom's house, and as normal, she had invited the whole family. I didn't get a chance to party in college (my only regret of dropping out) but I imagine this party probably rivaled some of the best. I was having a blast. The only problem: I had a conference call with the Saudi government at 1 am Texas time. You see, it turns out that fax I had picked up was a request for a quote for 100,000 toilet tank bags—a potential $100,000 sale. But I knew that there was more opportunity. The Saudi government had to have more plans for water conservation than these measly 100,000 bags. And I knew that I was the only one crazy enough to call them on Christmas Eve. I was sure our competitors got that same fax, but how many of them either threw it away or decided to wait until after the holidays? When the clock struck 12:50, I scurried up to the second floor and locked myself in the bathroom. Everyone was making so much noise, this was my only refuge. The call started promptly at 1 am. Eight government officials joined the call! This was obviously a big priority for them. I took them through the sales points I had carefully prepared, then I hit them with the big idea. What if you looked at a complete program? How could that change your country for the better? That moment was the moment that would change the history of the company forever. My career would catapult to heights I never imagined. After a short pause, the deputy minister replied; "That sounds interesting Carl. Why don't you fly to Saudi Arabia and let's discuss your plan."

It was a life-changing moment, the chance to put our company on the map. I should have been ecstatic, but instead, I felt something else: terror. The country was at war, and it appeared there was no end in sight. No one was flying domestically, let alone internationally. And definitely not to the Middle East! Everyone I told the story to thought I was crazy. No way, out of the question…suicide. The USA had just been rocked by the single largest terrorist attack in the history of the modern world. Everyone felt like that next one was coming any day. Americans were being targeted overseas, nowhere was safe. A quick Google search of Saudi Arabia travel gave me the state department website: "All nonessential US personnel should leave the country immediately, threats to American citizens imminent." All signs indicated I should gracefully bow out, retreat. But that wasn't the way I was brought up, and that wasn't the culture of the company. Our founder, Bill Cutler, had built his business on resilience. He knew that in order to succeed you had to do what others wouldn't be willing to do. You had to be a path blazer, a real entrepreneur. We sat for hours discussing the opportunity. Our mission was to save water, and where better to pursue that mission than in the Middle East? We were scared, but we weren't going to condemn an entire nation for the actions of the few. We were confident we could make a difference. After 48 hours of deliberating, I called the minister's office. We would be there next Saturday for the meeting. The preparation began.

We touched down in Riyadh, Saudi Arabia the following Friday. It was like being transported into an old Indiana Jones movie. Everyone was dressed so differently. The airport was dimly lit and customs officials wore military uniforms. This was not your typical "tourist" destination. We finally cleared customs after about two hours of shuffling through makeshift lines and haggling with the customs officer in broken English. We were out, and I thought the worst was over, until we got in the taxi. This was where the movie changed from *Indiana Jones* to *Clear and Present Danger*. The taxi driver sped us out of the airport onto a dark highway. It looked like the road to nowhere. Then it started, the chanting in Arabic, and it got louder and louder. Every time we tried to ask him a question, the chanting would just get louder and more ominous. I was sure this guy was saying our final words. He was preparing us to never be seen again. I was afraid I had already made a fatal mistake. But, in the end, he delivered us to our hotel. That was the longest 30-minute ride of my life.

The next day we entered the Ministry building. We had survived. We made our way up to the minister's office. The adrenaline was pumping. This was the big moment. All of the fear and anxiety of the trip was burning away and turning to excitement. We walked through the entrance to his offices, and the scene was like something out of the United Nations: flags everywhere, ornate furniture, and about 10 Saudi officials in their finest traditional Saudi attire. Time stood still for the next hour. I went through our proposal, our plan to save the Kingdom of Saudi Arabia a billion gallons of water. Forget the 100,000 tank bags, we wanted to supply every household with a water saving kit. This was something that could make a real impact.

At the end of the presentation, the minister leaned over, his English perfect, "I think this will work, Carl. How quickly can we get samples and put a contract together?" For the next three months, we prepared the plan to distribute 5,000,000 kits to the households throughout the Kingdom. The classroom desks were gone. We were expanding, and business was about to boom for the next seven years. In a time when businesses were closing their doors, we were thriving. The Obama stimulus plan was kicking off to save the economy; we were just fine on our own.

Some people think that fax was the lucky break for us, but I know otherwise. That fax was a tiny part of it. It was the decisions we made through the whole process that lead us to victory. It was our resilience. There were so many chances for us to drop out, to throw in the towel, but we committed. We had the burning passion to win. We knew that our moment was coming, we just didn't know exactly when. Too many times, people quit at the one-yard line. If you want to be great, and you want to make an impact, you have to keep pushing. You have to make that call on Christmas Eve. You have to risk it all and fly to a dangerous place. Most of all, you have to believe. You have to believe that what you're doing is worth it and that if you stay strong you will succeed. This was just the beginning for me. Since that fax, our business has exploded. We now have almost 200 employees and over 200 million in sales. We have locations all over the Middle East and continue to add more every year. On top of all this great success, I was recently a finalist for Entrepreneur of the Year. There are many more challenges to come, but I feel prepared now more than ever. The challenges of the past have paved the resilience of the future.

TWEETABLE

Most of all, you have to believe. You have to believe that what you're doing is worth it and that if you stay strong you will succeed.

A fearless leader in the war against waste, Carl Wehmeyer has dedicated his 18-year tenure to ensure that Niagara is known as a company that designs products that transform everyday acts into a powerful force for saving green. Carl has been a tantamount part of Niagara's growth and establishment at the forefront of the water revolution. Carl is an entrepreneur at heart and always looking to share ideas with other thought leaders. He can be reached at Cwehmeyer@niagaracorp.com

CHAPTER 7

Difficult Roads Often Lead to Beautiful Destinations

by Josh & Emily Houser

"If you must look back, do so forgivingly. If you must look forward, do so prayerfully. However, the wisest thing you can do is be present in the present…gratefully."

– Maya Angelou

Sometimes it takes losing almost everything you are familiar with to realize what's truly important in this life. When faced with challenges, will you allow them to defeat or define you? Or will you allow them to stretch and strengthen you?

EMILY: Our greatest story of resilience started long before Josh and I ever met. We both married at the young age of 20, just not to one another. In fact, it wouldn't be until several years later when I was 31 and Josh was 35 before our paths would cross in a way that felt like fate.

Nobody ever gets married thinking their relationship will one day end in the pain of divorce. That certainly was not something I ever imagined could happen to me. But, seven years into my marriage, the threat of divorce loomed over me. I remember feeling such deep emotional despair. How could this be my reality? I was in total disbelief and I felt betrayed. We had a young, beautiful daughter by this time, and I desperately wanted to protect her from being hurt. I wanted to fight to keep her family together.

I had begun to isolate myself. I didn't want anybody to discover the reality of what was going on. I felt ashamed and embarrassed. I eventually sought counseling, which ended up being a huge blessing. Over time, it helped me gain the courage to share what I was going through. I learned the importance of a support network, including my family and close friends. Looking back, I don't know how I would have gotten through it without them.

During this painful time, I started taking my daughter for long walks in her jogging stroller. These walks eventually turned into jogs, and then into longer runs. I can remember many times running, listening to encouraging music, sometimes tears streaming down my face, praying for God's help and strength. Running became an outlet for my stress and a positive way to be healthy and active. I began to love running, I even craved it!

The next three years were an emotional roller coaster, but I never gave up hope! There were times that I didn't know how I was going to move forward, but I put my trust in God, and He brought me through each day.

Despite my desire for my marriage to be saved, it eventually ended in divorce. My daughter was then four years old. It was time to move on. I had to let go of any resentment, bitterness, and anger towards my ex-husband. This was a process that didn't happen overnight. I had to accept that he was on his own journey and it was time for me to start mine. I could not let the failure define me. I needed to move forward in a direction that allowed me to be my authentic self. A quote that has since inspired me says, "Don't change so people will like you. Be yourself, and the right people will love the real you."

JOSH: When I discovered my wife of 12 years had left me, my world came crashing down. I couldn't imagine a more painful rejection than to have pledged my life and love to one who no longer wanted it. I felt alone, hopeless, betrayed, and at times even angry. The fear of divorce hung over me like a dark cloud. How would I explain this to family and friends? Was my life being reduced to a marriage statistic?

I couldn't see it at the time, but my negative thoughts and fears were self-inflicted. Never once did family or friends belittle or chastise me for the failure. I was the one talking down to myself, filling my head with negativity, resentment, and worry. My family and friends were a constant source of support and strength, and I am forever grateful to them.

In my search for strength and peace, I took up running again. Running offered not only physical benefits but also emotional and spiritual benefits. It provided an opportunity to pray and to reflect. I loved the serenity and calmness that running brought. Running allowed me to decompress and to see the world clearly. The more I ran, the more I could see I needed to make changes in my life.

As time passed, I realized that I had to let go. Bitterness and resentment were holding me back, keeping me from becoming the best version of me.

My prayers shifted to, "God, You are in control. Help me to be at peace with whatever happens. Please give me strength to move forward no matter what."

I still did not know what the future would bring, but I believed there were good plans in store. The Bible says, "For I know the plans I have for you, declares the Lord, plans to prosper you and not to harm you, plans to give you hope and a future." I discovered life is a series of second chances. God takes joy in allowing us to experience love, peace, and fullness. Along the way, something unexpected happened: my broken heart learned to love again.

You see, four years later, I met a girl (Emily). Our sisters were college friends and conspiring match-makers. When they leaked information about a dashingly handsome, single runner (me), Emily asked me to join her relay team. From that conversation, more conversations ensued. Eventually, we met, and our first date included a run! I was fascinated as I listened to this beautiful woman speak. We talked about running, relationships, and even resilience. I was amazed to hear how closely her story resembled mine. Even more amazing was the courage and inspiration she emanated. I felt I was being given a second chance. I was so mesmerized by this girl that I completely lost track of where we were going. Truth be told, we got lost, and so, naturally, we just kept going. Our short workout turned into an eight-mile adventure! It's a perfect metaphor for life. When you're lost, keep going!

EMILY: This became the first of many long runs together. Spoiler alert! We fell in love and eventually got married. I'm so thankful that Josh came into my daughter's life at the perfect time. They share a wonderful bond that continues to grow.

We look back on our painful trials as one of the best growth opportunities of our lives. As Napoleon Hill once said, "Every failure, every adversity, every heartache carries with it the seed of an equivalent or greater benefit." Without a doubt, our relationship is a "greater benefit" on the other side of failure. The love, acceptance, and joy we share are more than we could have imagined just a few years ago. The pain of the past was worth it. We would go through it again in a heartbeat to find each other. We are stronger today because of it. And for that we are grateful. In the midst of failure, adversity, and heartache, always remember there is light at the end of the tunnel. There is hope.

To this day, Josh and I still share a passion for running. There is something so refreshing about going out and running together. It gives us a chance to connect, brainstorm, and dream about the future. We've completed a combined total of seven marathons. I also just recently qualified for the

Boston Marathon! This is something I would have never thought possible when I first started running. I love this quote by Arthur Blank that says, "I run because it's so symbolic of life. You have to drive yourself to overcome the obstacles. You might feel that you can't, but then you find your inner strength and realize you are capable of so much more than you thought." If you set your mind to it, you can achieve almost anything!

JOSH: That drive and determination permeates into other areas of our lives, both personally and professionally. When I met Emily, I was already investing in single-family homes and small multifamily apartments. She quickly caught the vision with real estate. We started to network with other like-minded individuals about multifamily investing and eventually met Mark and Tamiel Kenney of Think Multifamily in Dallas, TX. They have since become our mentors, and we are blessed to call them friends.

We started our own real estate investing company, Houser Capital Group. Our focus is acquiring and improving multifamily communities and providing profitable investment opportunities to our partners. We have invested in over 800 units so far. Being a part of the Think Multifamily inner circle has opened up a world of opportunity for our business. Through the group, we've learned the importance of adding value to those around you. The more we focus on helping others and adding value to their lives, the more abundance seems to flow our way.

EMILY: We value the relationships we have formed through networking with like-minded investors and entrepreneurs. We travel on a regular basis outside our home in Oregon to be with our real estate mentors, fellow investors, and syndicators. With every event that we attend, we leave with more knowledge and insight, strengthened relationships, and new connections.

We have had the privilege of meeting incredible people along the way. Getting to meet Kyle Wilson, Bob Helms The Godfather of Real Estate, Robert and Kim Kiyosaki, Robert Helms and Russell Gray of The Real Estate Guys, George Ross, and many others has been amazing. Surrounding ourselves with inspirational and successful individuals has allowed us to expand our own vision. The future is bright!

You never know who you might meet while networking. We met Kelli Calabrese, a health and fitness expert, at a real estate investment conference, of all places. She introduced us to an amazing health and wellness company called Isagenix. The company's integrity, mission, and focus were all things we excitedly agreed with. We began using their nutritional system and immediately saw great results! We started sharing our results with others. What we found is that we not only enjoyed helping individuals with their financial goals through real estate but also saw the opportunity to help others with their health and fitness goals too. We have become healthier and stronger and feel privileged to help and inspire others to do the same.

JOSH AND EMILY: Our journey together has really just begun. Neither of us would go back and take away the struggles or heartache we've experienced. It has helped us become the individuals and team we are today. We are both still learning, still being refined, still works in progress. We don't have it all together; our relationship is not perfect. But to see how God has worked in both of our lives is humbling to this day. The opportunities and possibilities that are in front of us are nothing we could have ever imagined in the midst of our hardest storms. We know that we will face hardship in the future, potentially far more challenging than anything we have faced before. Jim Rohn shared this: "Don't wish it were easier, wish you were better. Don't wish for less problems, wish for more skills. Don't wish for less challenge, wish for more wisdom." We hope that what we have learned from our past will help us to rely fully on God and be resilient in whatever challenges come our way.

We know we are not alone. Everybody faces challenges in their lives: struggles, failures, devastation, heartbreak, and loss. Our desire is for you to be encouraged by our personal journey. Don't be ashamed of your story. You never know how it could impact others going through similar experiences. Have the strength and courage to take a step in the right direction for whatever circumstances you are facing today. We all have gifts and talents that we have been given. Don't let them go to waste. You can bless those around you every single day. If our story resonates with you in any way, our hope is that you will reach out to us. We would love to hear your story too!

TWEETABLE

Everybody faces challenges in their lives: struggles, failures, devastation, heartbreak, and loss. Don't be ashamed of your story. You never know how it could impact others going through similar experiences.

Josh and Emily Houser are real estate investors, entrepreneurs, and founders of Houser Capital Group. They welcome opportunities to invest alongside like-minded individuals to create passive cash flow and financial freedom. Together they share a passion for running, fitness, and healthy living. Their success with Isagenix has inspired them to help others achieve their own health and wellness goals while offering support along the way.

Learn more about multifamily investing and our team at housercapitalgroup.com.

Email: josh@housercapitalgroup.com and emily@housercapitalgroup.com

Connect: facebook.com/joshua.houser.75 and facebook.com/emilycrystal.houser

CHAPTER 8
Treasures in Darkness

by Mike Coleman

My wife and our girls were nervously waiting for the sun to go down as we sat on a dive boat off the west coast of the island of Hawaii. We were all certified scuba divers, but they had never been on a night dive. Some years before, my son and I had done one with manta rays. We had watched with wonder as our underwater lights drew plankton together, and then, out of the darkness, large manta rays appeared and swooped up their food. It was an amazing underwater ballet. Tonight I didn't know what to expect, but I knew this dive would be exciting.

I had arranged to have dive masters guide us tonight because they knew the local waters well and they increased our safety. My wife, Jeanie, agreed to do the dive, but only if she could hold the hand of the main dive master. Finally, the sun went down, and with some hesitation and excitement, we all entered the water. It was like descending into a different world. The ocean reef comes alive at night with creatures and scenes that you won't see during the day. Your handheld light reveals the things hidden in the dark. There are treasures to be discovered in the darkness, but you have to look for them to find them. I have found that the same is true in everyday life. When the darkness of adversity and pain comes to us, the way we choose to look at it determines whether we find treasure or just trouble.

I've experienced times of the light shining on my life through many opportunities, successes, and blessings. I grew up in Mobile, Alabama—a medium-sized city near the coast of the Gulf of Mexico. My dad used to say that we lived in LA, but in our case it was Lower Alabama, not Los Angeles. My parents were musical, and when I was about 12 years old, I began to take drum lessons (I wanted to make some noise!). I went on to play in the high school band and in a touring band. Over the coming years, I recorded three albums as a drummer, but I never knew that music would play such a pivotal role in my life.

After high school, I went to university and earned a degree in finance. In the early years of my career, I worked as the business administrator of a church and as the president of a nonprofit publishing organization.

Then in 1987, I co-founded Integrity Music, a Christian music company headquartered in Mobile, Alabama. After significant growth, the company went public in 1994, and its shares were traded on the NASDAQ stock exchange. The company grew into a global company with offices in the United Kingdom, Australia, South Africa, and Singapore. Its products were distributed in over 160 countries, and we received many Platinum and Gold record certifications for the sales of our music albums. Later we expanded further when we acquired the INO Record label. We worked with artists such as MercyMe, Darlene Zschech, Don Moen, Israel Houghton, Hillsong Music, Paul Wilbur, Paul Baloche, and Kari Jobe.

As the company expanded beyond music into books and other media, it was renamed Integrity Media. In 2004 the company went private. Then in 2011, Integrity Music and the other divisions of Integrity Media were sold. I had the privilege of leading this company as its president and CEO for 24 years, including 10 years as a public company. I had an amazing team of people working alongside me during those years. My time with Integrity Media was just some of the light and favor that I have experienced in my life.

But I have also experienced dark and troubling times in my life. After the sale of the company in 2011, I began pursuing new opportunities until I got some bad news from the doctor. I had been having real problems with the nerves in my body, especially in my hands and feet. I would have searing pain shoot through my body and it would wake me up at night when it was really bad. In 2012 I went to see my neurosurgeon. He examined me, reviewed my MRI and then told me that I must have surgery on my neck soon because my spinal cord was under pressure in several places. He said that if I had the wrong kind of impact on my neck I could be paralyzed. This news hit me hard, and I knew I was about to start an unexpected journey. I like adventures, but I was not looking forward to this one.

My condition was so complicated that I was referred to one of the world's leading neurosurgeons at John Hopkins Hospital in Baltimore, Maryland. He examined me and said that I needed surgery soon. He ended up doing two major surgeries on my spine in my neck, and he had to operate on my spinal cord. Ouch! The surgeries were a success, but later I began to have new problems which the doctors could not explain. I had serious problems with my breathing, sometimes causing panic attacks. I had always been a confident person, and it upset me that I couldn't remain calm. I couldn't lean over because my blood pressure would fall, and it would take four to six hours of rest for it to recover to normal. My equilibrium, digestion, body temperature, and heart rate were also affected. Finally, a neurologist diagnosed the source of my problems as dysautonomia. He explained that the automatic part of my central nervous system was out of sync. That is the part of the nervous system that controls much of what our bodies do without us thinking about it. Because I could not consciously control any of the things happening in my body, I could not fix them and neither could the doctors.

I went from being an active person who enjoyed scuba diving to someone who was confined in many ways and could no longer work. It was like I was taken out of the game of life and put on injured reserve. For the first time in my life, I was in a very long season in which I couldn't fight my way out of my troubles, change my circumstances, or understand what was going on in my life. These physical problems and adversities lasted about five years. My sweet wife, Jeanie, cared for me during my trials. My family along with a few close friends also stood with me. But, my greatest challenges weren't physical. I struggled deeply to find vision and hope for my future. I cried out to God to shine His light on my darkness and show me the way forward.

Slowly, God did begin to show me Himself in new ways, and I began to discover treasures in darkness as God shined His light into my heart and mind. I found peace that surpasses all understanding because of a deeper trust in Him. I learned to give thanks in a new way and to count my blessings. Hope grew inside of me, and I began to understand that adversity, pain, and unexpected change may look like setbacks, but many times they are a setup for your comeback. In fact, adversity, pain, and unexpected change are the doorway to your promotion into greater meaning and purpose in your life.

One of my favorite quotes, from Vivian Greene, says "Life isn't about waiting for the storm to pass...It's about learning to dance in the rain." I have found that to be true. We all want our circumstances to change for the better, and we want to be in control, but that is not what real life is about. Charles Simpson, my dear friend, said that "Life is defined more by the unexpected than by the expected." He is right. The way we view unexpected change will determine if we see it just as trouble or as an opportunity to find treasure. I have found that real life is finding joy and peace by trusting God, whether you're experiencing trouble or victory.

Even though my difficult circumstances did not change, a new vision and clarity of purpose were born inside of me. I knew that one of the keys to finding your purpose is to serve others. My passion and mission to help people discover and fulfill their God-given purpose became even more clear. I knew I had a new assignment for this mission, and I was exploring ways that I could pursue it given my circumstances. Then something amazing happened. God healed me in 2016 when some men were moved with compassion and prayed for me at a Christian conference. My autonomic nervous system problems were gone. Suddenly, my world changed.

Today, I'm back in the game and off of injured reserve. I'm now providing coaching for leaders, consulting for organizations, and speaking for events through Mike Coleman & Company. We help people and organizations find clarity, navigate change, and pursue purpose. My adversity was a setup for my future because it birthed a new vision and clarity of purpose. The light is shining again.

Just like our night dive in Hawaii, I saw things during my dark season that I would not have otherwise seen in normal daylight. I found treasures in darkness, and now I'm sharing those treasures with other people to help them navigate through challenges and fulfill their God-given purpose.

At the end of our night dive, I broke through the surface of the water, and all around me, the Pacific Ocean was as smooth as glass. I lay back and began to float. And then I saw the most amazing sight: the Milky Way blazing with millions of stars visible to the naked eye. It was overwhelming to see it so clearly while floating in the ocean. You can't see the Milky Way that clearly in most places because of the surrounding lights and atmosphere, but by being in an isolated place, in the darkness, I could see it in its stunning brilliance. When adversity hits, it is a chance to see things from a different perspective. Who knows, it may allow you to see treasure and not just trouble. Looking back, I realize that the ultimate dive master, God, had been holding my hand the entire time I was in darkness, and He showed me deep treasures that changed the way I view life and the world around me.

TWEETABLE
When the darkness of adversity and pain comes to us, the way we choose to look at it determines whether we find treasure or just trouble.

Mike Coleman is an entrepreneur, strategist, CEO, leadership coach, consultant, and speaker. He leads the Mike Coleman & Company which provides coaching for leaders, consulting for organizations, and speaking for events. He has worked with many leaders and creative people to help them find clarity, navigate change, and pursue their purpose. He co-founded Integrity Music, a global music company and led Integrity as the CEO for over 24 years, including 10 years as a public company. To contact him for speaking, consulting, or leadership coaching go to MikeColeman.com.

CHAPTER 9

From Busboy to Two-Time INC 5000 List of America's Fastest Growing Companies

by Adam Buttorff

The family tragedy that occurred in the summer of 1984 was the first of several events in my life that would shape my character and make me into the businessman I am today. The site I saw as I walked into my dad's room is something I will never forget.

My dad is throwing up blood. My mom and siblings are in a panic, grabbing towels to catch the blood. Shouting and knocking things over, we unsuccessfully attempt to carry my six foot six ex-marine dad to the car. My mom screams out to call 911, and it seems like hours before the ambulance arrives. I watch my once strong marine dad, covered in blood and disoriented, be hauled out on a stretcher. After I finally get to the hospital, the next few days are a haze, but I do remember that my father dies within days of being admitted. Then, within a few days of the funeral, my grandmother dies as well.

At 11 years old, this would change the direction of my life forever.

With a large family of seven kids, losing our dad would not only devastate us emotionally but financially too. We had no savings, no life insurance, and my mom had not worked in 20 years. So, we sold everything we owned and moved into my grandmother's house where all three of my brothers and I shared one room. This is also when I got my first job washing dishes and bussing tables for my friend's parents who owned a restaurant. I needed a job to help pay the bills because we were destitute after losing my dad.

I discovered that I don't think like everyone else. I really struggled in school. In high school, they did a ranking system based on grades which told you not only your class ranking but also which quarter you were in. My friends would tell me they were in the top quarter of the class and ask me what was I ranked. I would make a joke and say, "My quarter is what makes your quarter possible." Truthfully, I was in the last quarter of my class. I struggled with dyslexia and almost all my friends said I was so hyper that I needed to be on Ritalin, but my family was too poor for that. Needless to say, I was not a teachers' favorite student. However, after high school, I went to college, because that is what you do. I only went because my mom pushed me hard to get a degree. And after six different schools and a short, "very quick" seven years of college, I just barely graduated. During my last semester, my grades were not very good, and I was one point away from graduating. So, I did what any rational person would: I begged my teacher to let me write an extra paper for the point I needed to graduate. She did, and I graduated, finally.

After graduation, I thought I was going to set the world on fire and that businesses were going to be fighting over me. That was not the case. Again, society told me, get an education, get a great job, and life will be great. My current boss did not even give me a raise. As a matter of fact, he told me, don't expect a raise just because you have a degree. However, what he said did not phase me because I have always been an entrepreneur.

I started my first business in fifth grade. It was my birthday, and I asked my mom for bandanas—as many as she would buy me. I then proceeded to go to school wearing them on my legs and arms to sell them. Thank goodness I was a tall kid or I would have been unbearably teased. The good news is, I sold out the first day. And I repeated this process four times until I saturated my market. Later, my mom worked for American Chicle, a gum company. I got free gum, so I started selling it in school. One of my proudest moments was when I got three detentions. The reason for the detentions was, and I quote "using the publicity of the school to make money." Those of us with an entrepreneurial mind think I should have gotten an award and recognition, but no, instead I was punished. I realized then that I was a non-conformist, even though I didn't have the word for it at the time.

As a non-conformist, I go against how society tells us to live life and work. Society tells us: get a good education, don't think outside the box, stay in your lane, and do what everyone else tells you to do. This is okay for getting by, but not for being successful and having a secure future. I needed help, so I sought out the only help I could get, books.

As I became an adult, I started reading anything I could get my hands on that would feed me positive emotions and grow me personally. I had to flood my mind with positive thinking so I would believe that I could do something extraordinary. Everyone around me was struggling just to get by in life, and

I wanted more than that. I knew there had to be a better way. When I was 10 years old, I remember standing in the kitchen with my dad. He knelt down to me, looking me in the eyes, and said to me, "Son, you are going to do well in life." I kept those words with me and listened to that saying in my mind over and over again. While reading tons of self-help books on attitude, actions, and goals, I realized I needed a mentor to help me in life. Since there was not a place in the phone book called mentors, I found them in books.

I have always been and still am an avid reader. I heard at a young age that leaders are readers and I took it to heart. Through their books, my mentors became people like Zig Ziglar and Jim Rohn.

This really helped me grow and learn to be the leader I needed in business. With my mind fed and expanded, I did everything from striping parking lots to selling long-distance phone plans door to door, to being a personal trainer. Then I launched a real estate business flipping houses and an in-home personal training business with a business partner. Everything was going great until the market crashed and I could not sell the properties. At the same time, my business partner took action to push me out of my ownership portion of the fitness company. I lost everything in a matter of months. I was at the lowest of low. Here I was, married with two young kids, and we had to move into one of our rental townhouses because we had to sell our own house. I remember weeping and wondering what I was going to do. I had many feelings of, "I am not man enough," "I do not have what it takes." I finally told the Lord that I was willing to do whatever He wanted me to do.

The Lord humbled me enough to ask my brother-in-law for a job selling roofs. Before then, I would have been too proud to do such a job. Turns out that was exactly what I needed to do. After working for a year and a half, I realized I was 70% of the revenue of the entire company. So I launched my own company. This would be one of the best decisions I ever made.

The first three years I paid myself hardly anything, and we lived on rice and beans. It was rice and beans, but I had a goal, and we were going to make it. Remember, I learned that society told me to just get a job and work for others. And society told me to spend everything I made because I deserved it. But I did not listen to society. I knew from losing it all that I was going to build this company right. I did it debt free and nothing was going to change that. There were several times I remember talking to myself about the fact that my sales guys made way more than I did and they had none of the stress I was carrying. I learned from the other failed businesses that I needed to be smart and only pay myself what I absolutely needed to live and nothing more.

I started building systems and hiring people to put in the system. I learned to love people and put my staff first before me. I focused on hiring the right staff and started testing personalities to make sure they were a fit. I focused on what they were naturally strong in and putting them to doing those things. That was the magic sauce that changed everything. That is when our growth started to skyrocket and we hit the INC 500 list of the INC 5000 list. This is the elite of the elite. My company, Renown, was ranked 187 of 5000 of the fastest growing companies in the nation in 2017.

In 2018, we hit the list again. People ask me how I grew so fast, and I respond with a quote by Jim Rohn: "Discipline weighs ounces but regret weighs tons." I have had that quote up in my office for years and read it regularly. The truth is, if we would do what we know to do, in every area of our life, life would be amazing. If you read about what you need to learn, and implement, you will have life in the fullest. After losing my dad at such a young age, I was not one to wait around. I truly valued moments and time.

In the start of all this success, I suffered personal tragedy. I lost my sister to throat cancer, then three years later I lost my 26-year-old nephew to cancer, and then a month later I lost my wife to brain cancer. This rocked my world. I will never forget the day my wife fell over with a seizure. Prior to this incident, she was healthy, happy, and loving life. First came the seizure and then the diagnosis of stage four brain cancer. They gave her 4-6 months to live. I knew in my heart that God was good and God could heal her if that was His plan. But it was not. After battling cancer for 13 months, she finally passed away. It was surreal to see my best friend and love of my life deteriorate right before my eyes. She went from fun-loving and having loads of energy to losing her ability to write. Then she lost her ability to speak, so we communicated through a lot of hand motions. I was honest with our boys from the start. They were only 9 and 10 when my wife was battling brain cancer. I would gather my boys and just cry, realizing we were going to lose Mamma. My boys asked a lot about why this was happening and why God would allow this to happen. I kept reminding them that we were blessed with all our amazing years with Mamma and lots of kids have no parents at all.

This loss helped me out with perspective when it comes to life and business. It made me enjoy every moment as a precious gift, not to be run with fear but with excitement for the life and the blessings that I have. I remember the last picture I took of my wife just a week before she died. She could still smile, and you could see her love and passion for me and the boys, as well as the fun that so filled her life. In her own way, she was telling me to have fun with life and not be so serious.

I took that philosophy to my business as well. While all this was going on, my business was growing like crazy because I had poured into my team so much prior to this and found the "secret sauce" for business. My team all stepped up in so many ways. I no longer tolerated negative people in my personal life or business; **if you are in my life**, **you will be positive**. Life is too short to be dragged down by negativity. This experience has made me have a zest for life and realize it is so precious. I am even more positive now than I was before because I really know what the value of a day is worth.

Life has been hard since my wife's death, no doubt. There are times I am lonely, and there are times I miss her like crazy. But I have realized that life is about living it to the fullest, pursuing my dreams, investing in my boys, and growing my team. That is what really matters. Knowing this makes me passionate about helping other companies grow and invest in their teams. And now, I have the pleasure of speaking for large and small audiences on how to hire, grow, and invest in their teams. I love showing others how to become surrounded by superstars. I have an attitude of gratitude.

So, in conclusion, I encourage you to face that fear, go after that dream, start that business you have been talking about. Just get out there and **LIVE**. You were created for greatness. Do not let anyone tell you any different. When you do **THAT THING**, let me know the positive result from you **TRULY LIVING as God created you to**. No matter what you are going through, you are not alone. **Your past has been preparing you for SUCH A TIME AS THIS**.

Let me know how I can help you grow your team by hiring superstars and caring for and investing in your team in ways that resonate with them.

TWEETABLE

Do you want things to change? Are you sick and tired of being sick and tired? Change lanes and really make a difference.

Adam Buttorff is an entrepreneur, sales trainer, speaker, and business coach. He is a fun-loving father of two boys and an avid sand volleyball player. He is passionate about helping others build sustainable businesses, growing people wherever they are in the business chain from owner down to secretary. His company has hit the INC 5000 two years in a row, while Adam has been a speaker at several business conferences, featured on radio shows, and a coach for several businesses.

Contact him at Adam@TodaysChangeAgent.com

CHAPTER 10

From Military to Medicine to Making Millions in Real Estate

Why You Should Keep Searching for Your Purpose

by Thomas Black, M.D.

Setbacks come in many forms. For example, some people experience financial setbacks. Some people experience physical setbacks. Some people experience psychological setbacks.

I experienced academic, professional, and emotional setbacks. That I now can look back on my entire journey and laugh is amazing, because during the times of my greatest disappointments, of which there were many, it was difficult to look beyond how I felt and what was happening in that moment to even imagine the possibilities—but eventually, I did. And what I learned from each disappointment strengthened me in ways I never would have imagined at the time. Perhaps this has happened to you once or twice. Convinced you would prefer to zig rather than zag, turn left not right, or go down and not up, you were handed the opposite, so you begrudgingly accepted the undesired option presented to you...and you thrived. As did I.

Passion Has Never Been My Problem

I've never lacked passion. In my youth, I had an insatiable appetite for everything baseball, from baseball cards, to watching and dissecting Major League games as often as I could, and to eventually playing for my high school team. I would drop everything to do anything that had to do with baseball. Unfortunately, the main thing I dropped was school. My grades were horrible. By the time graduation rolled around, I wasn't sure whether I'd be included in the ceremony. Fortunately, I did graduate, but my poor, dare I say, pitiful academic performance and test scores left me with no options for higher education.

Then, the Navy recruiter called. The thought of joining the military wasn't new to me. In fact, my dad had been nagging me to join the armed forces for some time. At his insistence to "at least learn more about the opportunities and keep an open mind," I reluctantly headed down to the recruitment office.

Clean-cut men in neatly pressed uniforms filled with purpose enthusiastically welcomed me and painted pictures of glory and personal satisfaction. They convinced me I was needed and I could and should make a valuable contribution to our nation. I agreed and underwent the extensive physical and Armed Services Vocational Aptitude Battery to see if I even qualified. Imagine my surprise when the recruiter proclaimed that my scores were excellent, and according to him, I could be anything I wanted. This was the first time I'd ever considered my options to be limitless. Initially, the idea of becoming a medic appealed to me, but after my dad informed me I'd be cleaning up puke for the next five years, I moved to plan B: electronics technician.

In the Navy

About 100 of us headed to Orlando for dreaded boot camp. After a few weeks, the company commander selected two people as company leaders, and one of those selections was…me! This unexpected honor was a pivotal moment. I tasted the pride and accountability of leadership—and I liked it. I surprisingly enjoyed the structure, camaraderie, and deep sense of patriotism that came with being in the military and realized I hadn't been fulfilling my potential.

Bootcamp ended, electronics tech school began, and my motivation and upward momentum was gaining speed. I applied myself and discovered a capacity for learning I'd never experienced in the throes of surviving public schools. My performance, to my family's surprise, was stellar. I gained respect from my peers and instructors, and my new status inspired in me lofty goals that, although unthinkable just a few short years before, were now within reach. I was determined to become a Naval officer and a fighter pilot.

I put everything into attaining my new future, and it paid off. My hard work and high performance earned a chance to attend Naval Academy prep school, a one-year intensive program to compensate for my not-so-great high school performance. Equally encouraging was being awarded a Broaden Opportunity Officer Selection in Training Fellowship. These rewards meant that after I completed the coursework, I would receive a full scholarship to any college that offered a Naval ROTC program. That was quite a leap for a guy who, in the previous year, was essentially locked out of higher education. I was voted class president of the Phase I and Phase II class. My turnaround would be a key reminder that even our darkest hours quickly can be redeemed with focused effort.

Work Hard, Play Hard, Fall Hard

I couldn't help but daydream about my accomplishments and the quickness with which I'd accomplish them. I carefully balanced work and studies and made new friends, most of whom were a few years older. Although we were connected by so many shared experiences, there was one experience I didn't share with them: the ability to legally drink. It felt like a deficit, the one thing that separated me from my peers. I was a worldly 19-year-old after all! Why should I not enjoy the occasional after-class beer or drinks on the town? So, I did what many young, underage kids did and got a fake ID. Despite looking well under my actual age, it worked, and just like that, for a while, life was about as good as it gets.

I continued doing everything within my power to secure the future I'd dreamed of: volunteer work, drill team, leadership roles—you name it. I even retook the SAT, scoring much higher than in high school, and checked all the necessary boxes for a Naval Academy appointment.

The week before graduation, my company formed up outside to perform our regular drill as a demonstration of leadership, discipline, and teamwork. In less than a week, I would be graduating at the top of my class and preparing for my first assignment in Japan—I thought. Unfortunately, during this drill, I left my backpack in the hallway of the training facility. In the process of searching for the backpack to identify the owner, they found my wallet with my ID—and my other ID. It was not good under any circumstances, but it was particularly bad considering I was supposed to have been a leader among my peers with integrity beyond reproach.

Justice is swift in the Navy. Within a just a few days, I was dressed down by my officers in a formal hearing and demoted two ranks below my fellow graduates. In that same setting, my long-awaited appointment to the Naval Academy was presented to me and then ripped to shreds before my eyes. It was devastating. I was humiliated in front of my peers. Two years of hard work and dedication were essentially erased. I still graduated, but the future I'd dreamed about now was in the past. I'd been demoted and demoralized, and I was ashamed.

Inspiration on a Destroyer

My post was changed from Japan to a guided missile destroyer in the Pacific, cleaning toilets and mopping floors. Although this was perhaps the least glamorous job on the ship, it gave me plenty of time to reflect on my very public and humiliating fall from grace. I now understood my potential and was keenly aware of how much I could accomplish if I applied myself. But to what? Lavatory sanitation?

Soon, I was placed in the officers' quarters to suffer a three-month reminder of what could have been, but instead of defeating me, it renewed my drive. I would spent the next three years working my way back up the ranks.

Then, during one of my two deployments in the Persian Gulf, I was assigned to a team that boarded vessels looking for contraband being exported from Iraq. On one occasion, we intercepted a boat that had been afloat at sea without fuel or supplies for a prolonged period. The crew was severely dehydrated and emaciated. The gravity of the situation and the mortality of the individuals on board resonated with me. It was in that instant I knew medicine was my calling.

Again, I was single-minded in my pursuit. I utilized the remainder of my time in the Navy taking as many correspondence courses as I could in my spare time. By the time I left active duty in 1998, I had an associate degree and was one rank above the same group who started two ranks above me. Thanks to the GI bill, I immediately enrolled in college to continue undergraduate coursework. I lived for the competition and thrived in the studies. Finishing one class after another was like climbing a ladder of small goals leading to the ultimate reward of officially becoming a doctor. It was exhilarating. Three years later, I graduated magna cum laude with degrees in biology and biochemistry. Next stop: medical school.

Everything was going according to plan. I got into medical school and graduated in the top ten percent of my class. To scratch my earlier itch of becoming an officer, I joined the Army and accomplished that. After medical school, I did my residency at one of the top emergency residency programs in the country. There was no Army facility nearby, so I switched to the Air Force.

In a Groove? Or a Rut?
Again, life was good. All the years of sacrifice were paying off. By now, I was married to an amazing woman. We had just had our first child, and everything was going according to plan. After residency, my wife and I had more children, and I joined a practice in East Texas as part of an extremely busy ER. I enjoyed the challenge and learned my craft around some amazing practitioners. Things were moving right along. THIS was why I'd trained all these long years! Great! Right? Wrong.

Then the trauma and loss that inevitably comes with being in the emergency room began to slowly chip away at my enthusiasm for my profession. One event in particular was the turning point: a child drowning. Never had I let emotion creep in, but in this case, I saw my young daughter in her face.

Looking back, this was the first of many cases that changed me. Nights became harder. Doubt crept in. Had I made the right choice? Did it matter? I was in too deep. I had an amazing wife and four children and had to provide for them. On the outside, I was a well-trained and seemingly confident and aggressive doctor, but on the inside, I was miserable and knew something had to change.

From the Ground Up

It was around this time that a three-acre lot became available in the small town I lived in. By now, I had some real estate experience under my belt. The house my wife and I bought in residency at the peak of the housing market was undervalued by the time we were ready to sell, so we'd rented it in an attempt to mitigate our losses. When that worked out, we purchased a few more single-family homes, and our little portfolio of rent houses was providing some significant income on the side. If single-family housing could do that, what could multifamily housing do? The town didn't really have much in the way of apartments so what would happen if someone built one?

I bought the three acres and developed a 16-unit apartment complex as a side project. Looking back, it's obvious I had no idea how involved it would be. It was draining. The angst of the construction quickly dissipated when it immediately sold for a $600,000 profit, and suddenly, a whole new world of possibilities opened up. I realized that I didn't have to be beholden to the practice and my paycheck if I had another source of consistent, regular income, and real estate investment could be that source.

Moving On

My wife and I decided to leave the practice, pack up, and move closer to areas of growth where real estate investment opportunities were more easily accessible. I joined an emergency medicine group and started investing, and then an amazing thing happened. Our investments began generating enough cash flow to allow me to reduce the number of ER shifts on my schedule. My life gradually was coming into balance. My new real estate investing hobby was becoming more profitable. I was enjoying the profession I'd sacrificed so much for, and I was spending more time with my family.

When you are excited about something, your natural inclination is to share that excitement with others, which is what I did. After all, I wasn't the only physician who struggled with professional burnout. Countless conversations with my peers were the same: they were overworked, tired, and not enjoying the profession they spent years training for. The only solution, they thought, was to keep going and to work as hard, as much, and as long as possible until inevitably retiring with hopefully enough energy, time, and money to enjoy what was left of life. To find out there was another option was unbelievable for them. Many physicians I spoke with were enthralled with the possibilities, but still a little unsure. It didn't help that they also were overwhelmed with the details of the process. To help get their feet wet, I offered to partner with a few on some multifamily investments, and to my surprise, they were interested.

It must be said that, with the exception of my wife, my family thought the idea of getting involved in such large real estate transactions was insane. Although I'd proven them wrong with my apartment development, they were still apprehensive about the venture as a whole. My brother, Tim, who recently had retired, was included in my circle of skeptics. His most recent position had been with Great Wolf Resorts as their chief operating officer, and he had a phenomenal mind for operations. I'd spent a great deal of time discussing the benefits of real estate investing with him, but could tell he wasn't convinced. It wasn't until he experienced the income and tax benefits of real estate that he really understood the potential.

Investing Is a Team Sport

As I said, I've never lacked passion, and I was definitely passionate about this. By now, I had significant experience, knowledge, and industry contacts, but I did lack organization and operations experience, things that were second nature to Tim. It was a natural next step to put our talents together to help others change their lives, so we founded Napali Capital, a company with that exact goal in mind: to provide investors with opportunities to create wealth through cash flow and sustainable passive income. This was how we could help others find balance and flexibility in their professional commitments.

Our team of two got to work laying the foundation for the company. It didn't take long before we began growing, and pretty soon, we added to our team to keep up with the growth. By the end of the first year, we had five employees and had reached more than 250 investors from 19 different states.

Today, through Napali Capital, I'm in a position to help others avoid the professional pitfalls and burnout I encountered through a balanced life. The satisfaction in knowing my journey led to this is indescribable. I still practice medicine, but on my own terms, and I enjoy it again.

Looking Back and Looking Ahead

I realize that excellence is a decision, and once I decided to excel, I was unstoppable. Were there detours and the occasional dead stop? Yes.

At the time of each failure, did I feel defeated? Unquestionably, yes. But looking back, I learned something valuable from each setback. And what I learned led to a setup for something much bigger than anything I could have imagined at the time. Everything is an opportunity—an opportunity to learn, to make connections, to ask questions, to share experiences with others, to explore other ideas, to create something spectacular. Decide to be excellent. Take these opportunities. You'll never be disappointed.

TWEETABLE

Everything is an opportunity—an opportunity to learn, to make connections, to ask questions, to share experiences with others, to explore other ideas, to create something spectacular.

Thomas Black, M.D., is a practicing board-certified emergency medicine physician, author of bestselling The Passive Income Physician: Surviving a Career Crisis by Expanding Net Worth, *and co-founder of Napali Capital, a Texas-based investment company that creates wealth for investors through real estate-derived passive income. He is also a 13-year veteran of the US Armed Forces and a member of Forbes Real Estate Council. To learn about Napali Capital, visit napalicap.com, or to speak with Tom about creating wealth through passive income—contact him directly at thomas@napalicap.com.*

CHAPTER 11

A Trial That Transformed My Thoughts

by Julian Sado

It was 2003 when I was teaching my seven-year-old son boxing in the garage. I was hiding from my wife because I knew she wouldn't approve. It was exciting for him to learn how to hit and avoid punches. All was going great until…it happened. My son moved in the wrong direction and my focus mitt hit him square in the nose! It was at that very second that I had to think fast. I said to him, "Jordan! You just took a hit from me and you're still standing! You must have mutant powers. I knew you were a superhero when you were born." The tears that were beginning to well immediately dried up.

I was shocked to hear him say, "Hit me again!"

It's a funny story that illustrates how NLP works. My words to him invoked chemicals in his brain which incited particular emotions that sidetracked the shock of the punch. Feeling like a superhero was far better than feeling hurt. We both agreed that, like Superman, it would be best if he kept his identity as a superhero a secret from the world, and most especially from his mom.

As an only child to an absentee alcoholic father, I was raised by a single mom who had to work several jobs to support us. Spending countless hours alone in our apartment or being watched by an adult who was not trustworthy put me in situations where I was repeatedly abused physically and sexually. To cope with this, I created imaginative worlds where I could mentally flee.

By the time I was a teenager at the age of fourteen, I experienced teenage depression before it was recognized to the degree it is today. I lacked discipline in school, my grades dropped, and I became disrespectful and rebellious towards my mom. Her disciplinarian ways were not effective, so she felt forced to kick me out of the house. I had absolutely no place to go, so I ended up living with my alcoholic father in East LA. At the time, this seemed like a great idea, but looking back, I can see that I was only trying to escape the abuse.

One Friday evening, my dad came into my room after getting a letter from the school informing him of my truancies. He was drunk, as always, and I showed no interest in what he had to say. My indifference only infuriated him further. He left the room and returned with his sawed-off double barrel shotgun. Before I had a chance to think, he grabbed me by my arm, threw me against the wall, and pointed his shotgun directly at my face only an inch away. He had this crazed look of hatred in his eyes and said with a deep evil tone, "I should kill you right now."

I had already experienced being beaten up countless times, once even while my father sat and watched as a form of entertainment like he was at a fight-club. I had already been shot at twice, robbed at knifepoint, and was an eyewitness to a man shot to death right in front of me. These were the everyday stories in East LA, but this instant with my father would become a pivotal moment for me.

Time seemed to pass like a slow-motion movie as he stared into my eyes. I could smell the alcohol on his breath mixed with sweat and an unclean odor he always carried. Then, I can only assume a miraculous moment of sanity overcame him. He lowered the gun and began lecturing me on the importance of school and education. My only focus at that moment was the shotgun. After finishing his rant, he left my room. I was left there feeling faint and like I couldn't breathe. At that moment, I was convinced that I wanted to die. I drank several cans of my dad's Colt 45 Malt Liquor and smoked a lot of marijuana. I found that shotgun to see if it was loaded…. It was. All of the suppressed hurt from abuse and feeling like an outsider came rushing in. I knew then that I had always been a burden to everyone, including my mom who always struggled to support me. I felt completely alone and ready to die.

This all took place on a Friday night around 7:00 PM. The radio station always played romantic love songs at that hour. I could hear it in the background, and it only fed my suicidal thoughts. As I put the gun to my head, I felt that I finally had some power. I had the power to end my life. As I sat in my room sobbing and trying to get the nerve to pull the trigger, a song called "Jesus Is Love" by The Commodores came on the radio. If you've ever heard that song, you'd know that it's not a love song, but one of hope. Looking back, I have no idea why the DJ would play such a song for couples trying to get other things on rather than think about church. The song had me crying even more, but for help, not death. I eventually cried myself to sleep with a numbness to what had happened that night.

The next morning, I felt a sense of resolve. I made the decision to completely reinvent myself. I watched the movie *Rocky* over and over again. It hit a chord with me because I could relate to his loneliness. I imagined myself to be like him. I worked out religiously every day to the soundtrack. That same week, I took up boxing in downtown LA. I changed my name from Freddy to Julian. I chose my name because it represented someone who was cool, calm, and in control, which was what I desired to be.

I could end the story here and share how that trial was what made me resilient and how overcoming it changed my path from brokenness to complete success and fulfillment; however, that was not the case. It had become my determination to *survive* my world, but not *master* it.

At the age of sixteen, I signed a record deal with a subdivision of Capitol Records. It did not pan out for me, so I had my fun as a *Soul Train* dancer. Later in my twenties, I worked as a talent agent with Bobby Ball Agency. This opened opportunities to befriend up and coming stars like Lenny Kravitz, El Debarge, and Jennifer Lopez. I eventually quit the talent agency and cut people out of my life for trivial reasons, while later watching their careers soar.

After leaving the entertainment world, I took advantage of the cardio-boxing craze in the mid-90s and developed my own kickboxing program which was unlike anything else out there. It wasn't very long before my notoriety grew and I had contracts with many health clubs throughout California with instructors teaching my program. Having a history as a talent agent also gave me the leverage to work with several well-known entertainers like Bill Bellamy, Sugar Ray Leonard, and Sylvester Stallone. The money and the attention I received was great; but even through it all, I couldn't shake the ongoing depression and loneliness.

It was while I was teaching one of my kickboxing classes that I met the girl who would eventually become my wife. She and I attended pre-marital counseling with a pastor at my church. He challenged me about topics unfamiliar to me like a savings, 401k, medical insurance, etc. In his point of view, I wasn't successful as a fitness business owner, while I thought I had a stable career. Because the depression and anger persisted, I questioned myself and thought maybe he knew something I didn't. After all, he went to college, grew up in a well-to-do home, and appeared to know who he was; so I took his advice and impulsively gave up my fitness business to delve into a new industry in sales.

For the first ten years in my new professional career, my past became exposed. I was now married and with two kids. I was depressed and emotionally unavailable for my family. I appeared to be reliving all of my past childhood emotions.

In business, I moved from sales to management then to consulting. I never felt successful. The focus was to put on a facade of success and happiness to impress our social circle, yet I was truly miserable. I was working 70+ hour weeks. My health was not optimal while living off junk food, having little sleep, commuting through traffic, and having little to no exercise. Not surprisingly, I gained weight and developed health issues. This perpetuated the depression. These subconscious emotions continued to creep into almost every work position I held.

Now with two kids, one wife, a dog, a house mortgage, and having to dress professionally every day for a job I didn't like, I became a victim of fear. I got, what I call, the "what if" virus. I say virus because the fear would remain dormant until some outside force, like the economy, a project, a choice to cut costs or downsize would threaten my position. The fear of losing my job but having to provide for a family of four would grow like a virus, taking over my mind and terrorizing me.

At the end of my rope, I was introduced to books and motivational tapes of well-known speakers like Jim Rohn, Brian Tracy, and Napoleon Hill. I began to listen to those tapes every day while commuting to work. Not long after, I began to work harder on myself than I did on my job. This was an ideology Jim Rohn shared, and I live by it to this day. I continued reading and attending courses to learn and grow. I began sifting through all the information I was attaining and began studying the science of thoughts, energy, and emotions.

These new ways of thinking helped create new choices. By making new choices, my behavior began to transform, and I attracted different people in my life. These people lived in the way that the motivational tapes taught. Their energy was so powerful that I knew just being in their presence would help to change my life.

I never considered the power of my own thoughts and emotions. I simply reacted to them.

Growing up in a theological church, I had studied a lot of biblical theology and world religions. I shifted my focus and began to read books on the spiritual connection between subconscious emotional thoughts and life. These books helped me understand that there is more to life than my past experiences, like the traumatic one I had with my father. They do not have to dictate who I am. I learned to redirect my thoughts away from the past and align them to the experiences I want to have in my life today and in the future.

I gravitated my attention to emotional intelligence, NLP, behavioral coaching, and neuroscience. The more I learned, the more I desired to share. I could not hold back what I was discovering because I could see myself in so many others. Learning how to be street smart, as I did growing up, taught me how to be instinctive by sensing others' intentions and motives. As a consultant, I began feeling the subconscious fears people were hiding in their everyday roles at work, much like I had been doing. At the same time, I realized that the companies' employee retention and satisfaction was being impacted by the employees' emotional triggers. It had less to do with the inadequate job metrics or responsibilities and more to do with each individuals' subconscious perception of self. What a revelation!

Combining the sciences I've studied with my passion for music and fitness, I developed a program called NeuroWhyology®, helping my clients pivot their old ways of thinking by becoming conscious of their subconscious triggers in order to change their habitual behaviors. I initially tested my program on employees of the company I worked for. I won their leadership award eight out of the nine years I was there. I now certify leaders to specialize in this method, becoming NeuroWhyologists®. At last, I found myself and my niche! This prompted me to write a book, *NeuroWhyology®: The Street-Smart Approach to Reinventing Yourself*, soon to be released.

I leave you with these remaining thoughts:

- We are not defined by any type of profession, education, trade, or color of skin.

- We are defined by how we subconsciously feel about ourselves. Those feelings emanate and are what people subconsciously pick up.

- We are all spiritual beings disguised as whatever we are doing at this time.

- To pivot, to change, you have to become conscious of your unconscious self, which is only reacting to survive.

- Resilience has nothing to do with your past.

As Jim Rohn said, "We are the only creature on the planet that lives by choice." I hope to inspire you to turn all the experiences from your past into instinctive opportunities to *choose* your life as opposed to *reacting* to it.

TWEETABLE

If you realized how powerful your thoughts are, you would never think a negative thought again.
— Peace Pilgrim

Julian Sado is a keynote speaker, transformational leader, and behavioral coach who empowers others to understand their true selves. Through Pivot 2 Change, LLC, his personal and business coaching company based in Dallas, TX, Julian infuses behavioral coaching and neuroscience with NLP combined with kickboxing and music to explain the why behind the way you think and act. Knowing your "why" will not only help you grow personally, but also guide you to understand how to better develop your business and brand.

jsado@pivot2change.com

Facebook: Fred Julian-Sado, @pivot2change

LinkedIn: Julian Sado, Pivot2Change

CHAPTER 12

Breaking the Rules and Finding Yourself in the Process

A Hollywood Actress and Producer's Journey

by Lisa Haisha

I moved to Hollywood when I was 22 years old. I'd wanted to be a star since I was ten when my maternal grandmother told me and my four sisters that an intuitive told her that our mom (a Southern belle) would marry a foreigner (which she did), that she'd have five kids, and that one of them would be a star and very rich. I claimed it on the spot, and that moment never left me. I just didn't know how that would work; having an Iraqi father who was very strict—we weren't even allowed to move out of the house until we were married.

My parents ended up divorcing when I was 19 years old, but I was still living under my father's rules. It was tough but doable because of my bigger goal of being an actress in Hollywood. Living at home gave me a chance to stay focused and read and study the biographies of the great actresses of the day and the past as well as save money.

Then one day, a friend told me that Madonna was coming to our school, San Diego State University, to perform her very first live concert, The Virgin Tour. I was ecstatic. Madonna was my hero. She'd broken all boundaries and had a similar situation to mine. Her father was very strict and Italian, but she'd broken through and expressed herself in a way that was groundbreaking at the time. She was self-actualized, while I was still stuck in my cocoon, dying to burst free and fly.

I ended up going to the concert, and afterwards, my friend and I found out where the band was staying and decided to go to their hotel. We sat at the bar, waiting for them to arrive, and finally, an hour later, they showed up. We approached them and told them how much we'd enjoyed the concert, and they invited us up to their room.

We had a great time being in this rare situation. We felt like groupies… really living life. It was a big deal for two small-town girls with no real life experience. I ended up connecting with one of the band members, and we exchanged phone numbers.

Over the next three months, we kept in touch with late-night calls. He kept inviting me to concerts all over the country, but I wasn't allowed to spend the night (even though I was pushing 20 years old). Finally, I decided to meet them at the end of the tour in New York for the grand, five-day finale. I started to save money and decided to add a two-week European vacation. And my Dad's "overnight" rule? I rebelled. I knew it was time to strike out on my own, so I left him a note while he was at work. Sure, he'd probably kick me out when I got back, but I wanted to move to LA anyway. Besides, I knew he loved me and would get over it. Our bond was strong, as I'd been there for him after the divorce; but right now, it was time to let the chips fall where they may.

When I arrived in New York, my "boyfriend" picked me up, and we immediately went to a gathering where I got to meet Madonna. It was the moment I had been waiting for. She was rude at first, not paying me much attention, but after a few days, she warmed up.

I was confused by her behavior. We had such similar conservative upbringings, but she was so liberated! So when I got my chance to have a conversation with her, one of my first questions was, "How did you self-actualize into 'Madonna' from being one of seven children in a patriarchal family?" We spoke for 15 minutes, and here's a paraphrase of what she said:

> "It's hard when you don't have freedom to think the way you want or to experience life freely, but the advice I would give you is to travel. And you have to travel alone, so you can make all the decisions yourself, be brave and meet people, and explore ideas and activities with no judgment from your family or friends. We're so brainwashed from birth and indoctrinated into our parents' viewpoint on life. You have to dig deep and learn who you are—what your soul came here to express."

I took her advice seriously, and that's what I did. I went straight to Europe for a two week exploration of my new ideas. I went with my best friend, but we were very independent on the trip and did our own thing throughout. But, since then, over the past 25 years, I've been to over 80 countries, and in probably 50 or so, I've traveled alone. I meditated in Nepal for days, studied with the Sufis, went to Peru and did ayahuasca, and met with aborigines in Australia. I asked a lot of questions and put myself fully into the experiences that were presented to me.

I soaked up all this knowledge to self-actualize and was told to trust my intuition and expect miracles, because they are everywhere. I was told that everything has already happened and that we just need to claim it. I took that to heart. I felt it meant that if you want something, ask for it, because if it's a strong desire, it is Fate. But be careful what you wish for.

After I returned from my whirlwind vacation, I moved to LA to become an actress, fueled by the memory of my grandma's prediction that I would be a star. I ended up meeting an agent on the train ride up from San Diego (of course, it was meant to be). She got me work right away, and I was booking small jobs and then bigger ones, earning good money. However, I was an ingenue, and everyone wanted me to do eight seconds of nudity (or three seconds) or a love scene, and I had several #MeToo moments. I was way too conservative for all that and had to quit because it was getting too depressing, not being able to take great roles because of the R ratings and the casting people or producers wanting favors on the side.

When I realized acting wasn't for me, I met with the owner of my favorite 24/7 restaurant in Hollywood and suggested we start an open mic night called Hollywood Underground. He got on board and said he was open to it. It would be from 1:00 am to 4:00 am, when business was slow. Almost immediately, we welcomed stars like Chaka Khan, The Brat Pack, and Iggy Pop, since the restaurant was already a hot spot for celebrities. Watching these stars create material each week to perform and test inspired me to write. So I started writing my first screenplay with the help of a book called *How to Write a Movie in Twenty-One Days* by Viki King.

Then, just as funds were getting low, I got invited to go to Japan for a three-month modeling gig. I took it and pitched the idea of investing in a Hollywood movie to everyone I met. I ended up raising a million dollars. That lead to me producing, writing, directing, and acting a part in an independent feature film called *Psycho Sushi*. It wasn't the best film ever made, but the experience was invaluable.

After making the movie, I realized that we do all have a destiny to a certain extent, but achieving our desires is about whether you take the torch and follow through with it, whether you're able to see the miracles presented to you, and whether your mind is free from chatter enough to hear the whispers of your higher self guiding you toward your dream. You have to be brave and believe in yourself. You don't have to know "how" you'll get there, but you do need to follow the breadcrumbs.

When the film project was finished, I had a lot of questions about my Iraqi heritage, which I felt had held me back my whole life, especially in the areas of decision-making, people-pleasing, and relationships.

My childhood was still affecting my life, like it does for most people. I felt I was still just rebelling or conforming, but nothing was real, from my soul. So I read self-help books and attended workshops, but it seemed like going to Iraq and learning about my father's culture would be most beneficial— so that's what I did. I asked family members and friends to join me, but everyone thought it was too dangerous or didn't have the patience or time. So, I decided to go alone and booked a plane ticket for a month's stay.

The year was 1998. I booked a ticket to Jordan because at the time there were no flights into Iraq because of the "no-fly zones" due to the Gulf War. I made my connection in New York. At the airport, I met a woman who was also going to Iraq. She was an attorney from Michigan a few years younger than me, and we connected right away. We both were looking for an adventure and to be inspired. We knew we were heading into danger, and it didn't really matter to us what happened. I asked why she was going, and she said, "I want to die but can't commit suicide because it'll hurt my family."

And I said, "I want to get kidnapped so I can escape and write a tell-all book about the experience." We both laughed.

Though we were both somewhat successful and high-functioning, we were both broken in other ways, feeling depleted and dead inside. We wanted to see action, to put ourselves in a situation that would wake us up. At heart, we were both funny, alive, and adventurous people, not so much depressed as just wanting to feel alive again. She wasn't really suicidal, and neither was I. We could even laugh at our horrible states of mind, and yet it was serious enough to cause us to set out for Iraq alone—until we found each other.

We landed safely in Amman, Jordan, and learned that on the bus ride from Jordan to Iraq there were five stops where people were often robbed or kidnapped. Whenever we stopped, everyone was quiet, but we made an extra effort to start a conversation with the Generals checking our bags for paraphernalia or anything not allowed. They couldn't be nicer—all five stops. We made it safe and sound to the El Rasheed Hotel, where all the journalists and media stayed because it was in the Green Zone, in the center of Baghdad. So, now we just had to figure out how to meet Saddam and ask him questions and meet his sons, or somebody in power.

My dad and my new friend were both born in Tel Keppe, an Assyrian town in northern Iraq (the same town where Saddam was born). When we visited, all they had was caves connected to each other where people lived, a school, an ice cream truck, a liquor store, a church, and an orphanage.

We went into the orphanage and started talking to the kids. They asked us, "Why does the world hate us? Why doesn't anyone love us? Why do they let us hurt like this?" I fell in love with these kids. I saw myself in them. I had felt the same way. I wanted to give them a voice and memorialize their words.

I visited more orphanages in Jordan and then Israel and talked to the children there. Over the next five years, I went to 15 countries to visit orphanages, and I asked the children the same three questions: Is God fair? If you had one wish, what would it be? Who in the world would you want to meet and why? That ended up becoming a book, *Whispers from Children's Hearts*. That book launched my speaking career. I spoke in schools and gatherings across the globe, sharing the words of the unheard children.

I continued traveling the world and aiding SOS orphanages located in 135 countries. Soon, other people became interested in getting involved. That turned into a non-profit. I didn't charge money, but rather everyone who joined had to bring a suitcase of stuff and help. We'd visit orphanages or just knock on poor people's homes near the orphanages to ask them what they needed. If they needed a new roof, we'd hire a local roofer, so every penny spent went to the community and the kids.

After doing that work for years, I decided to adopt a daughter. It was a magical experience and helped me heal in more ways than I could ever have expected. I got to put my energy into giving to someone else and focus less on me. She was so full of joy and love and made me laugh so much...still does!

However, I couldn't travel as much now that I had a child, so I transitioned to using my reputation to highlight other people who were doing amazing work on a grassroots level locally in the US. I put on an annual Legacy Gala with over 300 guests, raised 20k for their non-profit, and gave them a lot of publicity with over 30 media outlets present.

When I did travel, I brought my daughter to do social work, helping build and repair schools and playing with the kids in various orphanages. Watching my daughter make friends with kids in different countries has been incredible. I want to pass the torch to her so she can continue to live her life with an open heart, be aware of all the diversity in the world, and not be threatened by other cultures or religious beliefs.

This part of my personal journey has helped me let go of my "shoulds" and my desire for achievement and material things. Now it's all about what I can give back. Once you make that switch, your whole life changes.

Feeling so overwhelmed that you can't give back is a warning signal that something is not right in your life. No one should be overwhelmed. When you break it down, getting through life can be challenging; but when you layer it with insecurity, self-doubt, self-loathing, excuses, and no discipline or focus, everything can feel unmanageable.

Perhaps it's because you're not going within and saying, "If this is the goal I want, will this choice move me closer or further away from my goal?" You have to be present, meditate, and go within. Before I went to Iraq, I had many setbacks in life despite my successes. I second-guessed myself and couldn't connect deeply with others. I didn't know who I was, so I flew whichever way the wind was blowing.

But in Iraq, by listening to the children's voices, I found my own voice and took back my power. I made the conscious choice to learn about my heritage, give back, and be of service. Then I starting doing TM (transcendental meditation) to help me stay grounded in my values, beliefs, and who I am. I was no longer indecisive, insecure, and living with a closed heart.

If, like me, you've gone off course, know that you can get back on track. But first, you have to know what you stand for, because when you discover your core values and belief system, you will not waiver. It won't matter how much someone tempts you. But if you don't know what your values are, you just blow with the wind and then beat yourself up when you don't achieve what you desire. You realize that you're not trustworthy, so you have to rebuild that relationship with yourself. You must stop chasing no's and start embracing yes's.

Today, I teach clients how to do this through a process I call Soul-Blazing. We talk about the "eight Impostors" who live on the stage of your brain, wreaking havoc in your life, and about your Authentic Soul, who lives on that very same stage. We have to train the Imposters and put a leash on them. Our Authentic Souls know who we are, why we're here, and our mission on this Earth. Once you discover this, you get solid and grounded. Then, through meditation, you can keep it steady. Going within, not without. Digging deeper, not wider.

Awareness is an essential ingredient in a fulfilled life. If you would just spend 10-15 minutes in the morning planning your day, if you would just set your intentions—even in just a two-minute meditation; if you would just do your affirmations, stretch, look in the mirror and tell yourself that you love you—or whatever it takes so that you feel you're showing up for you, then the rest of the day will just run itself.

I delve into this in my show, *Soul-Blazing with Lisa Haisha*, on Amazon. I interviewed thought leaders, trailblazers, and *Guinness Book of World Records* holders to get their story of how they made it, the choices they had to make, and the obstacles they had to overcome. It's about the baby steps they took, how they showed up for themselves, and how other people showed up for them. If you have one person who believes in you, that's really all you need.

Now I'm back in LA, writing my travel memoir, which I'm hoping to turn into a feature film. It's a way to share my adventures around the globe and help others discover their life purpose without traveling all the miles.

I also continue to run the Whispers from Children's Hearts Foundation, healing children worldwide through international humanitarian missions.

People say I'm lucky, that life just works out for me. I am not lucky. My life is very conscious. I show up for myself, and when I do, my choices are different.

Your obstacles are all in your head. Your success is determined by what you believe you can do and you stepping into opportunities. Success is about not having fear of the unknown, not having fear of people, not feeling that you're "less than." It doesn't matter where you are in life, it's who you are. If you don't show up for yourself or give yourself self-love, you can never be there for others and others can't fully be there for you.

TWEETABLE

You don't have to know where you're going. You just need to go inward each day and connect to your higher power, and the answers will come. Follow the breadcrumbs and your life will unfold.

Lisa Haisha, M.A.'s mission is to revolutionize global consciousness. She is an experienced life coach who founded The SoulBlazing™ Institute and the nonprofit foundation Whispers from Children's Hearts. Lisa teaches women, men, and couples how to "show up" in their lives with her fearless expression as a globally sought-after life counselor, life coach, and mentor. She helps people discover answers to perennial, soul-searching questions through SoulBlazing™, a process she created using her Impostor Model™. Her popular, decades-old work has garnered the attention of Hollywood's elite, helping them deal with ego, fear, and shame, which gives her unique insight into the minds of powerful leaders.

Lisahaisha.com | Twitter: @LisaHaisha

CHAPTER 13

The Three Lessons of BE DO HAVE

by Michael Blank

At The Real Estate Guys Investor Summit at Sea in 2018, Robert Kiyosaki came on stage to talk about BE, DO, HAVE. It wasn't about making more money, paying less taxes, or how messed up our school system is, it was about getting your BEING right before you can do anything of meaning.

You have to BE someone first before you can DO and HAVE. For example, if you want a million dollars so you can quit your job, the DO part is completing your first deal so you can then HAVE more. The doing part is clear. The more fundamental question is, who do you have to BE before you start to DO and HAVE the things you want? That question is something I discounted as hooey for a long time. But if I reflect on my own past, this is so profound.

A lot of the BE has to do with your character, and frankly, your relationship with God and your spirituality. Over the last 12 years since I became a full-time entrepreneur, there have been three key lessons I had to learn before I could be successful.

When I started entrepreneurship in 1997, I joined a software startup called webMethods. It was the right place at the right time. Three years later we had gone from zero to $200,000,000 in revenue and had the most successful software IPO in history.

It was an unbelievably heady time, putting a bunch of money in my pocket and making me appear and feel successful.

As I was reading biographies and autobiographies of numerous important and famous people, I noticed that all of them had failures—sometimes massive and repeated failures. I really hadn't failed at anything. I was successful; I had all this money in the bank, I had a family, I had a nice house. So I felt something was wrong either with those people or something was wrong with me.

So, I read *Rich Dad Poor Dad* in late 2004, and in 2005 I left my job in pursuit of passive income. Looking back now, my being was not ready. It was so far from being ready that I ended up losing my entire net worth in the next seven years.

Lesson 1: I don't control anything.

I felt very successful. I felt like I controlled my destiny. I did a good job with my career. I was climbing the ladder very successfully. But when I went out on my own, I discovered the truth.

My big idea wasn't real estate as I am in today. It was a series of pizza restaurants. I knew people involved in franchises, and the idea was that someone else would run everything while I sat back and counted the passive income. That's exactly what I wanted. I did a little bit of everything after I quit my job (flipping houses, apartment building boot camp, trading stocks and options), but franchise pizza restaurants were my big idea.

We built our first restaurant in 2006, then bought a franchisee out, and then built another one. In 6-9 months, we had three restaurants. I hired a capable, experienced multi-unit operator. We were doing really well, except for that second restaurant we bought. That one we struggled with. It had poor sales when we took it over, $6,000 a week, and was losing money. But I felt I had a knack for marketing and my operator had a knack for operations, customer service, and team-building. It was working in the other two restaurants, but in this one we just couldn't seem to move the needle. In fact, we were losing more and more money.

It was unbelievably frustrating. Nothing I tried did anything. In six months we had moved the needle from $6,000 to $6,400 a week in sales. I had to start making money. The first restaurant wasn't really making money because it was new, and losing money every month was putting me in panic mode. I could see this turning into a complete nightmare. I wasn't used to losing $10,000 a month. I was used to making $10,000 a month on a salary.

I got the strong sense that, despite my best efforts, I couldn't control the outcome for the first time in my life. It was the most unbelievably painful experience. I thought I was successful; I thought I was ready, and, all of a sudden, nothing I did worked or mattered at all. It was my first lesson in: you don't control anything.

I remember having a conversation with God: *You got me into this! And I refuse to believe that you are going to let me fail.* In that moment I took a pause. Instead of being angry with God, I started asking myself, what should I be learning? I got the strong sense that I needed to learn something. It was that I needed to give up control.

Once I gave this up, I got a sense of peace around me. And then, you're not going to believe this, a week later sales went up to $7,500! The week after that, we were going into December (which is usually slow in the beginning then picks up towards the holidays before dipping again in January), sales were still at $7,500. The week after that they went to $8,500. The week after that they went to $9,500. And then, the slowest week of the year, the first week in January, sales went up to $10,500! Sales increased by $4,000 in just four weeks! Insane, right?

It was so clear that I had nothing to do with that. It was God telling me He exists. And that He is in control. And that, yes, I had done a good job. I grew up Christian, and I went to church all the time. But I had never really tested or exercised my faith. I never really had to. If you're successful all the time, why do you need faith? This was one of the biggest faith experiences I have had.

Lesson 2: Find peace regardless of what is going on around you.
I finally purchased an apartment building in 2011, and it was a complete nightmare.

It was the worst case scenario. I had a tenant who was not paying rent, but worse than that, he was a professional tenant who used the system. He was trying to make my life difficult for me by making me go bankrupt.

My first apartment building was also my first syndication, which was really cool. Then this happened. This tenant wouldn't pay rent. Then, every time we walked in there to work on our renovation, he would call the permit guy who would come out to the property and, of course, would always find something wrong, resulting in fines. In the great district of Washington DC, to replace a fixture, you actually need a permit. And it takes four hours to pull a $25 permit, and only a licensed plumber can do that. They will happily wait in line for a $500 fee. And if you don't get that permit and you get caught, they charge you $1000.

My tenant was doing this among other things, including persuading other tenants not to pay rent, on a consistent and frequent basis. He would sue me in housing court over these ridiculous things every six weeks! He made our lives miserable. This went on for almost two years. The judge realized we had better do a mediation.

It was my first apartment deal, my first investors, and things were not going well at all. In fact, I was going to run out of money. A lot was riding on this. My goals depended on me successfully moving into multifamily. Even though I had learned that I don't control anything, I was getting really tense again.

A week before the hearing, I got this strong sensation that I was supposed to learn something. The lesson I found and felt very strongly was that I needed to learn to be at peace regardless of what was going on around me. Now that I knew I didn't control anything, I needed to see how I reacted to things I couldn't control. I was reacting in a very stressed, high anxiety way. I was reminded, you don't control everything, give it up, be at peace.

It was like a physical weight was lifted from my shoulders. I slept all night long, and I was fine all the way to that hearing.

The day of the hearing, the judge was reviewing the cases the tenant had brought against me. The tenant knew the law well and caught me in technical details again and again. He was a smart guy. The judge looked over at him and said, "Are you serious?" Each of the charges were so ridiculous and over the tiniest things. I didn't say anything, at peace. After a half hour of review, the tenant stood up and requested a few minutes to speak alone with me. I was startled. Before I knew it, the judge and my property manager were out of the room. Within five minutes, they came back, and when the judge asked my tenant what he wanted to do, he said he was going to drop all charges.

Next thing I know, I was down in the cafeteria chatting with my tenant like long lost friends. I just couldn't believe it. The tenant told me, "I'll take care of the back rent. You don't have to worry about me anymore." I was there, but to this day, I don't know how in the world that happened.

I'm not saying there was cause and effect, I'm only stating what happened. It was nothing I did or anything anyone else did. By the grace of God, he stopped doing what he was doing. It was amazing. These things happen and you start developing a peace around yourself.

This prepared me for the third lesson.

Lesson 3: Give rather than get.

The restaurants became a real problem. In 2012, the margins had shrunk.

I had gotten very complacent. I had six restaurants, and I was meeting with the manager once a week so we could pat each other on the shoulder and counting my passive income. I was in a state of semi-retirement, flipping houses, having a good ole time.

In the meantime, I hadn't noticed that our sales had kept going down and our costs kept going up.

All of a sudden, we bounced a payroll check. I was perplexed. There should have been $30-40,000 in the account. What the heck was going on?

I looked into the business, and oh my gosh, we were in trouble—serious trouble.

Within three months I had to let my vice president go. He was doing a great job, but I just couldn't afford him anymore. Suddenly, I was running six restaurants.

I had no interest in running restaurants whatsoever, that's why I set it up as a passive investment from the beginning. But I decided to focus on turning this around. I worked with the managers. We did customer service. We introduced core values. But it was like trying to catch a falling knife. Nothing I did mattered.

We started getting to a break-even point, and I knew it was time to sell. I listed all six for sale. They weren't selling. And the situation was worsening.

Before you know it, I was losing $10,000 a week. This time, I didn't have any money left. I started to run out of any kind of liquidity, debt or otherwise. Shortly, I was going to lose everything and probably be sued on top of it.

It was this really, really stressful situation. Even so, I was relatively calm. If this had happened three years earlier, it would have been really bad for me. I couldn't have handled it.

This time I knew to ask, what should I be learning?

Leftover from the software days, we have a vacation house an hour out of town. I planted a bamboo grove out there. I decided to spend a lot of time sitting in this bamboo meditating, praying, and thinking about what I should be doing next.

I spent hours and hours reflecting. I think when you get silent, you think much more deeply. You become aware of things you were not aware of before. One of the things that kept coming up was all the times I was teaching something. I taught tennis after college. I developed an adult literacy class for a community college that was built around Robert Kiyosaki's Cashflow game. I rolled out a financial literacy course at our church. And I gave a one day course on how to buy apartment buildings three years prior. Every time I did that, I felt truly alive.

I got the strong impression that I needed to help others become better entrepreneurs and become financially free. That was the path I was on. I was struggling at the moment, but I had learned so many things that could help others, and I had also had measurable success. I felt like I could spare other people a lot of grief by sharing things that worked and things that did not work.

Of all the things I have done, the apartments buildings, from a startup and passive income perspective, checked off more boxes than anything else I have done or seen other people do. In that moment I decided I would share how to raise money, how to buy apartment buildings, and how to build from there.

The only problem was that the business plan sucked. I researched the online business. I knew you had to put out content, you had to do guest posts, you had to build your list, and maybe two or three years down the road, if you're lucky, you could monetize and it would grow into something—maybe.

And so, I did it anyway.

I started blogging on BiggerPockets. I put up a website and an ebook. People were asking me how to analyze deals, so I polished up my deal analyzer which I used for over 300 deals in Texas back in 2007. People loved it.

It snowballed. As I was raising money for apartment buildings and sharing with others, the whole venture became more and more successful.

Today my company is one of the leading authorities on teaching people how to invest in apartment buildings with a special focus on raising money.

We offer online training, coaching, and live events and have helped people purchase over 2000 units.

That moment in the bamboo when I switched from getting to giving is when everything changed.

I didn't have my BEING right, and so the DO and HAVE parts weren't working. I had been a selfish control freak who had a knack for worrying. At the heart of this lesson was a huge dose of surrender.

Work on your BEING first so that you can DO and HAVE whatever you want.

TWEETABLE

Work on your BEING first so that you can DO and HAVE whatever you want.

Michael Blank is the leading authority on apartment building investing in the United States. He's passionate about helping others become financially free in 3-5 years by investing in apartment building deals with a special focus on raising money. Through his investment company, he controls over $30 million in performing multifamily assets all over the United States and has raised over $10M. In addition to his investing activities, he's helped students purchase over 2000 units valued at over $55M through his unique "Deal Desk" and training programs. He's the author of the bestselling book Financial Freedom with Real Estate Investing *and the host of the popular* Apartment Building Investing *podcast.*

To learn more about Michael, please visit www.TheMichaelBlank.com.

RESILIENCE

CHAPTER 14

From Jail to Millions

by Chad Kneller

turned 30 on July 18, 2003, and little did I know, my life would radically change the very next month. I was singing with One Shot Twice, and our drummer's son's best friend had just died in a car wreck. We decided to do a benefit at a little bar in Hudson, Illinois.

I was focused on the band when she walked in—a beautiful stranger. When I saw Jaree, the sight of her took my breath away because she was so incredibly beautiful. She didn't fit in at that little place and was completely out of my league. All I could mutter to my friend Tim was, "She is my future wife." He elbowed me and said, "No, she's my future wife."

I knew I had to meet her but was nervous about the how. Shortly after my band played, she thanked me for volunteering to play and assist with the benefit. I asked for her phone number, and she gave it to me! Later that night, I called her and asked if she would meet me out for karaoke.

That was 15 years ago, and we have been inseparable since. Jaree had traveled two hours to attend the benefit because the guy who passed was a close friend. Meeting Jaree lit a fire that I didn't even know was in me. I thought I had already missed my opportunity.

Why was I given a second chance in life? I don't know. Maybe it was because shortly before this encounter, I sent up a desperation prayer. I said, "God, I need your help. Trying to do this on my own isn't working." I believe saying that prayer was crucial. I believe that God heard me and sent the woman who would give me the courage to change.

Jaree will tell you that meeting me saved her life too. When she arrived at that benefit she was looking for a way to escape her abusive boyfriend. She had already been wounded, broken, and fractured by other men, but this guy was the worst. She had also recently prayed, and I was part of the answer that she needed.

About two weeks into our relationship, we went out to sing karaoke. You can imagine my embarrassment when I was taken away for having six warrants.

One was for public urination and the others were almost as bad. Without hesitation, Jaree went to the ATM and got the money to bail me out. That's when I knew I had found the right woman. If she would walk with me through my past mistakes, then I knew we could build a future together.

At the time I met Jaree, I was earning $2000 in a good month, and she had started waitressing at Cracker Barrel. What had started off being a few hundred dollars in tickets would end up costing us thousands of dollars and a two-week stay in jail. Going to jail was a wake-up call for me and was not helpful to our financial situation.

Jail was a culmination of all the bad decisions that I had made over a decade. Time exposed every area of my life during this season, and I got to sit in the big house for two weeks and reflect and reset. I see now how perfect the timing was in all this. Without jail, I'm not sure I would have ever slowed down enough to focus on my life and what needed to change.

During those two weeks in my cell, I picked up a Bible and read the entire book for the first time. I had heard some of the stories, but this time the book came to life. I felt my heart begin to change. I knew that when I left jail, I would implement major life changes, and things would be completely different.

I've always heard that behind every man is an amazing woman. This is 100 percent true in my case. My bride has consistently stretched and challenged me in every way. God knew it was going to take an extremely strong-willed woman to change me, and that is exactly who He sent. She didn't put up with any crap. She has always loved me fiercely, stood firm in her convictions, and not compromised on her beliefs.

We needed each other to grow, but I needed her more. My greatest accomplishment in life was getting Jaree to marry me. I'm dedicated to proving to her for the rest of my life that she made the right decision.

When we got married, she was already eight months pregnant. We lived in a spare section of her grandparent's house and were living on around $500 a week. I bought her a cubic zirconia ring that cost less than $150 and my ring was even less.

After marriage, having faced my past, and having child #1 on the way, I was truly excited about the future. Jaree and I had decided to become Christians and make the life-changing choice to accept Jesus Christ as our personal Lord and Savior. I was thirty years old and felt like life was finally beginning.

After we started our family, I had the idea to join the military. I soon finished my degree and became an officer. I originally thought that I would serve for twenty years and retire, but God had other plans.

After serving for eight years, things started to happen which opened my mind to a career change. It started with mandatory 10-hour days, and then one- to two-week training periods that caused me to miss important events such as my daughter's birthday.

In 2012, three things happened that would drastically alter our family's future forever. These three things quickly opened my mind to a drastic and immediate career change. At the beginning of 2012, I intended to serve in the military until I was forced to leave, and by the end of the year, I couldn't leave fast enough.

I met Chase Prasnicki for the first time while going through field artillery officer training in 2011. He was a rare individual who was amazing in every way. It seemed as if everything he touched turned to gold. He was all-American in every sense of the word.

Chase was a West Point graduate and football alumni who could have done anything in life but chose to serve in the Army. Everyone who knew him loved him. He was a natural-born leader, incredible athlete, extremely intelligent, and he genuinely loved people. I cherish the time I had studying with him and our long conversations about leadership and marriage. Chase was married in November 2011, right before reporting to his first duty station in Germany.

In late June of 2012, I was in Fort Polk, Louisiana, training for an upcoming deployment when I got the tragic news. Chase had been deployed to Afghanistan, and on the fourth day, he selflessly volunteered to lead a patrol. During the mission, his vehicle hit an IED, and he suffered catastrophic brain trauma. He passed away on June 27, 2012.

When I heard the news, it rocked me.

Chase was the last person I thought this would happen to. He seemed invincible like some sort of superhero. This news rocked my world and reminded me of my own fragility. For the first time, I began to ask myself some questions. What if this happened to me? What would that look like for my family? Should I serve another ten years in the Army?

These questions led me to the realization that I wanted to do things that mattered with my family in a stable and safe environment.

First Lieutenant Chase Prasnicki was a true all-American who willingly laid down his life for his friends. He sacrificed himself so that our families could sleep in peace at night. I wear a memorial bracelet in honor of his sacrifice that reminds me to make each day count. Your days and mine are numbered, and we don't know how many we have left.

After I learned of his death, I viewed my upcoming deployment through a whole new perspective. This was not some video game where you get extra lives. This was a real enemy, with real bullets, in a country where most people did not like us nor want us there.

Should the unthinkable happen, I decided to take the family on an epic vacation before deploying. What better place to go to than Disney World? You can imagine my children's excitement when I shared the news that we would be heading to The Magic Kingdom of Disney in October 2012. My kids were counting down the days, and we had less than two weeks to go when I got the news. Some unexpected pre-deployment training came up, and I would have to cancel my vacation and save it for after.

I could live with the vacation being canceled, but breaking the promise to my kids was rough. I will never forget the alligator tears rolling down my daughter's face when she said, "Daddy, you said we were going. Why can't we go?" Her little mind could not comprehend why I had to break my word to her. It was heartbreaking to cancel those plans with my kiddos. Due to my military commitment, I had to break trust with the ones I cherished the most.

The harsh reality was that as long as I was a soldier, I would not have time freedom. The military demands your best and your first. I enjoyed leading soldiers but wasn't sure I wanted to continue for another decade.

At the end of October, I deployed to Afghanistan. My mission was to lead a small squad of six men and train the Afghan Army on how to operate their artillery. We would be responsible for three different locations and have to travel periodically to train, qualify, and oversee our Afghan artillery operations. During a layover in the Bagram airport, I jumped on the Wi-Fi to check on friends and family. My wife had made a post on Facebook about our son Elijah. Here is the post I read on December 21, 2012:

> *Elijah has Meckel's diverticulum. He is getting his blood transfusion now and is headed back for surgery. Please pray. This surgery is extremely risky because of the croup he was just diagnosed with on Tuesday. The doctor said the only reason they are doing the surgery now with all his breathing complications is because he's bleeding out faster than they can get blood in. Chances are he will have to be put on a ventilator for several days in order to keep him in stable respiratory condition. That means the machine will breathe for him while he's sedated. I'm a wreck and really need my spiritual family to cover us.*
>
> *Love you all and will update soon.*

I immediately began to make arrangements to leave Afghanistan to go support my family. I assumed the plane ticket could be rerouted, and that I could sign my weapon over to my platoon sergeant then begin the journey home. But that wasn't the case. I had to fly the wrong direction, have a 24-hour layover, and fly back to the airport all to sign a couple pieces of paper. I could not believe it. At that point, I mentally retired from the Army. I knew that I would have to make some serious changes before I could officially leave. I had a lot of time on the way home to do some thinking and began to formulate a plan.

I arrived home on Christmas Eve of 2012, just hours after my son had been released from the hospital. I remember being so thankful to wake up on Christmas with us all back together.

A few months before I deployed, one of Jaree's friends reached out to her about a health product she was excited about. Jaree began to investigate, and the more she learned, the more excited she became. She said she wanted to try the products, and if we liked them, we could start our own business with the company.

We tried some of the health products with this new company and immediately fell in love with them. We jumped right in and started telling the world about what we had discovered. In our very first full month, we earned over $2000 with the five ways the company paid.

Because I was able to come home, we were able to attend a business conference in January of 2013. Towards the end, our CEO put out this crazy promotion. He said, "If you can promote twice by March, you will earn a $25,000 bonus."

So Jaree looked at me and said, "Is that even possible?"

I said, "Honey, through Christ all things are possible." I had heard that over and over, but I finally believed it. We went home super motivated to build something that could get me out of the military.

Over the next 101 days, we promoted three times and earned all kinds of bonuses. We went from never earning six figures to being a multiple six-figure family ever since. We got so excited about this business that we earned over one million dollars in less than three years.

I was recently honored to be on a leadership panel to share about the importance of a *why* on stage in front of 20,000 people in Tampa, Florida.

When you have a strong *why* and are willing to put in the work, you become unstoppable, and your success becomes inevitable! The *why* is essential.

Most people spend more time every year planning their two-week vacation than they do thinking about their life. Our *why* is what gives us the fuel to make serious changes. Our *why* is what makes our reasons strong and excuses very small. It's where our passion and our excitement come from. When someone has a really strong *why* and they put in the work, they will literally become unstoppable, and success becomes inevitable. That's how strong the *why* is.

Between my buddy Chase passing, my family vacation being canceled, and the struggle to get home from deployment during the emergency, I had all the reasons I needed to transition out of the military. Resigning my commission took about six months, and I officially separated from the military on February 1, 2014. We have been a full-time family who have experienced total and complete time and financial freedom ever since.

Through this process, I learned the important lesson that if I would change then everything would change for me. My wife and I are living, breathing examples that if you dream big and work hard then anything is possible!

TWEETABLE

When you have a strong **why** and are willing to put in the work, you become unstoppable, and your success becomes inevitable!

Chad Kneller is the founder and CEO of Made For More Inc., a company dedicated to bridging the gap between reality and possibilities for aspiring entrepreneurs. Mr. Kneller served as an Army officer after pursuing a music career in the rock and roll industry. He represented the US Army in 2009 in Operation Rising Star and was a top six international finalist. He's had the opportunity to speak in front of tens of thousands of entrepreneurs over the last six years and is a highly sought-after sales trainer in the field of health and wellness. You can learn more about Mr. Kneller and his family at www.made4more.biz or reach him at madeformoreinc@gmail.com

CHAPTER 15

Practice and Grow Happy
Your Angst is Your Liberation

by Greg & Daniel Zlevor

When my kids were still young and needed me, my marriage ended in divorce. I moved out and into a one bedroom apartment. The kids visited infrequently, our relationship strained by the divorce and my feelings of failure. On weekend nights, glum and alone, I regularly traveled into Boston to feed and meet the homeless because I too felt alone and homeless without my family. The pain of the divorce not only tore us physically apart, it tore us mentally, emotionally, and spiritually. My kids became remote and separated by the hurt and loss. They were feeling pain and confusion. Living alone, I could do little to repair the broken tie. I needed to keep active by doing something meaningful. I struggled. A lot. It was a painful time for all of us.

Can you make it through anything no matter what?

Resilience is a superpower, but you don't have to be born with it. It can be learned; it is a habit like any other. We learned through challenges. You can too.

Daniel and I are a father and son who have been on a journey to become more resilient. Together, we've been learning how to embrace challenges, see obstacles in a new way, and grow from even the toughest experiences, including divorce.

But how did we end up where we are today? It all turned a corner when Daniel called and said, "Dad, this is my last year in college, and there are a lot of things I want to learn from you before I graduate. Let's spend the summer together."

Stunned, I didn't talk for three hours. Wow! This was a big step. This was every father's dream. But the stretch over the last ten years was tossed waters—times of memories and connection interspersed with misconceptions, indifference, arguments, and missing moments.

Four things got us through that choppy period—hope, encouragement, time, and eventually clarity. Hope sprung from the desire to be together. We shared experiences like homework, evening workouts, or sports. For me, encouragement came from friends—"Healing takes time. Reach out again."

Daniel told me, "Even if we kids don't want to be with you, it doesn't mean we don't want to be loved by you. Please keep loving." Encouragement from family and friends picked me up. Over time, the pain lessened. Finally, clarity ensued. I found new strength. Daniel saw that it's healthiest not to take sides. The subsiding fog allowed us to grow again. Today we have clarity. Today we deeply love, care, and support each other.

So, and with those words "Let's spend the summer together," our potential for love and connection grew. All the work and mature effort of the past ten years materialized in this phone call. We decided on a theme of growth and resilience, and we spent several days together that summer, reading and discussing ideas around resilience, building our "resilience muscles," and learning to see things from a different point of view. At the end, we participated in a silent retreat that helped us crystallize a lot of these ideas.

What we discovered this summer has been life-changing. These are the six most valuable lessons we've learned about resilience:

INSIGHT #1: Resilience is a mindset.

Daniel: I started thinking about resilience during my semester abroad in Barcelona. At the time, I was surrounded by people who spent most of their time going out, partying, and enjoying themselves in the moment. But every morning at 6 am, as they were coming back from the clubs, I was getting up for a two-hour workout.

"They're all about happiness in the present," I remember thinking, "But I care more about creating future happiness." That's what I told myself as I ran dozens of sprints or knocked out a hundred push-ups. I had decided that life was a trade-off between present and future happiness, and instead of being happy now, I was going to be happy later when all my hard work paid off.

But you know what forced me out of bed all of those mornings? Honestly, it was mostly the massive sense of anxiety and pressure that I was putting on myself. It's safe to say that I was definitely not happy at that point, and I had talked myself into believing that was okay because it would all pay off later.

But one day, I stopped long enough to ask myself, "Why am I choosing anxiety?" Why was I stuck in this mental tug-of-war between present and future happiness? Why couldn't I be happy both now and later?

I knew I needed to change something, so I changed my mindset.

First, I refocused on the "why" behind all those early morning workouts. Knowing my "why" allowed me to enjoy the journey, even on those mornings that I just wanted to stay in bed. Yes, I kept waking up at 6 am, but instead of focusing on how tired I was and how tough the workout was going to be, I began to focus on the fact that I really wanted to get into great shape. That was my "why." It allowed me to be happy in the present, even as I worked towards happiness in the future.

I learned that knowing the "why" behind what you're doing can help get you through even the biggest challenges. If you can change your mindset, you can transform any challenge from something that you dread to something that gives you a sense of purpose—and with that, maybe even a little happiness.

Greg: When Daniel figured out his "why," even the hard things became a little easier and more enjoyable. Being able to shift your mindset really is the key to resilience. But I think this isn't something that comes naturally to most people. Often, when we're confronted with a challenge, we turn away from it instead of facing it head-on. But if we face it with the right mindset, we not only transcend the problem, we transform ourselves.

When I think about the value of cultivating an open mindset, I think of the story of Ishi. He was the last remaining member of his tribe, the Yahi, and had lived alone in the California woods for a long time before an anthropologist named Alfred Kroeber invited him to come to San Francisco.

Ishi agreed, but as they were about to board the train, he vanished. Searching high and low, Kroeber eventually found him hiding behind a pillar. He talked Ishi out from behind it and convinced him to board the train.

Later, when asked why he hid when the train approached, Ishi explained that he and his tribe had believed that trains were demons that devoured people.

Kroeber was astonished. "If that's what you believed, then why did you agree to get on the train with me?"

"Well, living alone, I realized that it's better to be curious than afraid," Ishi replied.

It's better to be curious than afraid.

When Daniel asked why he was doing those morning workouts, he was following his curiosity. When Ishi decided to board that train, he was doing the same. That curiosity allowed him to do and experience things most people wouldn't.

INSIGHT #2: Resilience is a daily practice.

Greg: It was 4:30 am on September 24th when I bolted out of bed in a panic.

"I'm late for my flight!" I realized, scrambling for my things. I had missed my 4 am alarm. Fortunately, I was already packed, so I jumped into my clothes, got in the car, and headed to the airport.

Three miles out of town, something suddenly flashed in front of me—a deer! I slammed on the brakes, but it only took a second: both the deer and the car were dead. I couldn't do anything to restart the engine.

"Great!" I thought, as I opened the door and stepped into the bitter cold. I trudged to the construction site I'd passed just moments ago and asked for help.

The workers called a friend who came to pick up the deer within a few minutes. I called AAA, who came to pick me up two and a half hours later.

When the tow truck finally arrived, the driver couldn't get into the right position to get the car on the truck bed. He asked me to stand on the other side of the road, face oncoming traffic as it sped towards me at 50 miles per hour, and signal people to stop so he could maneuver to the car.

"OK," I said and turned to face the oncoming lights. "I'm going to get killed out here," I thought.

By the time we finally towed the car to the dealership, I had already missed my flight.

"This can't get worse," I thought. Just then my phone buzzed, an email came in from a client: *The project budget has been cut and we don't even know if we can do it anymore. Also, we need a proposal for [a smaller project] three days early.* Three days early was in the next 24 hours! It meant that I would have to work a whole lot more for a whole lot less.

At that point, I wondered if I should just cancel the whole trip. But I was supposed to meet a close friend who was going through a tough time, and I didn't want to let him down.

By the time I finally landed at my destination, I was five hours late, had four urgent emails to deal with, was starving because I'd skipped lunch, and had to delay seeing my friend by another two hours.

But after we finally sat down to dinner that night, he told me, "Wow, you've had quite a day and you're still hanging in there. You were really focused during our meal, and I really appreciate that."

That's when I realized that my habit of a daily morning meditation, as well as the work I had been doing with Daniel, had helped me to take one difficult thing after another. Because I had been building up my "resilience muscles" a little each day, I was strong enough to handle everything that had happened on this day—and still have energy to give to my friend at the end of it all.

When Daniel and I set out to become more resilient, we wanted to never turn away from the difficult things in our lives. So each time we faced a challenge, we would practice turning towards it, not away. For example, each morning I spend a minute taking a shower with the water on full blast cold, just to wake myself up and remind myself that if something's going to happen today that I don't want, it's important for me to deal with it head-on.

For us, resilience has become a daily practice.

Daniel: We practice on small things so we can be ready for the big things when they happen.

One big insight we had during our silent retreat was that problems are necessary. There's no better opportunity than that to practice resilience!

Problems make you stronger by forcing you to face challenges and issues directly and work through them with everything you've got. If you can get to a point where each time you face a challenge you change your thought process around it, you eventually get to a point where resilience becomes a habit.

Instead of having a problem arise and sulking about it, you can turn to it right away and say, "Okay, how am I going to deal with this?"

Resilience, like everything else, takes practice.

Greg: I have a story about that. When Daniel was in 5th or 6th grade, there were two basketball teams: the A team and the B team. The first year, Daniel was one of the better kids on the B team. The next year, he made the A team. So he went from being one of the best kids on the B team to the bottom of the A team.

He came to me one day and said, "I like being on the A team. It makes me want to play basketball when I'm in high school!"

"But I realized something," he said. "When you're on the A team in grade school, if you're one of the top five or six players, you'll play. But in high school, you need to be the best or second best player in your grade to play."

I told him, "Okay, that means you've got to get better faster than your classmates. One of the toughest things in basketball is dribbling, so if you want to play in high school, let's practice that."

We got a couple basketballs, came up with some drills, and I told him, "Do this each morning and each afternoon, and you'll get better faster. None of your classmates are doing this before and after school, using these drills."

So a couple weeks went by and I asked him, "How's the dribbling going?"

"I haven't gotten to it yet."

Then a week later, I asked again.

"Haven't gotten to it yet."

And I knew that Daniel wasn't going to play basketball in high school. (He did end up being a great lacrosse player, though.)

The message here is that if you don't practice, you can't get better. And if you want to be more resilient, you have to practice. You don't get better by thinking about it, you get better by *doing* about it. And if you're not "doing about it," you're not "getting better about it."

So build the *practice* of resilience into your day. Create habits and systems that prepare you to face big challenges as they come up by practicing on small challenges first.

For me, an important habit is meditating the moment I get up in the morning. I set up a system to help me do it. As soon as I turn off my alarm and return from the bathroom, I hit "start" on my meditation app. Try setting up systems like these to support your own resilience habit.

INSIGHT #3: Your angst is your liberation.

Greg: While Daniel and I were on the silent retreat, one of the leaders shared this line with us: *Your angst is your liberation.*

In other words, no matter what you're feeling during a challenging time—whether it's anger, frustration, disappointment, worry, or fear—there is a message in that emotion. If you can understand the message, it will help you through the challenge.

Try this. Any time you feel yourself starting to get angry or frustrated, stop and ask, "What's the message in this emotion?" Usually, you'll uncover what's really important to you and understand the next steps to take.

For example, when I got into the car accident with the deer, I first got angry that the car wouldn't start, and then anxious that I'd miss my flight. In that anger, I remembered to ask, "What's the message here?"

I was angry because I didn't want to miss seeing my friend, and that's why I didn't want to miss my flight. As soon as I understood that message, I could let go of the anxiety and ask, "Okay, what can I do to connect with him and get on another flight?"

Then, when I got the email from the client and started to feel anxious, I asked, "Now what's the message?" For me, the answer was that it was important to take care of my staff and keep my business going. That allowed me to move past that emotion and take action, rather than letting anxiety and anger compound.

Knowing how to find the message within the emotion makes you more resilient. Once you can do that, you don't have to get stuck feeling whatever you're feeling. You can acknowledge it, learn from it, and take action. Positive action.

When I look back on the day I hit the deer, I see that even though it was filled with challenges and disappointments, I actually handled it well. A lot of my ability to handle it came from the work Daniel and I had been doing together.

INSIGHT #5: Forgiveness is freedom.

Greg: Resilience is also about *forgiveness.*

As Daniel and I completed the silent retreat, I realized that there were a lot of people in my life that I needed to forgive. One by one, I began to do just that. But I was surprised to see that the more I forgave, the happier I became! By the end of the retreat, I wondered, "Why haven't I forgiven these people sooner?"

When you forgive someone, you are the first one to benefit.

There is a trap in thinking that the world should be fair, and I had lost so many years to thinking this way. I would think, "Wait! Why I am forgiving this person? They should apologize to me!"

But resilience really isn't about fairness. It's about finding a way to persevere even when life is difficult or unfair.

I realized that I could wait forever for the world to become fair and for people to come forward and apologize. But that meant giving away my own power to take action *today.* I didn't have to wait for anyone: I could just *forgive* and move on.

INSIGHT #6: Community makes you stronger.

As the summer progressed, we both realized how fortunate we were to be on this journey together. Not only did we have a great summer exploring ideas and building new habits, we also learned that we could rely on each other through difficult times.

Greg: For example, Daniel and I had spent a week that summer trying to live as healthfully as we could. We ate healthy food and exercised, did hot yoga followed by ice baths, completed a juice cleanse, and meditated every morning and several times throughout the day.

By the end of that week, we both felt fantastic. Our relationship was strong. We were both making good decisions and living a healthy life, and we were committed to keeping up our good habits. We couldn't stay together forever, but we decided to have a couple phone calls each week to help each other maintain momentum.

However, I really struggled after we parted ways. I couldn't keep the pace up. At some point, I got busy, missed a workout or two, went to bed late, picked up a couple of Diet Cokes, and was far from where I wanted to be.

Daniel had been struggling, too. So when we spoke on the phone, we made a commitment to each other to try again and enjoy the journey.

That made me realize that it's so valuable to have people who can remind you of who you want to be and what you want to accomplish. Even when you slip and fall, you can help each other back up, in a very loving way, so you can keep going.

If you have friends, family, or a group that can push you in this way, it makes all the difference. Very few of us are good enough to push ourselves, and most of us will need a coach, partner, friend, team, or community that can help bring us back up, remind us of what we're capable of, and keep us moving forward.

FINAL INSIGHT: True resilience is a practice and a journey.

How we travel determines the rhythm, the path, and even the destination. Anger travels differently than joy or curiosity or wonder. Each attitude maps a unique pattern and experience. Each experience takes us somewhere. Do you like your somewhere? If not, then practice. Practice on challenges both small and large. Resilience is bigger than bouncing back. Resilience is never turning away. It's facing everything. The more you face, the more freedom and joy you will discover. Don't just bounce back, bounce on and on and on. Practice builds true resilience. Let your somewhere be remarkable.

"What love does to us is a Gordian knot, it's that complicated." **– Mary Oliver**

TWEETABLE

If you don't practice, you can't get better. If you want to be more resilient, practice.

Greg Zlevor: *Greg Zlevor is the President of Westwood International, a boutique firm reimagining what it means to lead wisely in a global age. He is the co-founder of the Global Community for Leadership Innovation and founder of FOG. Westwood's signature leadership programs and initiatives have energized global brands like Johnson and Johnson, Volvo, The Singapore Police Force, and GE. How can we help you lead wisely in a changing world? Send a note to Greg at gzlevor@westwoodintl.com or call 802.253.1933. You can find him on LinkedIn at Greg Zlevor.*

Daniel Zlevor: *Daniel is a senior at Franklin and Marshall College. He is a four-year member of the varsity lacrosse team, consistently recognized on the Dean's list, and is a member of both the Financial and Delphic Honor Society. Over the last four years, he has worked with PWC, America's Cup in Bermuda, and Champlain Investments.*

CHAPTER 16

From Insecure to Influencer

Creating Opportunity, Success & Legacy Through Intentional Conversations

by Tammy Thrasher Mitchell

The art of authentically connecting with people and being an influencer is natural for some, challenging for many, and impossible for others. Or is it?

Several years ago I was asked to speak on this thing I do. This thing I do? There wasn't even a name for it. It was just how I showed up. It was what I did, who I was, and people noticed.

"It's common sense," I thought. "Who wants to learn more about networking and connecting?"

"Tammy, you do a great job of connecting with people, building strong, authentic relationships with amazing people, and then you do a fabulous job of making warm introductions between people. Can you speak at my upcoming event and help my attendees learn how to do what you do?"

"Hey, Tammy, can I hire you to coach me and teach me to be a better networker, to connect with people and be more effective at events like you?"

"It would be great if you could train our team at our upcoming sales event and help them focus on techniques that will help them grow their database and close more deals."

These questions and requests just kept coming at me. Initially, I was curious to understand what exactly they wanted me to help with—what they wanted me to speak and coach on. When we do what we do, when we are in our element, it's easy for us to simply be who we are and hard to see the uniqueness others may observe. When people wanted to learn more about what I did and how I could help them do it, I had to step back and process what I was doing, why I was doing it, and how.

The more I reflected on my connections, my relationships, and how I approached networking, the more I realized that my approach was so common sense, it wasn't common anymore.

However, one of my truths is, I didn't feel qualified to fill these requests. I was a simple girl choosing to show up and connect, choosing to show up in my excellence, and adding value with each encounter. As much as people saw me as a social butterfly and power connector, what they didn't see was I had my "showman" persona on and was choosing to manage my introvert and bashful tendencies.

Have you ever heard the quote, "Life is 10% what happens to us and 90% how we respond to it?" It's amazing how, over time, that 10% can seem pretty significant. We have to choose to be bigger than our circumstances a whole lot to excel at how we respond. This is truly how we prosper in life.

As a teenager, though I was shy, I was generally surrounded and welcomed by the who's who of my peers. I had grown up and gone to school with the well-off, the gifted, the popular, the athletes, the fun, and the interesting. And for some reason, maybe because I let them talk for hours without interruption or because I gave honest feedback and counsel when they dumped their teenage first world problems on me, I was always surrounded by something to do and somewhere to be. In spite of being welcome, I wasn't comfortable with myself, and the shy, insecure, broken me ventured to an unknown place, a foreign language, a new family, and new friends.

Prior to heading abroad, I had reached a point of hopelessness, despair, and uncertainty that so many teenagers feel as a result of many "life happening to me" moments, and I had not quite developed the skills to cope well or grow through them. During my junior year of high school, I chose to leave the comforts and discomforts of all I knew—my family, friends, and school—and moved to Denmark.

My family was very middle class, and a struggle at that, while I was growing up. Being the oldest of six children, I had very typical oldest child strengths, skills, and personality traits. Bossy, demanding, organized, decision maker, big picture observer, and at home, I had the confidence of a dictator. However, outside of the home, I was insecure, uncertain, shy, and did a great job of blending in with wallpaper and decor. I didn't want to be seen.

I was not quite prepared to be such an anomaly in Denmark where blending in, being the wallflower, was not really an option anymore. I did my best to stay out of the limelight and enjoyed the people watching, taking in a whole new world, trying to understand even a fraction of the conversations happening all around me. For the most part, everyone let me be. However, I quickly became friends with Thomas Gadegaard, and he frequently invited me over to his home to spend time with his family, who were all fluent English speakers.

"Show up, step out, and engage. No one is really going to care if you don't; just think about all of life that you will miss out on by staying on the sidelines."

Ouch! At 17, the shy, broken, insecure, introvert me did not like these words, but I knew he was speaking the truth.

"Why do you sit back? Why are you watching everyone around you and not participating in this thing we call life?"

Mr. Gadegaard, Thomas's father, was the most direct, wise, informative person I had been counseled by, other than my own father, my whole life. I spent most of my free time with the Gadegaard family, and Mr. G took every opportunity to parent and mentor me.

Why did I hide in rooms full of people? Why did I prefer the comfort of anonymity? Mr. G was a persistent man. He repeated the question, "Why are you watching instead of being part of the experience?"

"I don't know what to say. I don't know everyone. I'm not interesting. I don't have anything to talk about. I don't want to bore people. I don't speak the language…."

This clearly was not going to be a quick or pain-free discussion. In fact, the conversation stung. I went home and reflected on the conversation deep into the night, wondering what it would be like to feel brave when I walked into a room. What would it feel like to connect with people, to freely smile, laugh, and engage in conversations confidently?

I decided I would step up and be part of experiences and conversations and I would create memories by engaging instead of just watching the world pass me by. And it was not easy. It did not happen overnight. In fact, it was somewhat gradual. The more I showed up, the more I engaged with people, both friends and strangers, the easier it became. I became fascinated with people as I got to know them better and as I learned other people's stories.

Over time, caterpillars become butterflies, sand becomes pearls, and coal becomes diamonds. Time and pressure can create spectacular results.

Life is a series of events, and it's up to us to choose to make them intentional. They are not always comfortable, and that is okay. The greatest experiences, memories, and relationships are developed through growth.

It was 7 am. The event was scheduled to start at 9. Connecting does not happen while speakers are on the stage, connecting happens before the day starts and after the day ends, with limited opportunities on breaks and lunch. I had two days in Chicago with some great minds, and later that day I would get to interview George Ross, Donald Trump's real estate attorney for over 20 years.

As I entered the room (it was a limited event with less than 100 other entrepreneurs attending), I boldly walked towards the front and was greeted by all sorts of new faces along the way. I scanned the room, people were still slowly making their way in, and I spotted Mike, whom I had met in Dallas a couple of months earlier.

"Tammy! I have to tell you...every single time I see you, you look so energized and refreshed! How many cups of coffee did you have this morning, or what's your secret?"

Insider secret, I don't drink coffee. I choose to be high on life. I'm excited to connect, learn, and bring value.

Today, the day in the life of Tammy Thrasher Mitchell includes countless phone calls, scheduled Zooms, occasional podcasts interviews, conferences once or twice a month, speaking or emceeing from stages all over the country, and connecting with new and old friends all along the way. I am frequently asked to coach or speak on various aspects of real estate businesses and investing, but more and more the requests are for me to speak on the power of relational capital.

What is relational capital? It's social capital, collaboration, understanding, referring others, connecting, and networking, but not. It's a series of intentional connections with people and businesses, adding value, and nurturing strong and viable relationships to be able to refer to and do business with. Relational capital is going beyond networking and is essential for all who aspire to grow in business.

So many introverts have the same story. Our childhood was filled with people and places that overwhelmed us. We were commonly viewed as the sweet, quiet kid by teachers and friends' parents.

I was the epitome of the wallflower. Actually, I considered myself part of the wall I blended in so well. Today, when people meet me they are quick to assume I am an extrovert and may even think that I naturally have great social skills.

Being an introvert and a recovering wallflower, as shy as one could be, I understand the challenge of connecting with other people, the challenge with showing up and shining in a crowd. Yet, once I got out of my own way, I realized and embraced the power of intentionally engaging in life. My business would not have gotten off the ground if I had not been willing to step out of my comfort zone and become an expert at building authentic relationships and adding value through random acts of intentional connecting.

Because I made a choice to step up, I have what I have today. I consult with professionals and retirees to help them create multiple streams of income through passive investing in commercial real estate and businesses. In more than 25 years in real estate, I have closed over $100 million in transactions and participated in hundreds of deals personally. Because of my integrity, insights, and authenticity, I've partnered with cofounders of Fortune 500 companies, CEOs, thought leaders, and international investors on a variety of projects.

And, much to my joy, in addition to helping people become intentional investors, I speak and consult on the power of relational capital.

In my spare time, I travel the world, participate in masterminds and live events, and spend every moment I can with my children, family, and friends. Yes, the introvert in me absolutely requires recovery time from these adventures in life, and I plan accordingly. It's a life I am grateful for.

TWEETABLE

Show up, step out, and engage. No one is really going to care if you don't; just think about all of life that you will miss out on by staying on the sidelines.

Tammy Thrasher Mitchell is a real estate investor, speaker, relational capital consultant, and the podcast host of The Influential Conversations. *With over 25 years of real estate experience, she has closed over $100 million in transactions and participated in hundreds of deals. Relationships, conversations, and her trademark "random acts of intentional connecting" set her apart as an authentic connector bringing value to her community and her projects.*

To learn more, get free bonuses, and connect with Tammy, go to: www.tammythrashermitchell.com or text "resilience" to 80800.

CHAPTER 17
Juliette's Wings

by Matthew Hayden

"It's called acrania," the doctor's voice crackled as it came through the speakerphone. "It means the baby's skull hasn't developed."

I turned to the ultrasound tech, confused but hopeful, "Ok," I said, "What do we do?"

"Nothing," said the voice down the phone. "There's a 100% mortality rate after birth—if baby survives that long. I'm sorry. It's probably kindest for everyone if you just end this now."

Our children—Niamh, 14 and Gabriel, 12—had been ushered out of the room before the doctor was put on the phone. I asked for them to be brought back in. I held on to my wife as the room started to spin around us. How could this be? 30 minutes ago we were full of hope, excited to see our newest addition; two years earlier my wife had suffered a miscarriage that had almost broken us all into pieces. How would I tell the kids!?

My wife, Paola, and I love being parents and absolutely adore our kids. We always wanted to build our lives around our family, not build our family around our lives, but I had suffered a crisis of confidence and had walked away from my career as a personal development coach and ended up in restaurants to pay the bills. Now I had made the move from the food service industry, and we had built a successful nutrition focused network marketing business. For the past two years, we had been the most present parents we could be and enjoyed a level of closeness with our children that I had never thought possible.

"What are we going to do?" Paola sobbed.

"Baby, I don't know," I replied. "What do you want to do?"

It was a little girl. We had chosen the name Juliette Lily. I thought about our delight at watching those long legs kicking and her fine pianist's fingers (both just like her mother) curl and uncurl. "Termination's not an option, is it?" I asked, knowing the answer.

"No…no," she replied. I don't pretend to have any answers or wisdom. We're not pro-life or pro-choice, we're just pro-us, and this was what our hearts told us. We hugged, silent tears wetting both our faces.

Our children were brought back into the room, confused and apprehensive. We hugged them and told them that Juliette was perfectly designed to be happy and healthy right where she was inside Mummy, but that she wouldn't survive being born. We told them that we loved her so much that we were going to stay with her until it was time for her to go. The knowledge that it was the right thing for our family did nothing to assuage the pain of watching my wife and children—my entire world—in such agony; it is something I can never forget. We sat, huddled together and cried for what seemed like, an eternity. The drive home was a blur, as was the rest of the day. That night we pulled all our mattresses into the living room and camped together on the floor. I sat and watched my family as they finally succumbed to the relief of sleep, but there would be no sleep for me. I was raging! My angst had been replaced by a sense of complete injustice.

"Why?!" I silently screamed at the sky, "Why this? Why us? Really, you want to take another one? This again, but worse?! I have to watch this one grow, to love her and then just hand her over!? This is some sick bullshit!" I looked at Paola, sleeping peacefully "Why do this to her!?" That's when I heard the voice; this was the fifth time this voice had spoken to me, the last time was after Paola's miscarriage.

"What do you mean?" the voice said.

"What?" I said.

"What do you mean?" the voice said again. "What part of this is bullshit?"

"Listen," I said, "I'm not in the mood for some mystical, f$&*ing experience right now," I yelled silently. "How dare you do this? How dare you make us love her, make us watch her grow, then take her!? That's sick!"

"That's true," the voice said. "That is what I'm asking you to do. And it will be difficult for everybody, but what you're describing are all your problems. What about her?"

"I'm talking about her," I raged, motioning to Paola. "How can you do this to her?"

"I'm talking about Juliette," said the voice. "What about her? What about what she needs? While you're busy complaining about how hard it will be for you, have you thought about her?"

I was stunned into silence.

"Matthew," the voice continued, "as a parent, if I offered you the chance to have a child who would always be warm, always be fed, always feel loved, always be close, always be in comfort—never be cold, never be hungry, never be alone or feel scared, never know pain or heartbreak....if I offered that for your child, would you take it?"

"What?" I stuttered. "What does that have to do with anything? That's what everyone wants for their kids, isn't it? But that's impossible!"

"Matthew, that's what Juliette will have. That's the life that she needs. She will pass from my arms to yours and then straight back to mine. She will have a life filled with nothing but love. How many can say the same?"

I stumbled into the bathroom and stared at myself in the mirror. I hadn't even thought about Juliette. My anger immediately dissolved. Then the tears came.

"This is too big for me," I said. "I'm afraid it's going to break me."

"It will if you stay rigid, and hold on to your old ideas. If you're willing to be flexible, it will grow you. I know it hurts," said the voice, "but it is what she needs. Will you do this?"

"Of course, I will," I sighed. "But I don't know if I'm strong enough."

"You will be. I'll be with you." The voice said. "She'll help too."

Just like that, the conversation was over. Suddenly, I was clear on what I needed to do and who I needed to be. I shared what the voice had said with my family, and our course of action was decided. The mission was clear: we would love, nurture and cherish our little one until it was time to say goodbye. We would make sure she experienced as much love and good feelings as possible, however long or short her time with us might be.

As Juliette steadily grew bigger and more active, she kicked like no baby I'd ever felt! With every kick, roll, and elbow, our family's love for this little bundle of perfection grew. "All I want is for her to open her eyes and see me," said Paola one day. We shared that hope with our amazing doctor, Melissa. Unfortunately, she was clear that, because Juliette's brain wouldn't form without a skull, she wouldn't have any higher brain function, so that couldn't happen. Still, it was a lovely thought, and neither Paola nor I could help but fantasize about the moment, however impossible it may prove.

As Paola's belly grew, we would sing, talk, and read to Juliette, and she would often kick in response to a nearby voice. I was so clear that this was what the voice was talking about—Juliette was having an incredible time! She would actually chase me around Paola's belly: I would poke and she would come and find me. I tried to convince myself that I was just inventing stories to feel better, but she would actually "play" with me for 10-15 minutes at a time!

We continued our lives as normally as possible. The two biggest parts of our lives, our nutrition business and the rugby club that I had founded, Okapi Wanderers RFC, meant that we were surrounded by a beautiful support group that constantly rubbed Paola's belly and talked to Juliette. Everywhere we went, we were met with hugs and love. We had announced Juliette's condition on social media, to avoid awkward conversations wherever possible. What we weren't expecting was the outpouring of love and concern from friends and even total strangers! We were able to connect with so many people with similar stories, sharing experiences, tears, hugs, and love. As the delivery date approached, we were cocooned in love from all directions.

The date finally arrived when we would meet our Juliette, and we were welcomed by the wonderful team at the hospital. Paola was being induced, so, with the IV in place, all we could do was wait. I will never forget, as the endless day wore on, and the moment for us to say hello and goodbye to our little girl approached, the constant presence of family, friends and business partners. At one point, all the maternity unit waiting rooms were full of people waiting to see us, bringing with them hugs, tears, love, and even some laughter.

When, many hours later, Juliette was born, we were as ready as we could be. In the quietness of the room, our little girl came into the world, tiny and perfect with her mother's long legs and those same pianist's fingers. But her fingers, like her, were blue and lifeless. Paola and I held her, kissed her tiny face and those little hands trying to burn every feature into crystal-clear memory, and cried as she lay there looking as though she was peacefully sleeping. She was so beautiful, but the doctor was right, the birth process had clearly been too much for that frail little body. We cried as she lay on her mother's lap: tears of joy, tears of relief, tears of gratitude, and tears of sorrow that she wouldn't be able to see us.

And then, she opened her eyes!

Juliette Lily Hayden stayed with us for 1 hour and 3 minutes. She got to be held by her parents, siblings, and grandparents whilst being surrounded by nothing but love and then slipped, silently, to sleep. The voice had been right. Our son, Gabriel, held me tight as we cried together, "No-one ever told me you could be so happy and so sad at the same time." He was right; it was the most beautiful, difficult, humbling and joyful experience I could have ever imagined.

Our beautiful Juliette has taught—and continues to teach—me so much:

Juliette's Lessons:

Life is beautiful.

Just because it's difficult, doesn't mean it's bad.

Miracles are real.

You're more ready than you think.

Wishes are granted.

It is life's brevity that gives it its sweetness.

Our youngest daughter, Chloe Emma Hayden, born in June 2017, is happy, healthy and looks just like her big sister.

In the Tao Te Ching, Lao Tzu writes "What the caterpillar calls the end, the rest of the world calls a butterfly." In her short time with us, our own little butterfly brought love, understanding and a clear vision that there is a plan for all of us that exceeds anything we thought possible. Today our family is passionately reaching for our dreams, creating opportunities for love and promoting butterfly-thinking in a caterpillar world.

TWEETABLE

There's a plan. If you would only allow yourself to trust, in yourself and the beneficence of life, you will find purpose and love in all things. In the Tao Te Ching, Lao Tzu writes "What the caterpillar calls the end, the rest of the world calls a butterfly." Decide to think like a butterfly.

Matthew Hayden is one of the most engaging visionaries in the world; he is as likely to be hilariously irreverent as he is truly profound whilst creating simple strategies that move you effortlessly to the life of your dreams. Matthew is the creator of the 6 Day Uplift and Life: A Beginner's Guide and has helped thousands become more vital, energized and awesome! Matthew's work has been featured on TV, Radio and in print all over the world. If you're ready to see your heart's desires become a reality, follow Matthew at https://www.facebook.com/thepathetofreedom/.

CHAPTER 18

Living My Passion Through World Travel & Investing

by Tim Hubbard

We finally landed in little Salamanca, Spain. It was the first time I had ever stepped foot outside of the US. I was 16 and eager to explore. The next few weeks I'd be living with a family I had never talked with let alone met in person. I wasn't even supposed to be staying with them. Another student in my high school class had decided she didn't want to fulfill the return part of her foreign exchange program, and since the family was expecting someone, I jumped at the opportunity to take her place. I remember how initially everything appeared so different. The buildings, the cars, the language, the weather, the food, and the fact that they actually took mid-day naps; it appeared to be a dreamland away from home.

I was young and easily influenced but still recognized how the subtle changes in our environment and culture can change our whole lifestyle. After returning home and reflecting more on the most amazing trip I had had to date, the idea of living the rest of my life in my hometown without first exploring as much as I could almost seemed unfair to myself. Maybe there was a place out there more suited for me. I've been exploring that idea ever since.

I've traveled to nearly 60 countries and stayed in over 120 cities within those countries, many of which I've visited two, three, four, or more times. It's been an interesting journey, to say the least. I've found myself in the best of times and in some not-so-pleasant times. I've been stranded in a small coastal town for days by tropical rainstorms where the roads had flooded over and the seas were too rough to leave by boat. I've been deported. I've had food poisoning more times than I care to remember. I've been threatened in languages I didn't understand and for reasons I'm still not sure of. I have had a gun pulled on me and I've even had a machete waved madly at me like a scene from a Rambo movie.

On the flip side, I've seen and explored some of the most beautiful places and met some of the most amazing people. I've dived along beautiful ocean floors and stood atop the world's tallest buildings. I've tried foods that were more delicious than I could imagine and have seen genuine smiles I will never forget from people living in cultures with next to nothing compared to western standards. And I'm certainly not finished. Looking back, it's easy for me to see now that the majority of my life-defining events, including changing careers, pursuing higher education, moving to different cities and eventually out of the US, and running my own hospitality business, stem from the drive my first travel experience instilled in me. It left a spark inside me that keeps me pushing forward even when the uncertain future has me intimidated and uncomfortable.

After finishing high school, I started a degree in international business, thinking, if any degree was going to allow me the opportunity to travel, it would certainly be a degree with an international focus. Well, not exactly. It did, but just for a short time. Traveling abroad for one semester was a requirement, and so I spent one semester back in Spain. I managed to explore for a few months before and after the semester began with a few bucks saved up and some soon-to-be debt. I was broke, so I stayed on couches in homes of people I didn't know, bunked up in massive dormitory hostels, and traveled around as cheaply as I could, always noting in my journal the different environments and how I felt living in them.

I finished my degree in international business hoping to find a position that would allow me to continue traveling and discovering the world. After exhausting my resources, I realized that just because my degree had "international" in the title didn't automatically make me a prime candidate for an international position. Most of the positions available were entry level sales jobs either behind the phone or in an office cubicle. After going back and forth between options, or lack of options, I ran things over with my dad and luckily, through his previous work, we uncovered an opportunity for me to work as an independent contractor selling software to automotive repair shops.

For the next few years, I drove door-to-door representing the software company, and while it didn't explicitly involve travel and it was quite stressful at times having an almost entirely commissioned-based income, working independently allowed me to sneak in trips to foreign places, and so I did whenever I could. Being a salesman was difficult for me at first, but I began to realize that the anxiety I had in selling was much the same feeling I often had traveling alone to unknown places. Being alone and in unfamiliar places has toughened me up quite a bit, but more importantly, it has forced me to become a better listener and a student of body language. Many times throughout my travels, that was the only option I had. From struggling to communicate in small Japanese neighborhood stores, to Moroccan street vendors, to talks with an elderly host in Bosnian while I stayed in Sarajevo, my ability to communicate effectively has undergone a barrage of tests and trials.

I believe that all of these interactions helped to propel my sales career, and I was doing well, but I certainly wasn't working my dream job. However, the upside to the long hours behind the wheel was that it did provide me the opportunity to listen to many very influential audiobooks. My car became a mobile university, and through these "lectures," I discovered real estate. It seemed like exactly what I was looking for. Investing in real estate could be very passive and lucrative, but it's also a REAL asset. It's land. It's new buildings and homes and environments, which was such a big part of what I enjoyed in traveling. I had a newfound excitement for real estate but realized after purchasing my first investment property that it was a slow path to progress. So in an attempt to broaden my opportunities, I enrolled in an MBA program.

As the program was nearing an end, I began to realize that it was only offering me what seemed to be an elevated set of the same positions I had been offered years prior with my undergraduate degree. So here I was, a new diploma in hand, and not a thing had changed except for the depletion of my checking account balance. But on the bright side, my travels had continued throughout those years. I had purchased more investment property, and I had new experiences in many new countries that I would never forget. So once again, I went back to the drawing board in search of the perfect position.

In an effort to expedite my real estate investments, I started looking for a position as a commercial broker. From my research, commercial brokers were the top dogs making all the big bucks and thus the people who had the most freedom to explore. I purchased a fine new suit and set out to all the local offices, bombarding their phone lines and emails until I got an opportunity with a small team of six that had an amazing track record. They had completed past transactions exceeding $2 billion and it was of the top investment brokerage teams in Sacramento. I jumped right in.

On the first day walking through the big glass doors into the modern office with my newly purchased suit, I met everyone who was eagerly awaiting the Christmas party. We would all soon be flying down to the Newport Yacht Club near the company headquarters, and I questioned myself, "Wait we're flying down just for the day? That's crazy." I had been frugally living below my means to fund my travels and real estate investments, but now would soon be flying down to Orange County with a group of some of the biggest deal makers in the Sacramento area just for the day? It was an amazing opportunity and a crash-course in commercial real estate investing, but it had to come to an end. On one hand, I was learning from the best and on a clear path to being successful, as I was already working on deals over $1,000,000. On the other hand, I knew that getting to the place where I wanted to be would take a lot of time, most likely years, and the position didn't allow me the flexibility to travel how I had grown accustomed to. It was a pivotal point in my life and a point where I realized I would probably never be working in a position that would keep me from what I was really passionate about again.

Everything went back to normal afterwards, and I continued selling software and searching for my next investments. I ended up going out of state, and while staying in a short-term rental accommodation, I realized the returns I could earn from catering to other travelers as well. Once I got back home, I started furnishing some of my existing properties and converting them to short-term rentals, and before I knew it, I was operating my own little hotel! It was simple to me, I just created exactly what I looked for in accommodations in my prior travels. I then turned around and offered it to my guests who were thoroughly enjoying it.

That trip to new markets also reminded me that good properties in good locations didn't always come with a price tag like I was used to in California. The fundamentals of the real estate I was looking for had changed in California, and so ultimately I moved away from my hometown and continued building my real estate portfolio, spending another couple of years expanding in Tennessee. My mission is buying, renovating, and furnishing properties and developing a great team that, between us all, gives our guests great service and keeps things running smoothly.

Fast forward another couple of years, the air is dense with dust, and the sound of a rotary hammer is making it hard for me to talk with my contractor. I'm almost yelling over the machinery in the background. Trying to get a better idea of our construction timeline, I blare out to my project manager "When are we tearing this wall down?" My travels had brought me to Medellin, Colombia four years prior and I had fallen in love with the people, the culture, and the beautiful year-round weather, so I had been coming back every opportunity I had. I am just getting started here but feel fortunate to have found a place that not only makes sense for investing and diversification but also offers an amazing lifestyle. I'm looking forward to continuing to expand my business here and providing more accommodations with the same concept as I have in the states.

Along this journey, I became financially free in my twenties. As of today, I have acquired a multi-million dollar real estate portfolio, and with the help of my team, have provided short-term accommodations to thousands of guests coming from dozens of countries around the world spanning from Chile to Saudi Arabia. We receive reviews every day from our guests of their travels, and it puts a big smile on my face to read them and see how they so often resemble much of what I've written in my past travel journals: the excitement of experiencing a new environment.

Looking back, I can clearly see the series of small decisions that have consciously and, many times unconsciously, guided me. I had always thought that I would need to become successful to sustain my travels, but looking back I can see that it has actually been my passion for travel that has made me successful. Travelling has provided me direction. It has broadened my perspectives, it has taught me to work with personalities and people from many different backgrounds, and most importantly, it has provided the drive in me to keep pushing forward. I couldn't be more excited to continue exploring while at the same time providing the opportunity for others to do the same, one reservation at a time.

TWEETABLE
Sometimes the journey becomes the destination.

Tim Hubbard is an international real estate investor and entrepreneur with holdings in multiple cities. He is a travel advocate and CEO of Midtown Stays, a short-term rental company that has accommodated thousands of guests from dozens of countries around the world focused on providing sophisticated and comfortable accommodations in excellent areas.

Tim lives in Medellin, Colombia and continues to travel on a regular basis exploring new cultures and ways of life while keeping an eye out for unique investment opportunities to share with others.

Contact: timhubbard@midtownstays.com.
www.midtownstays.com

CHAPTER 19

After Football, I Still Had Purpose

by Steve Fitzhugh

Growing up in "LA," that's Lower Akron, Ohio, I had the kind of childhood in which I did not know I was poor until I was told so by a classmate. Though my parents grew apart and divorced when I was in the second grade, my mom was an everyday blessing. To this day I don't know how she raised three boys and a teenage daughter on her own. Mom made life fun and interesting. She had an engaging sense of humor and no qualms about sharing it in any situation that needed brightening up. She was a meticulous "interior designer." Walking into our home was like walking into one of those expensive homes of the "well to do people," as she would call them, on the other side of town.

I can still smell the crisp summer Saturday mornings when she'd get the *Akron Beacon Journal*, pull out the classifieds, and we'd circle all the garage and yard sales we'd be going to that day. She had a knack for figuring out the best ones to go to and the order in which to travel that would conserve the most gas. She was a master negotiator. That was my mom, doing the best she could with what she had, and what she had was always very little.

My mother only had a high school education. She was my hero, a divorced mother of four on welfare, struggling to feed, clothe, and raise her children. My dream was to have the kind of success that would relieve my mother from the weighty burdens of poverty.

Although I was an honor student, athletics seemed to be my ticket out, like so many young boys from the hood. My older brothers were great athletes. Raymond, the oldest, was the most talented and smart. He was the reason I played football. He was a strong honor student and standout running back. He was an outstanding track athlete as well. I tried to emulate Raymond. His senior year of high school, he was recognized as one of the top running backs in the state. He earned athletic scholarship offers from universities all around the country. Because of him, it was football I began first, then baseball, and finally in high school, track and field. My success on the track outshone my success in football and baseball. Every weekend during track season I'd show up in another *Akron Beacon Journal* sports headline. Expectations began to rise. Then the scholarship offers began to appear, LSU, Purdue, Notre Dame, and Ohio State among others. I accepted a full athletic scholarship to Miami of Ohio University. I was the first in my family headed to college. I was the first of my siblings to start and finish college.

I dreamed of making it to the National Football League. But even after making it to college, it seemed like a long shot. My mom continued to struggle. As a domestic, she spent her entire life cleaning up after people. Even as captain of the football and track teams at Miami University, while at home on semester break there were occasions I'd help Mother on her jobs. To earn a little extra money, she'd spend a day at a home cleaning and washing clothes. There I was, with Mom. I was her big strong college football player doing all the heavy lifting of laundry and vacuuming the bedrooms of the family she was working for that day. After pausing in one bedroom and noticing the Miami of Ohio University paraphernalia, I thought to myself, "I'd bet this kid would get a kick out of knowing the captain of the football team at his university was washing his dirty laundry and vacuuming his bedroom over Thanksgiving break." I promised my mom that if I made it to the NFL I'd make things better. She wouldn't have to struggle her whole life.

Draft day came quickly. Both the Denver Broncos and Dallas Cowboys sent scouts. I waited to hear my name called as one of the top picks for the Denver Broncos. Instead, they traded picks away to move up in the draft order. After not being selected, I was in the driver's seat as a free agent. Sitting in my dorm room with a few close teammates, my agent on the phone, and the scouts from the Denver Broncos and the Dallas Cowboys both prepared to sign me, the negotiations began. I chose Denver. I believed it gave me the best opportunity to begin my professional football career.

The team flew me to Denver to train all summer with the draft choices as if I were one. It was a delight, but my rookie season was short-lived. I beat many odds, did well, managed the very quick NFL free safety learning curve, but didn't survive the final cut. After preseason, my career was over, and I was on a flight back to where it all began: Akron, Ohio. It was certainly fun while it lasted. Besides, no one in my family was a Denver Bronco fan anyway. At Denver's invitation, I was determined to return next year, with improvements, to accomplish my dream of competing at the top of my field, professional football.

Of the 10,000 college football players each year who dream of playing in the NFL, only 3.3% will ever play at least one down. Of that 3.3%, 80% will only play 3.5 years before retiring at around 28 years old. And then, after a lifetime of athletics as their core identity and having reached their life-long goal, they'll find themselves forced to begin the pursuit of a secondary career.

My families' disappointment was more profound than mine. I tried to console my mom and siblings by sharing my invitation by the Broncos to "stay ready" and to proceed with the short list of improvements that would increase my chances of making the roster on my next attempt. Their courtesy smiles could not mask the deep disappointment in their eyes.

I approached the next draft season in my best shape. My agent was excited about interest in me from a few teams who needed a big, strong, and fast free safety. Then something totally unexpected happened. The CLEVELAND BROWNS called. The HOMETOWN TEAM. They wanted to come down to Akron and work me out. Everyone was ecstatic. Season after season since I was a kid, everyone in our family cheered for the Cleveland Browns. I tried to give the family pause about my prospects. "It's a real long-shot," I told them. Let's first see if this scout will even show up. He did. Let's see if I can impress him. I did. Let's see if they offer me a contract. They did. It was special.

In a matter of just two days, I went from possibly traveling back to Denver for a second chance, to an opportunity with the hometown team. What a change of fate. In fact, their contract offer was 15% greater than my last contract with the Broncos. My agent called and said that Denver had been trying to find me. Two other teams had interest as well.

I had a decision to make. Would I go back to the team that first signed me? Believed in me? And wanted me back? Or would I play for the hometown favorite where my mom would get to see me play? I signed the Cleveland contract. Everyone celebrated. My brother Raymond was so proud. That was important to me. He was the greater athlete but chose not to go to college but into the military instead. It changed his life. My good news spread quickly. My classmates from high school were congratulating me. I was cautious. Signing is one thing, making the final roster is another. I was very confident though. My pastor who was a father figure in my life announced from the pulpit that one of the church's "sons of the gospel" signed with the Cleveland Browns. I was eager to prove myself.

Mini-camp was the next week. I was one of about a dozen veteran free agents mixed in with the rookie free agents and draft choices. The Browns wined and dined us for a day. We had a big steak dinner, a trip to the NFL

Hall of Fame in Canton, Ohio, and a tour of the practice facility back in Berea, Ohio. Day two was scheduled to be the first workout and signing bonus delivery. We were to wait for a call to our hotel room before coming down to the lobby that morning to pick up our signing bonus check and Cleveland Browns warm ups for the day's workout.

I was so ready. One training camp and preseason experience already under my belt, I was bigger, stronger, and faster, and my technique was sound. The phone rang. It was my turn. Exiting the elevator and walking into the lobby, I passed a few young, giddy free agents who had already peeked at their signing bonus check amounts. I was next in line. The Cleveland Brown warm ups were stacked neatly on the table. I had already spied the XLs. Also, on the table was a stack of white envelopes with "The Cleveland Browns Football Club" printed in the return address window. These were the signing bonuses, the easiest five-figure paycheck I had ever made. I was next. I tried to conceal my smile. Inside, I was grinning ear to ear.

At my turn, the director of player personnel said, "Steve Fitzhugh, the team physician is not going to pass you on your physical. Your shoulder is a risk. You are free to go home." I pleaded my case, to no avail. Time stood still. The devastation of this surprise declaration was paralyzing. No bonus check. No warm ups. No mini-camp. Smiles of excitement were still pasted on the faces of other young athletes as I headed to the elevator to return to my room and collect my things. I felt their same zeal and excitement a year before with the Denver Broncos and lived an entire year preparing for my second chance. I immediately called my agent. All other teams interested in me had already filled their rosters in those few short, critical days after the draft. I was crushed. How could I tell Momma? What would my brothers, my sister, my pastor, my friends, the congregation say? I didn't have the courage to go to my car while the guys were still milling around in the lobby for fear of having to explain why I would not be joining them on the field of play that day. I peeked in embarrassment from my hotel window as everyone clad in their Cleveland Browns warm ups boarded the charter bus for the practice facility. I would soon be headed the opposite direction on Interstate 77 for the quick 25-minute drive to Akron, Ohio.

What do you do when the rug is pulled out from under you, out of nowhere, and your feet fly into the air and you crash to the floor? What do you do when the door slams in your face and you are left to deal with the humiliation of life's letdowns? How do you respond when you feel the dream that you almost had fully grasped in your hands crumble through your fingers and fall to the ground? My NFL experience faded away as a cloud disappears into a clear blue sky.

It's defining moments like these that break us or build us. We cannot predict the seemingly random catastrophes that life hurls against the canvas of our hearts. We cannot anticipate the unwarranted betrayal of a close friend or ally in our time of need and support. We can only decide how we will respond. For some, these disappointments become the death knell of dreams, extinguishing the passion of the pursuit of a meaningful goal in one's life. Out of our disappointment and depression, we surrender to the death of that which we had hoped to be, to do. For others, setbacks are simply setups for comebacks. For true champions, leveraging learning in times of loss is one of life's quintessential skills.

Driving down Interstate 77, with watery eyes, I had a choice to make. Zig Ziglar says that we are born to win. I am a believer that although we all in some dimension have the capacity to truly win, every day we must choose to be a winner. With the Cleveland Browns in my rearview mirror and my entire life ahead of me, on that bright and sunny Sunday morning I made my decision. My life had value, I would value it by choosing to be a winner through this.

How did I become one of those overcoming over-achievers in the wake of gross pain and disappointment? How is it that some land on their feet time after time when life's wicked curveball strikes them out while others never recover from a broken heart, an injured spirit, or the pain of both? Maybe it is because of pedigree, those inherent family success traits that are part of one's DNA. Maybe it's tied to the resources at one's disposal and the confidence that if all else fails, money can buy almost anything. Is there a link between power, influence, and fame when asking why one may experience fortune rather than misfortune after tragedy? Not necessarily. I didn't have any of those things. What I did have proved to be more valuable than a combination of all those things.

I had a mentor. I had a human resource who, above all else, validated me and convinced me at a young age that regardless of what happens in life, I matter. It was not just what he told me that taught me so much about life, but indeed, it was how he lived life and treated me. He came to my track meets. I didn't have to win for his approval. He was proud simply because I ran my best. He came to my football games and cheered as if I was the only one on the field. His words were always full of encouragement and acceptance. It was always okay for me to be me. Because of my mentor, I learned to bat again after the strikeout, to run again after losing that last race, and to love again even when loving isn't easy. I have continued to employ the lessons I learned from my mentor, Dr. Ronald J. Fowler, many times over.

The Denver Broncos gave me another chance. It culminated with a Super Bowl finish. I was able to bless my mother with each paycheck. Not many years later, we lost Momma to brain cancer. She left us way too soon. I miss her. My brother Raymond succumbed to cocaine abuse, tragically. He never played football after high school. My sister is gone too; she lost her battle with multiple sclerosis. My brother Chucky's on the right track though still with challenges. And me, Lil' Stevie Fitzhugh from "LA," I am still standing.

There are many who may have achieved success in their lives yet are unfulfilled. They are destined for a life described by Tom Rath in Strengthfinder 2.0 as a journey "from the cradle to the cubicle to the casket." They never become what they intended to be, remaining devoid of the impact they could so easily have had. Never healing from what wounded them, they bitterly live a life of bleeding on those who did not cut them. The setback is winning. Although I have traveled throughout the world and have spoken to a million students— Although I have conducted devotions at the White House, encouraged troops on military bases across Germany, and rallied students in Zimbabwe, it's my role as a mentor that has produced my life's greatest dividends. And now, professionally, I'm afforded the privilege daily to export my distinct life lessons to a rare clientele. Today, as a certified transition coach for the NFL, I assist NFL retirees in transitioning into their secondary career. Like I once did, they will face an uncertain future in the wake of a devastating setback. Their identity as a stellar athlete and the reward of achieving the elusive status of professional athlete will screech to an end. They will be faced with starting a new profession at roughly 28 years young. I lived this transition. My setback became a comeback because I learned that football was what I did, it was not who I am. My mentor taught me that. After football, I found my purpose, my work. Football was my job, it was not my work. My job is what I do, my work is who I am. These lessons are principle-based and translate to professions beyond sports. Ultimately, we all must discover our purpose if our goal is genuine fulfillment.

As a mentor, I have generational impact. Outside of my treasured time with my wife, daughters, and grandchild, I value most today my time mentoring those who one day will have the rug pulled out from under their feet, the door slammed in their face, and a dream crumbled in their hands. Who knows? Perhaps one of my mentees may one day be that resource for another in need of discovering the resilience necessary to move from a setback to life's next great opportunity, their comeback.

TWEETABLE

For true champions, leveraging learning in times of loss is one of life's quintessential skills.

Steve Fitzhugh is president of PowerMoves, boldly mentoring leaders. After parlaying his two-sport NCAA success into a short career in the National Football League, Steve has been unstoppable. As an author, master motivator, and international force for change, Steve's words make a difference. His assignments have included The White House, Department of Defense, schools, and Universities and Corporations throughout America. Today Steve is a consultant for the NFL, helping rookies and retirees to succeed. www.SteveFitzhugh.com

CHAPTER 20

Stumbling Upon Success
The Inspiration of Desperation

by Glen Mather

There are greater tragedies in life than I have faced. I didn't lose a family member at a young age, nor did I have to overcome a great handicap or being unfairly incarcerated for a crime I didn't commit. No, my issue had to do with my self-worth and providing for my family, and in the moment, it was crushing.

I was in my mid-40s, living and working in an affluent Chicago suburb, with my wonderful wife, Loida, and three young children. Most weekdays would find me in distant cities, serving as a strategy consultant with a small consulting firm that was a significant player in the early days of the cellular industry. Loida was a registered nurse at a nearby hospital working in labor and delivery.

For the previous seven years, we had slowly built up our finances after the disastrous decision to venture out and start a new cellular company with a few friends. This first business failure soured me on the concept of believing that I could be successful with my own ideas. I was more than willing to forgo the promise of stock options and revenue multiples for a steady paycheck and a reasonable challenge.

Then, Michael, the owner of my consulting company, approached me with the idea of starting another company, this time, largely focused on what was changing everything in business—the internet. We were to raise over $90M from an equity partner, and then our management team would purchase and integrate the operations of regional software implementers for customer relationship management. Here I was with a second chance of being a big success, with the potential of a sizable financial payoff. Perhaps not learning my lesson, and because Loida was always so supportive, I jumped in with both feet.

Whatever we had saved up went right back into this newest adventure, but this time with a twist...an assurance that should anything happen, I would be promised a soft landing with a one-year severance package. Having lived on Top Ramen and anxiety after my first venture failed, I was not about to repeat the same mistake.

As part of my newest venture, I had the responsibility to prepare our Boston office for integration with the rest of the company. My routine was to fly out of Chicago O'Hare early Monday morning, spend most of the week in Boston, and fly out of Logan back home Thursday evening.

On September 11, 2001, less than a year after starting the company, as the world knows, four jets left Logan airport, two of which flew into the World Trade Center, one into the Pentagon, and the fourth diverted into a Pennsylvania field.

As this news filled the portable color TV in our Boston office—I realized, even at this uncertain time, that I would not likely be able to fly home to Chicago, especially since the terrorists hijacked all four planes less than ten miles from where I was sitting. I grabbed the nearest phone and started calling for any means to get me back to Loida and my three children.

After sharing a ride with five strangers in a rental car, we arrived back in Chicago in tears. I was hugging Loida and the kids and telling them that I would not leave them a week at a time again. I went into the office the next day, but most of us were far too distracted by the happenings to concentrate on integrating software companies.

As day after day passed, it became apparent that commercial flying would not be restarting anytime soon. Without travel, we would not be able to effectively build the company, and if we couldn't build, perhaps its very survival would be threatened. Our CEO Michael pleaded with our equity partner to trim back personnel in order to ride out the short-term disruption, but the partner refused. By January, the company was dissolved.

What was worse, that promise of a soft landing, that one-year severance agreement, that was gone as well.

Now we would have to sell our home and move, somewhere, anywhere less expensive to live—and start all over again.

I felt like such a failure! Why was I so willing to gamble with my family's well-being to foolishly chase a dream that was so elusive and that I probably didn't deserve? The worst part of this tragedy was that I had been through it before, and I should have learned to be content with a more ordinary position with a stable company.

After a quick inventory, I realized that God hadn't abandoned me—he had given me Ashley, Albert, and Alyssa, three wonderful kids, and a wife who was constantly supportive. With that foundation and all the "wisdom" I had gained from two spectacular failed businesses, there was little that we couldn't do if we were willing to keep our options open.

To cut our costs, since we had little money coming in from side consulting jobs, we sold our home in Hinsdale, IL and moved the family to Orlando, FL. A smarter person may have lined up a job first, but I wanted to get to a warm place with a lower cost of living as fast as possible.

Prayer became a daily necessity for me, as the days of taking God's blessings for granted was over. I needed to figure out what his purpose was for me, and I was ready to get started (and make some money).

One habit that I always had was starting every morning with reading the paper, both the local as well as the *Wall Street Journal*. Although I was not working steadily as a consultant, I was afraid I would miss something important. In the *Journal* that day, I read about a financial services company that permitted individual IRA holders to direct their retirement into individual real estate properties.

I was fascinated and somehow mustered up the courage to call the CEO of the company referenced in the article. After a quick exchange of pleasantries, I asked him if I could open an office of his company in Florida, as he was based in California. He asked about my experience in financial services, which was none—yet still agreed to meet with me during a future visit to Orlando.

Why did I make the call? Because 10 years before I had read somewhere that I could buy real estate with my rollover IRA and talked a Chicago Bank into being my custodian on the deal. I owned a lot on Seabrook Island, South Carolina in my IRA and it had doubled in value, so it wasn't much of a stretch to think that other people in Florida might share my fascination.

Four months later, after meeting with the CEO I meet through the *Journal*, I opened the doors of what would become NuView IRA and later NuView Trust. At age 47, here I went—the two-time failure starting yet again. What gave me the drive, ambition, and faith that I could make it go this time? It was just hunger and the fear that my family would suffer without me figuring it out. and of course, God's blessing and lots of people that believed in me.

Fifteen short years later, I am surrounded with an amazing group of employees who have helped build NuView Trust to custody well over a billion dollars in self-directed retirement assets, with clients doing incredible things to build wealth for their security.

These experiences have caused me to think a bit differently than the crowd—and now I am surrounded by thousands of clients who also march to the beat of a different drummer. With NuView, they invest their retirement into investments that they find outside the hustle and high fees and commissions of Wall Street. Investments into new ventures, lending money, tax certificates, joint ventures, private placements, and really creative deals are made in IRAs, Solo 401K, and other plans, with the gains sheltered from taxes as they grow.

We even provide ways that our client's children can grow their Roth IRA tax-free, eligible through earned income, and managed by their parents—a great way to teach the power of compounding and investing. That was inspired by my fourth child, Adam, who joined our family during the building of NuView.

Despite the tens of thousands of people we have helped to better prepare for their retirement, the greatest sense of accomplishment for me is the stellar performance and career growth of our 40 employees at NuView. If I had given up after my last failure, where would they be, and would they have been challenged and risen to the same degree?

Throughout the time we have been growing our business, our clients and our employees have embraced the idea that with financial gains comes the obligation to serve others, so we founded a charity to help those with ambulatory issues. *Chair the Love* was born initially to buy and donate wheelchairs to everyone in Central Florida that was discharged from a local hospital and couldn't afford one. Together we build ramps and modify homes for those with special needs. We also deliver container-loads of thousands of new wheelchairs each year to countries in Central and South America and often ask our clients to join us in these amazing distribution trips.

I believe that nothing gets in the way of great success more than some success. Generally, we will all become content at a certain point of our lives. Someone may reach that with their first employer, and others may spend their lifetimes passionately driving toward a particular goal. The key for me is to quantify that goal, measure against it periodically, and celebrate the success of achieving each milestone.

I've had quite a few mile markers in my working career. I thank God for the failures of my cellular company because I had so much to learn about strategy and operations from my seven years in Chicago. The tragedy of 9/11 and the second company shut down taught me not to rely on severance packages and other future promises, but instead to place value on learning new things and developing new skills.

Who knows, perhaps an earlier success for me might have caused me to be less thankful, more accepting of the accolades of others, or just plain self-absorbed. What a joy it is to be surrounded by great employees, inspiring business friends, and the best family a man could desire. God gave us two arms: one to be pulled upwards by someone who sees more in you than you ever could, and the other to be that mentor, perhaps to someone who just lost their business and wants to start over.

TWEETABLE

God gave us two arms: one to be pulled upwards by someone who sees more in you than you ever could, and the other to be that mentor, perhaps to someone who just lost their business and wants to start over.

Glen Mather is CEO and Founder of NuView Trust, a leading custodial company for self-directed retirement plans including IRAs and QRPs. For people that love real estate, private placements, new ventures, and lots more, NuView unlocks your retirement plans to access investments most never thought possible.

Glen welcomes your comments at gmather@nuviewira.com. Visit Chairthelove.org to learn more about an incredible rewarding cause. Come join us!

CHAPTER 21

From Trauma to Purpose with a Little Magic In Between

by Chelsea Newman

To be frank, parts of my story aren't the prettiest.

I guarantee that looking at me, a holistic healer and therapeutic nutrition coach who teaches The Chakra Method, you wouldn't guess my "story." Most people don't. You would probably think I grew up munching kale, meditating on a mountain, and dancing under the full moon. You would be wrong.

At times I still have to find the courage to sit with my scars and find their beauty. Some parts I can laugh off, others I want to hide.

But we all have stories. The true magic is in their lessons.

My magic? Well, it really didn't look like magic at the time. I was 19 years old, alone, crying in the parking garage of a hospital in my beat down, rusted car. At the time, I was a full-time college student almost $50,000 in debt with no medical insurance. I had three jobs, couldn't afford school anymore, and was struggling to make rent. I felt a mounting panic at the thought of the medical bills.

I had reached a point, very early on, where my body was backfiring and I didn't know what to do. I remember sobbing after sitting through yet another appointment with a doctor who had put me through a series of exams with little regard for my delicate state. I was confused by what I had just heard and frustrated with what I was going through.

Until then, I had never really stopped to give my body a second thought. It was my tool, I was the boss, it was merely a vessel that carried around my head and obeyed my wild, unruly, and usually self-sabotaging brain.

If I had known better, I would have clearly seen why my body was rebelling.

Up until that point I had been through a lot. The fact that my body started to tell me very clearly, "No, you cannot go on until you pay attention to me," is no surprise to me now.

My life, from 14 years old on, had been a total mess. It was filled with drugs, alcohol, extreme stress, and abuse. By 15, I had moved between England and America six different times, had lived in 19 different houses, and had two spiteful parents dragging themselves through a nine-year-long divorce headed straight for poverty.

My stress level was beyond what I can now fathom.

I was never the girl waking up early for lacrosse practice and studying. I was the girl that was still up from the night before, working herself to the bone, bartending until two in the morning, when I was still just a baby.

For the most part, I kept it private. I was embarrassed and ashamed. I was angry and alone. To say I grew up fast is an understatement. I would say it was more like I was dragged up quickly through the mud, body and soul in tow.

I wish now, looking back, that I would have been able to understand what was happening to my body, but going to that place was just too painful. I was in such emotional turmoil and so afraid of the depth of that hurt, that I couldn't even stand to face it. I remember trying to sleep my way through the loneliness, popping a sleeping pill as I walked down the stairs to the couch I slept on in the basement I called home, the only place I could afford.

I didn't know at the time that sleeping through the pain wasn't the answer. Emotional scars stay in our body and etch themselves deeper and deeper into our tissues. Our body holds the hieroglyphs of what has happened to us, and it is our job to face them, learn from them, and release them so that they aren't carried on in our DNA.

When high school ended, as a result of an almost daily cocaine habit (supplied by my bosses and a slew of colorful boyfriends) plus an unnoticed case of anorexia, I weighed, at best, 95 lbs. Traditional therapists will tell you eating disorders are about control. As someone who's been through it, I can tell you part of that may be true, but most of it was a way to starve myself out of existence. It was a way to avoid a place that had become painful, the dinner table. As a little girl, eating was the only family time we really had. I clearly remember my dining room with a view of the garden and my favorite birch tree, the one I careened into while learning to ride my bike without training wheels. I remember the wood walls, the radiator that used to heat the old brick house, and my father sitting at the head of the table drinking a large glass of milk, something very American and very unacceptable to my British mother. The dining room used to be a place of joy, but as the family began to break down, it started to feel like poison. Dinner became a stressful, angry, and sometimes even dangerous time that I dreaded. When that disappeared, so did my appetite, and it didn't return till years later and after a lot of soul-searching.

By 17, I remember feeling that I would die if I stayed in that East Coast town. More than a handful of my friends did, the drugs were out of control. So, I struggled my way through school, hardly having time for it on top of three jobs. I applied to one of the only colleges with a free application. Thanks to a recommendation from my high school state trooper, a man who had seen (and arrested) first hand what I was dealing with, some killer SAT scores (my grades certainly weren't getting me anywhere), and a scholarship from the Boston Red Sox received on national TV, I managed to attend college in Hawaii, a place I had never been and knew nothing about. All I thought was, "Get me as far away as possible."

But here I was, two years later, sitting in my car in a tropical paradise, the place I thought I had gone to heal, dealing with a health crisis.

Every month, during my menstrual cycle, I found myself in debilitating physical pain to the point of hospital visits and passing out. I had been diagnosed with extreme polycystic ovarian syndrome (a condition considered "un-fixable") and recommended surgery as well as a lifelong prescription of birth control. PCOS, as I would later come to find out, is one of the most common hormone conditions in women and, as I would come to experience, very fixable.

But this story isn't about my diagnosis, it is about the medical system. It's about the "diseases, disorders, and symptoms" that are managed by pills and surgeries without ever looking at the root cause, without ever seeing what your body is trying to tell you, and without ever being given hope that you can fix them.

As I headed back to my crappy little apartment that day, the one with the slanted floor and the toilet slightly hanging off the hinges, I decided to stop at a funky little shop.

Natural medicine was foreign to me at the time, but what did I have to lose?

I remember the smell as I walked in the door. It felt soothing in a way I couldn't quite understand. The place was small and white, the shelves stocked with supplements, incense, candles, and crystals. A salt lamp glowed next to the register with a hallway leading to a treatment room in the back. A very tall, and surprisingly handsome, man came to the front—not at all what I was expecting.

The doctor and I got to chatting, his manner was a stark contrast to what I had just come from. He was kind, he listened, and he seemed genuinely interested in fixing my problem, not just masking the symptoms. At that time I had been subsisting off of a diet of microwave meals, snacks, more caffeine than any fully grown man should have consumed, and the occasional granola bar. He suggested to me a 21-day cleanse. It wasn't cheap, roughly $300, but I was desperate, and it turned out it was exactly what my body needed.

As I started to flood my body with the nutrients, herbs, and spices it needed, I finally began to understand what it was to nourish myself, and I began to heal. It was a process of self-love and the start of a long-overdue apology to my body, but it was just the beginning of the magic.

As I detoxed that month, I went through a lot. It was physical, it was emotional, it was hard, but I can honestly say I have never done anything better for myself; 21 days later, my body had changed, my mind was clear, and my pain was gone. I had healed from a condition I was told was untreatable and something I would have to live with my whole life, all by changing the way I nourished my body.

It was a profound shift for me. My hormones balanced, my mood changed, my weight shifted. How had I missed the memo that I was made from the inside out?

But there was something even more that happened that day. The doctor had asked me a question I doubt he would even remember. He simply said, "What's your relationship with your feminine? You are manifesting this pain in your second chakra."

I didn't know what a chakra was, but I knew my relationship with "the feminine" wasn't good. My connection to these parts of me, my softness, my nurturing nature, my gentle flow, was non-existent. In fact, it wasn't even really "safe" to go there. That was where the true work began.

Over the next few years, I embarked on a healing journey. I quickly moved to Maui to become a holistic esthetician, studying Chinese medicine, facial mapping, plant medicine, and energy healing. I became fascinated with how a face could show me what was going on inside a body. Dark circles with a reddish hint indicated adrenal fatigue; a pimple on the tip of the nose was caused by heartbreak; rosacea meant there weren't enough healthy fats in the diet plus an A-type personality with perfectionistic tendencies. These ancient secrets fascinated me.

During that time in my life, I created my first nutrition program: "The No Make Up Wake Up," 21 Days to Flawless Skin from the Inside Out. It was a hit. I felt I was really onto something, but I needed more. I needed to go deeper than just diet.

Over the next 10 years, I went on to study Western nutrition, Eastern nutrition, psychology, aromatherapy, biology, astrology…. You name it, I dabbled in it. I was privileged enough to sit and learn from Aboriginal, Hawaiian, Maori, Indian, and Peruvian healers and blessed enough to be able to incorporate these practices into my coaching with clients from around the world.

What I came to discover on my journey was a system, something that was hinted to me that day in the shop—the chakras.

As I studied, I noticed that every discipline, every religious text, every healing modality, and even Western medicine textbooks (whether they noticed it or not) referenced the chakras. In fact, the Western medical symbol of two snakes intertwining on a shaft is thought to be a representation of the seven different chakra points, intersecting along the vagus nerve.

The chakras felt like a system revealed to me that anyone could use to heal themselves. There are seven chakras in total. Each one originates from a section of the spine with a bundle of nerves traveling out to an organ system. Each chakra has an emotional body, and each one has a color. When they are aligned, when energy is flowing through the body, you begin to radiate health.

We hear hints about them in society all the time. "They have a dark energy," or "She lights up a room." This knowledge that we are made of light isn't new, it just isn't represented in the current medical system. We are more magic than we know.

As I developed my health programs, these chakras became a mini healing manual for body, mind, and soul. There was science, there was nutrition, there was mind, and there was spirit. I went through my own journey with each of them, learning to rest, finding forgiveness, learning to get out of fight or flight to let my body and adrenals relax, reclaiming my softness, and finding peace with my feminine self. Each chakra revealed a different layer of myself I had been too busy to explore. These were the little portals to my health and a way to shift the physical and emotional trauma I had been through.

We are given these amazing bodies to act as our ships for this time here, yet we know so little about them. I was forced to learn, but this knowledge is now my gift. When you understand yourself on this level, you can decide which diet is right for you and not be swayed by fads. You can actively participate in your preventative health, and you can work to create healthier generations. My biggest pleasure is children finding health from a place of fascination and awe, not deprivation and shame.

Learn about your health; don't give it away to a broken medical system. You can learn to release the "dis-ease" within your body before it manifests.

I remember, very clearly, the day this came full circle for me. A doctor, a gynecologist of all things, called me from her office in the very hospital where I had sat crying in my car. She was struggling to lose weight, her hormones were a mess, and she couldn't get pregnant. I reluctantly took her on as a client, scared that she would prove all my work wrong. Eight weeks later, she had lost 15 lbs, her skin had cleared, her sex drive was back, and she was asking me how she had never been taught these things in medical school.

I still don't know how we lost this knowledge, but it is my privilege to help bring it back. A little more fascination with the Earth we live on, the bodies we inhabit, and the food that creates us could really change the world.

TWEETABLE
Emotional scars etch themselves into our tissues. Our body holds the hieroglyphs of what has happened to us. It is our job to face them, learn from them, and release them.

Chelsea Newman is one of the nation's top-rated holistic health and nutrition coaches. Chelsea has been in the health industry for over 10 years and has educated some of the top companies in the US including GNC and The US Marshals. Her unique online programs and one of a kind coaching beautifully weave together modern science and ancient wisdom for a mind, body, soul transformation. Chelsea's work is frequently found in publications such as mindbodygreen *and* Tiny Buddha. *You can find her at www.withchelsea.com where you can book a phone consultation to find out if one of her holistic transformation programs are right for you or for wellness business consulting.*

CHAPTER 22

There Are No Sweet Journeys to Greatness

by A.M. Williams

never thought everything I had accomplished could be gone in a matter of hours. Twelve hours to be exact. That's how long it took to make a decision that would alter the course of my life—forever.

My journey began 20 years ago when I developed a noticeable limp. I went to the hospital thinking that I may have pulled a muscle in my leg or something. I would have never imagined that this doctor's visit would be the beginning of my new life—a life filled with new experiences that I never knew existed. After all, I seemingly had it all together. I had a great banking career, had emerged as a leader in sales, and had earned a high five-figure salary. I became a new father of my wonderful, smart, beautiful baby girl. Life for me was sweet. I was on top of the world, and I accomplished all of this at the tender age of 27.

I walked into the doctor's office explaining the complications I had with normal functions like walking in a straight line or standing still without holding onto a chair or the wall. There were times when I would be dressed up in my business suit (I love corporate attire), greeting my fellow colleagues while walking down the hall at work, and suddenly, I would lose my balance and fall. There was no apparent reason, but it was embarrassing and quite frankly a bit scary. In my pride, I'd get myself back up and joke about how my day was off to a great start, but deep down I knew something wasn't right. It wasn't until the doctor came back with test results that I would know what was happening to me.

"You have two cysts on your spine! This is life threatening! We have to operate immediately!"

I had no time to process the information, only time to react. My doctor told me that the cysts they found could be cancerous, but he wouldn't know for sure until he was able to operate. Before I knew it, I was heading into a five-hour surgery, not knowing what to expect. Honestly, I did not know if I would survive due to the delicate nature of the surgery. Even if I did survive, there was a high probability I would lose the use of my legs, arms, or both. Before that day, I had never heard the words disabled or paraplegic. I went from being on top of the world to the bottom of the pit in the blink of an eye.

Change can be scary. But being a Person with a Disability has taught me that adversity makes you stronger, and in the absence of adversity, you merely grow weaker.

The first surgery impaired my walking ability, but I did manage to regain the strength to walk with a cane and returned to work. I felt good about my progress and believed I had this thing beat, until a year later when we had an ice storm. I went into work like I normally did, but this time I stepped on a sheet of ice. My legs locked and began to spread apart on their own. I didn't have the strength to pull them together again, so all I could do was pray that someone would come along and help me. Sure enough, my brother came by to see me at my office and caught me in the parking lot. I told him what was happening with my legs, and he helped me stand again and walk into the office. The next day I went into work and lost the feeling in my legs. I told my wife what happened, and we rushed to the hospital to see my surgeon.

After running several tests, he said that the shunt in my spine had come out and that I had to have another surgery to replace it. I felt at that moment that I had just had the wind knocked out of me. "Not again," I said.

No one ever likes going through extreme adversity more than once. Oh, if only the journey went according to plan! Oh, if everything would just clear the path and let me get to my destination, life would be sweet! Let me dispel this myth now: there are no sweet journeys to greatness!

When I had my second surgery, there was no warning that I wouldn't be able to walk again. Yet, this time, the scarred muscle tissue accumulated had to be removed from my spine so that the shunt could be replaced. This time, the outcome was significantly different.

I still remember the anxiety I felt when the doctor asked me to move my legs, and I couldn't do it. He asked me to wiggle my toes, but I couldn't do it. I couldn't fathom what was happening to me. The simplest things I took for granted, like walking, were no longer present. What was once subconscious in nature now seemed impossible to perform.

It was painful not being able to do so, but I still didn't let it stop me.

Growing up poor in a small rural area, I was no stranger to limitations. We didn't have a lot of money, and I wasn't able to do a lot of things that other kids were able to do. However, those lean years taught us how to navigate the adversity of tough times and how to find happiness even in the land of "have-not."

Despite my challenges growing up, I had a burning desire to do something big that would transform life as I knew it and help countless others to do the same. Little did I know, this opportunity would come through my experience of disability and the adversity attached to it.

In the years to come, I would grow to perceive and embrace adversity as my greatest ally, for it contributed to my personal growth and my internal development of one of the most powerful gifts ever given to man by God:

the power of adaptive resilience.

Adaptive resilience is a term typically utilized in the framework of art. However, when examined, there is a worthwhile application of the term in the context of human potential. Mark Robinson, a Fellow in the Royal Society of Arts, in his famous paper *Making Adaptive Resilience Real* defined adaptive resilience as *"the capacity to remain productive and true to core purpose and identity whilst absorbing disturbance and adapting with integrity in response to changing circumstances."*

Life presents us with a series of experiences to allow us to fulfill our unlimited potential. Yet, many of us often struggle with the adversity that challenges us along the way. After my first surgery, my body became weak, and I left my banking career because I could no longer carry out my job function. However, I didn't stop working. I actually started my network marketing business, built a sales team, and was even recognized at both the state and national levels. I moved from getting paid bi-monthly to getting commission checks every two or three days. In fact, there were a few times that the office had to call me and say, "Andre, you've got a check down here; when are you coming to pick it up?" Good problem to have, right?

I walked with a cane at that time, and with the power of adaptive resilience, I hobbled into people's homes and gave presentations, hobbled into sales meetings and gave presentations, hobbled around in cars with my team to train them and help them close sales, and even hobbled onto a college campus and gave a lecture to a class of business law students! At our sales convention, I won so many awards that I had to have someone go on stage for me because my legs grew tired from all the walking.

I'm not trying to impress you, but rather to challenge you with a question: What are you willing to hobble around for? What do you want for you, your family, your career, and your company so bad that you would hobble around to do it?

It's important to conceive adversity as your friend. Why? Because, in the absence of challenges, you eventually grow weaker. Maybe the fact that you haven't been challenged lately is your greatest challenge. Maybe the fact that you haven't challenged yourself lately is what is keeping you stuck in the foyer of life with no gravitational pull to the next level.

After the second surgery, I learned that I had contracted an infection in the operating room that would cause me to spend several years in and out of hospitals. I was even told several times that I may not live through the surgeries I had to have.

In this period of my life, I lost a lot. I lost my business, the money I was making, the marriage I had, my health. I literally felt like I had lost complete control of my life. Still, something in me would not allow me to feel defeated or buy into the limitations that were being imposed on me by myself and others. No matter how bad it looked or seemed, I maintained a disposition that something in my life could be leveraged to create something I want, and that one day, I would come back from all of this. That is the power of adaptive resilience.

During my time in the hospital, I made it my business to serve every person I could in some meaningful way. I prayed for my nurses, aides, and doctors. I motivated, encouraged, empowered, and inspired every person I encountered while in physical therapy because no one deserves to hear it more than those who are giving it 110% every single day! After years of doing this, one day, I had someone tell me, "Boy, you are a great coach!" I told them thanks, but I was not a sports coach. They told me, "No, you are a great life coach." I didn't even know what that was. I looked it up on the computer, and a close friend of mine (who I am now married to) brought me a couple of books to read about coaching. I took an online course and became certified from my hospital bed.

Inspiring people became my magnificent obsession. I needed another way to get the word out, so I discovered online radio and started my online radio show from my hospital bed. The show eventually caught the ear of an international audience, and I started getting people to call in and listen from the U.K., Belgium, and even Tokyo. I scheduled the show around my therapy times, and the doctors told the nurses to put up a sign on my door so that I could record without being disturbed. Seriously.

You see, when you get to the point where you are willing to deny your circumstances to accomplish your dreams, then you're ready for next-level success. Sure, there will be times when you may experience great challenges. You may even encounter setbacks along your journey. But, with the power of adaptive resilience, you can adapt and pivot where needed without losing sight of your goal or (more importantly) your innate identity!

The true power behind adaptive resilience is that it turns you inward to access more of who you really are. Access more of who you really are, and you can optimize when needed to create more of the results you want.

Adversity is the catalyst! In Napoleon Hill's *Think and Grow Rich*, he makes mention of how every adversity carries with it the seed of an equivalent advantage. I have come to see adaptive resilience as such a seed in my life, for with it, I have escaped the realm of limitations, and have entered into a different dimension of success.

Not only did I receive my certification as a life coach and launch a podcast from a hospital bed, I also managed to go back to school and complete three college degree programs in which I graduated with honors. I have also coached, trained, and mentored international sales teams, entrepreneurs, and professionals—helping them step into the truth of who they are and accelerate their income, productivity, and well-being.

I have had the pleasure of interviewing and working with titans in the personal development industry—people such as Kyle Wilson, Bob Burg, and David Neagle who have poured richly into my life. I have touched many lives by speaking at entrepreneurial conferences in my home state of North Carolina and have even done a talk for a group of business law students at North Carolina A&T University.

Today, my *Yes, Go!* radio show is featured on BSRNradio.com and is syndicated across 300 different radio stations. My health has significantly improved, and my doctors believe that I should and will walk again. Despite spending much of the last 10 years of my life in a bed-bound condition, my heightened level of awareness has allowed me to build a six-figure business, impact business people across the world, and inspire everyday people who are tired of playing small to pursue their desires and become the best version of themselves. Still, I deeply believe that there is greater impact to be made, and I am determined to live full and die empty.

I'm reminded of my friend Louis Monsour, a wealth acceleration mentor and founder of *MakeitandKeepit Wealth Systems*, and a powerful statement he once told me. Louis said, "Impossibility is nothing more than a degree of difficulty." I have come to discover the truth in this statement, as the power of adaptive resilience has empowered me to achieve what I once considered both impossible and unimaginable.

When obstacles become limitations, the question becomes *"How do you make it to the top, when you can't take the stairs?"* How do you stand up when adversity becomes so great that it paralyzes you? How do you respond to the challenges that leave you with no other option than to journey the dark path of change? The power of adaptive resilience.

My life experiences convince me that fewer things will contribute to your success in any area than the power of adaptive resilience. Why? The power of adaptive resilience empowers you with the audacious energy you need to rapidly recover from setbacks, be vulnerable and adventurous enough to follow your desires, and make adversity your greatest asset. The power of adaptive resilience has served me well and has proven to be a meaningful key in my success journey. It will do much of the same for you, if you let it!

TWEETABLE

I have come to see adaptive resilience as such a seed in my life, for with it, I have escaped the realm of limitations, and have entered into a different dimension of success.

A.M. Williams helps high performing entrepreneurs to step into the truth of who they are and become the best version of themselves. He has discovered the gift of challenges and has mastered the art of transforming adversity into one's greatest advantage. A.M.'s powerful story demonstrates that it doesn't matter where you are in life right now, you have the ability to come back or come up from anything! For more on A.M., go to www.yesgo.live to check out his radio show and training programs!

CHAPTER 23

My Relentless Pursuit of Life, Love, and Legacy

by Sean C. Na

About three years ago, I received a call from one of LA's top real estate brokers. She said, "Hey Sean, I have a great investment opportunity, but you will need to look at it today as I am meeting with the seller shortly. If we don't have a contract on it by tonight, you may not win the deal." We quickly ran through the numbers and calculated a huge profit. I dropped what I was doing and raced over.

I went to the house where the seller and broker were waiting. It was getting late and I wanted to get straight to the point. We walked the property, sat down to discuss terms, and began negotiations. An hour later, we shook hands, I wrote him a non-refundable $50,000 earnest money check, and we had a contract. Score! This was going to be a great project.

Real estate in LA moved fast in 2016. I ran a successful real estate sales and investment business and was about to have a third consecutive record-breaking year. Work-life balance seemed like an impossible feat as I pushed harder to maintain momentum. What I didn't realize then was that I was driving off a cliff and I would soon have one of the absolute worst days of my life.

It was about 9 pm when I drove up to my home, excited to share the day with my wife. Working late had become a regular occurrence. I told myself it was okay since I was working hard to provide for my family.

I opened the door and was greeted by my two-year-old, Brandon, sprinting at me full speed in his Batman suit. I kissed Jane and my newborn son, Mark. As I was taking off my jacket and shoes, I began to tell Jane the exciting news. "This is going to be a great project to finish off the year!"

Before I could say another word, her eyes welled up with tears as she said, "I'm suffocating. I feel like a single mother, and the boys and I always come second to your career. If you will step into your role of being the husband

and father you are called to be, then I will love you more than any other wife loves her husband. But if you fail me, then I give you my promise that I will leave you, raise the kids on my own, and from that time on they will barely know their father."

I felt like I got hit by a bus. What a fool I had been. Jane had been trying to tell me for months that she needed me to be present, to love her and support her as I vowed to on our marriage day. The pursuit of money clouded my most important priorities, and I felt lost and empty.

That night, Jane took the kids to her parents' house and left me alone. I had hit rock bottom. I knelt in my empty living room and wept. I prayed a simple prayer, "Lord, from where I'm standing, it's so hard for me to see where this is going and where You're leading me. Whatever it takes, please bring me closer to You."

From that day on, I fought for our marriage. I realized that my biggest problem wasn't whether I worked more or less hours; my biggest problem was my inability to do it on my own. I would never have the patience and the selfless, serving heart for my wife without God's help. He has since been at the center of our marriage, and I am happy to report that Jane and I are at the best we have ever been.

After that fateful evening, I also realized that we needed to make a drastic change to our lifestyle—we would become free of the need to work by building up our passive income from our investments to cover our living costs.

This would allow me to pursue my passions: God, family, and business. I wanted to play the game of life on offense, not defense.

In early 2017, I went on a mission to find the best real estate investment opportunities in the nation. I didn't find them in LA, so I started looking out of state: Atlanta, Jacksonville, San Antonio, and Dallas. The energy in Dallas was electrifying, and I was immediately drawn to the city. We started buying real estate in Dallas while still in California, and shortly thereafter decided to move to the Big D.

Upon our arrival in late 2017, I fell back into the trap of working too much. Perhaps the difference this time was that the pressures of entrepreneurship were coupled with the pressures of building a life in a city where we knew not a single soul. I came to Dallas with a plan, but that plan was not moving nearly as fast as I wanted, no matter how hard I pushed. I didn't have the network I did in LA.

Fortunately, I had learned from my recent experience that working too much comes with severe consequences. Still, the anxiety of failure was paralyzing. Uncertainty plagues every entrepreneur. On one level the uncertainty and drama drive us to perform at our best; on another level, they cause deep insecurity. That used to be me. But as a Christian, I now fear the Lord more than the uncertainty. When I gained respect and awe for God and faith that He would lead me where I am meant to go, my fear of uncertainty became manageable. Business was no longer my idol.

I had to trust that things would work out. We visited a local church and quickly got plugged in. On Easter Sunday of 2018, I was baptized and reaffirmed my faith in Jesus Christ. When you ask God for something, He delivers. You don't need to know the Bible to feel the spirit of God move. I am grateful that in that conversation with my wife I prayed for God to bring me closer to Him. In the year that followed, I experienced the most intimate moments with God and witnessed miracle after miracle in seeing people around me come to Christ.

Today, I am invested in over 550 residential units. I have been blessed with an amazing network of key partners, alliances, and friends in Dallas. As I've become smarter with my money and the advantages of real estate investing, I've experienced firsthand how life-changing these financial principles can be. Investing has allowed me to play the game of life on offense, not defense. It has allowed me to be as present as I want to be in my family's lives, without limits, and to serve in various ministries and be obedient to God.

I am passionate about passing this knowledge along to others so they can invest in real estate themselves or invest passively alongside me. I continue to invest actively and passively, and if I can do it, so can you!

I am not sure where the road will lead me in the future. Where my family and I end up residing, whether it is Dallas, Los Angeles, or in a foreign country serving as missionaries, is less important to me than accepting that I will go where I am called to be. I do often wonder how God plans to use my gift of entrepreneurship to further His Kingdom.

Since I reaffirmed my faith in God on Easter of 2018, I've been excited and vocal about my becoming a Christian. Most people react with a mixture of mockery and intrigue. I know I am being watched to see if my life matches my profession of faith. People often ask if it's difficult being a Christian and a successful entrepreneur. I answer, "It's difficult being a Christian in any walk of life." The battle to conduct yourself in the ways of God is difficult for everyone.

I believe that every one of us, as we'll inevitably face death one day, will have to ask ourselves if we've lived our lives to the best of our abilities. I encourage you to start asking that question now so you can minimize the regrets and maximize the celebrations.

Ellen Goodman said, "Normal is getting dressed in clothes that you buy for work and driving through traffic in a car that you're still paying for in order to get to the job that you need to pay for the clothes and car and the home that's empty all day just so you can afford to live in it." It's sad for me how many people continue to live this way—to force themselves out of bed to live the same day again and again and call it a life when there are other options.

Ask yourself these three questions: 1) Imagine you have enough money to take care of your needs, now and in the future. How would you live your life? 2) Imagine your doctor says you have only 5-10 years to live. You won't feel sick, but you'll never know when death will come. What will you do? Will you change your life? How? 3) Finally, imagine that your doctor says you have only one day left to live. Ask yourself: What did I miss? What did I not get to be or do? This usually gets me thinking about how fragile life is and what I have yet to accomplish for God's Kingdom.

Has this inspired you to ask yourself some tough, but invigorating questions? Great! Now, go out and smile more, hug more, laugh more, and love more. Make your ripple in this world!

TWEETABLE

I believe that every one of us, as we'll inevitably face death one day, must ask ourselves if we've lived to the best of our abilities. Start asking that question now so you can minimize the regrets and maximize the celebrations.

Sean C. Na is the principal and founder of Brandmark Capital Partners, a successful real estate private equity firm. He is passionate about real estate and has been investing in real estate for over 10 years. Sean is more passionate about showing others his path to financial freedom and how that has enabled him to fund his passions in life. He loves talking about life, love, and legacy. To book a call with Sean, email info@brandmark.com or visit www.brandmark.com.

CHAPTER 24

Turning Discomfort into Mastery

by Nicholas J. Scalzo

For me, resilience is how well a person can adapt to their life situations or events. Like anyone else, there are events that have tested my resilience throughout the years. Some tested my resilience more than others.

May 19, 2006—it was a beautiful Friday afternoon in Washington DC. I was elated, feeling great, and on top of the world. Earlier in the day I went through the hooding ceremony at George Washington University and received my doctorate in counseling and human and organizational studies. I had just called my wife, and she told me the doctor said she was doing fine, her lungs were clear, and she would be able to come off of the oxygen. I was so happy and felt things couldn't be better as I drove back to my home in Long Island, New York. I could hardly wait to get there.

Little did I know, my world would come crashing down in two days. When I woke that Sunday morning, my wife had trouble breathing, and within an hour after speaking to the doctors, I carried her to the car and rushed to the emergency room. By the afternoon, she was unresponsive, and family members were arriving to say goodbye. By evening, she was gone. I was crushed, in pain, and shocked, and my world was shattered.

The grief was overwhelming. I spent months feeling a range of emotions from indignation, loss, sadness, grief, jealousy of other couples, and pity among others. I avoided being with family and friends. At times I felt forced by family members to attend holiday gatherings, which only made me sadder, and in some cases, angrier. I missed her terribly. When she was hospitalized, we discussed how we would finish the basement of our home—I spent the next year working on making it the way she dreamed. Spending time at work and focusing on home projects became my refuge.

I felt alone, losing my father a year earlier, then my wife, and months later, my mother. In less than two years, I lost my wife and both my parents. The people closest to me other than my children were no longer around, leaving me with a sense of isolation—and sometimes despair—like I had never experienced.

One day my father-in-law took me to the side and reminded me that I had a lot going for me, that I was young and should not be alone. He told me she wouldn't want that and encouraged me to live life. It was the wake-up call I needed. I reflected on what he said and thought about how to rebound.

I recalled helping a colleague through a similar situation years earlier. Using techniques and tools I had developed throughout my career and my own self-development, I worked with him through a devastating situation where he lost his job. We worked together on developing skills to increase his confidence, improve his leadership skills, and communicate more effectively. Realizing I had rebounded from hardships before—I knew what to do. I had already developed the knowledge, skills, and techniques needed to overcome obstacles. I had to step back and look at my situation, diagnose what I was doing, and how to take action. I had to change what I was doing to reclaim my life. Getting back in shape and running the Disney marathon were first, followed by reconnecting with friends and eventually dating. I was starting to feel confident, happy, challenged, reconnected, and alive. My daughter and I took dance lessons, thoroughly enjoying it, laughing at our missteps, and deepening our relationship.

Then it happened. A friend introduced me to a woman who had lost her spouse also. We hit it off immediately and rediscovered love. I felt I was alive again. We married approximately two years later and feel we are living for the four of us. I feel I have returned to being the "eternal optimist" my friends used to call me. I feel blessed being fortunate to find love twice in my life.

Feeling emotions of joy derived from our new adventures and our love reminds me of other times I overcame obstacles and how they changed the direction of my life. One obstacle in particular, a new position with new and unfamiliar responsibilities, had the most impact in the direction of my career.

I had always thought about becoming a math teacher and pursued my undergraduate degree in mathematics. However, graduating in 1971 proved to be a bad time for the hiring of teachers in New York. In my senior year at St. John's University in Jamaica, NY, I was working part-time in a major financial institution in the Wall Street area. Upon graduation, they offered me a full-time position in the stock transfer department. My initial strategy was to accept the position and stay there until I found a teaching position, but that never happened. I went so far as to take vacation days so I could serve as a substitute teacher in order to "get my foot in the door."

Then fate stepped in—I was enjoying my work and was rewarded with a promotion to supervisor of the department in less than a year. My original intention and desire to teach math was slipping away.

Another year passed, and I learned about an accelerated training program for college grads in another division. I went to my HR officer to throw my hat in the ring. When he informed me that the candidates for the training program were already selected—I was shocked and devastated. Later I found out that he had chosen his favorites, which made me suspicious and resentful of his motives. Being persistent, I wanted to know why I wasn't chosen. Finally, he revealed that the division was looking to develop a new training department. However, I would have to pass some tests to even be considered. I knew it would lead to developing new skills, more challenging work, and a better position. Even though I felt anxious about an unknown challenge, I wanted in!

I was overjoyed when I learned I excelled in the testing and was selected for the department. I didn't realize until I was in the position that besides developing training materials, job aids, and procedures, I had to teach other officers, managers, and staff in the organization about various topics! Now I became very nervous and uncertain about my abilities since teaching adults was quite different than teaching a math class to high school students. I was very uncomfortable presenting to management and large groups. I had a very low level of confidence and would go so far as to make excuses to my manager so I would not have to present at the seminars or classes. Subsequently, I would feel very apprehensive when I ran a class. I did not want to forget the lessons, say the wrong thing, or fall short of having the right answers.

In spite of my apprehension and discomfort, I was driven to succeed. I wanted to develop the knowledge, skills, and techniques to become an excellent corporate trainer. I wanted to do whatever it took to becoming confident and comfortable speaking and making training presentations. Among other things, I took classes in behavioral styles, presentation skills, and communication skills. It was hard work learning how to flex to other styles, move out of my comfort zone, present, lead skill practice, and manage group dynamics in the classroom setting. Learning about my developmental needs was, at times, embarrassing and eye opening. Many times I found the necessary study and practice difficult.

Looking back, though, it was all worth it. Quickly, I reached the point where I was speaking to groups of over 100 officers and managers with confidence. Over time, I became very comfortable designing training initiatives, making presentations, helping organizations create and manage change, and consulting or coaching senior executives. I was rewarded with various promotions up to Vice President of Corporate Training & Development in a time when Vice President titles were few and far between.

As I mentioned earlier, my friends have always called me "the eternal optimist," and I attribute much of my success to having a "positive attitude" and what I call "stick-to-itiveness," which I attribute to my dad always telling me to never give up—along with friends, family, and managers who supported my goals and development. My first manager provided opportunities for me to become aware of my strengths and development needs. Perhaps the most significant time was when my management sent me to Ojai California to attend a week long development workshop at the National Training Laboratories (NTL). There I learned a great deal about myself, which immensely helped me make a breakthrough in self-confidence. This awareness enabled me to focus my energies to become more flexible, versatile, and yes, resilient, and to change my professional behaviors. I am still an introvert at heart, according to my Myers-Briggs and DiSC assessments, but I learned how to flex to a style that helps me relate to, coach, and lead others.

My professional experiences facilitated my desire to pursue a master's degree and a doctorate in counseling and human and organizational studies. As a result, I developed my knowledge, skills, and abilities to the point where my career enabled me to present at international conferences, conduct numerous seminars for high-level managers and executive leaders both domestically and internationally, and write my first book on organizational change. Additionally, those same professional experiences, skills, and techniques were eventually instrumental in helping me rebound and overcome the challenges of my first wife's passing. They have truly blessed my life.

Today, I help individuals and organizations overcome obstacles, improve their performance, change direction, identify objectives, and set goals to achieve success. I also help others maximize their own potential through providing executive coaching on a personal level.

Looking back, this journey has taken me full circle back into what my initial career goal was—teaching (albeit not math) and much more. I now teach graduate and undergraduate courses as an adjunct professor in multiple universities on topics such as leadership, strategic planning, high-performing work teams, managing conflict, and human resources. To say that I am extremely satisfied and proud of my development, the skills

I developed, and the people and organizations I have helped reach their potential is an understatement.

Looking back, I can honestly say that even though some of the lessons learned and skills developed were difficult and trying at times, they have enabled me to enjoy what I consider to be a wonderful and fulfilling career which I still enjoy to this day. This is all possible because I learned the communication tools and techniques to enhance my resilience and versatility.

So, what are the lessons I would like to share with you?

Simply, each of us are going to have successes and setbacks throughout our lives and careers. The key is not to focus on the setbacks to the point where they hold us back, but to look at them as obstacles to test our mettle. To overcome those obstacles, we must:

- Step back and observe the obstacle or frustration.

- Diagnose the situation—what is going on or what has happened?

- Adapt to the situation by:
  - using the tools of resilience, flexibility, and versatility
  - using personal assessment and development to improve on our skills
  - accessing your family, friends, and supporting network for honest feedback.

- Take action and persevere to reach your goals.

Remember, being able to observe, diagnose, adapt, grow, and persevere are critical for your success.

TWEETABLE

The world will always present obstacles. It is what we do when we come upon them that allows them to make or break us. To overcome obstacles, we must step back and observe the situation, diagnose what is going on or what has happened, adapt to the situation by using tools or techniques to improve our conceptualization, and finally, take action and persevere to reach your goals and achieve success.

Nicholas J. Scalzo is the principal architect of OnTrack, a training, consulting, and coaching firm, which creates tailored solutions for select clients. The philosophy at OnTrack Training is to provide extensive expertise in leadership, interpersonal communications, organizational change, and executive coaching to help clients meet their business goals. In partnership with select clients, we help identify a client's present status and future direction, analyze the gap between the two, and select and implement the steps needed to bridge the gap. Many clients have consulted with Nicholas and used his tools and services for over 20 years.

CHAPTER 25

Let Faith Carry You

by Meredith Besse Maggio

grew up in a small town called Morgan City, Louisiana, 70 miles from New Orleans where I live now. Most of the time people refer to Louisianans with the idea that we have Mardi Gras daily or that alligators are pets to us. That is not the case, but I can assure you that my life has been a parade of success and I've bitten every opportunity that has come to me like an alligator.

Education and Southern manners were my upbringing since I was a young girl. My mother and father both taught school for 40 years. My mother was an English professor and my father was a history professor football coach at the local junior high school and everyone in their environment knew me. They were both my first teachers who taught me how to read, write, communicate and share with others. They instilled in me faith that I could carry myself and endure at a young age. "Greatness ought to be a habit" my mother would quote to me from Aristotle. She would say, "Never make Mum upset about your character. Go off into the world and experience all you can."

When I graduated from college, I got married at 23 and started working in corporate America. At age 24, I got involved in a well-known networking business part-time to help bring in extra money. Little did I know, this company would lead me to meet Jim Rohn himself.

Two years into this part-time business, I decided to leave my corporate America 9 to 5. Well, I am 110% proof that anyone can do it. I decided to leave my full-time job as a paralegal for a major global law firm to start the rest of my life as my own boss. And it was final.

I read *The Day That Turns Your Life Around* by Jim Rohn over and over. I listened to the cassettes so much that I wore out the tape and had to buy another copy! In September 2006, I was rewarded and honored by the chance to meet Jim Rohn at a convention brunch with the millionaire team in Las Vegas. I remember being so young. I still wonder if I wore the right outfit and shoes. I'm such a Southern belle when it comes to manners and fashion. Did I say "yes, sir" and "thank you, sir" to Jim Rohn?

The brunch was only for the team members who made the qualifications for the month and was an extra advantage that changed my life. Jim had this way as we all know, of taking over a crowd and making them feel how extraordinary FAITH was and that you could become a better you if you just started and held on. I was hooked the minute I saw, heard, and felt Jim Rohn. It was the best brunch I ever had in my life. Everyone at the brunch was listening to *The Day That Turns Your Life Around* non-stop after the brunch was over.

My Southern manners did kick-in at the end of the brunch as we all were thanking Jim Rohn for the wonderful, wise words of wisdom. I dashed to the elevator to personally shake his hand and make sure I got the chance to make eye contact with him. Wow, what an experience, a handshake that I will never forget. His smile was contagious, and I truly believe that's why I smile so much today.

As soon as the plane home from Las Vegas was in the air, I felt a strong need to come home. Fear and faith were the only two things that went through my mind. I had a fear of something, and I could not figure out why. Still, I had faith that I would face whatever came to the best of my abilities.

At the time, I was still married, but when I returned home from this convention I would not be married anymore. I returned home to an empty home and letter on the table. Yes, it was a Dear John letter from my husband explaining how he did not want to married to me. My heart dropped to the floor and my faith flew out the window.

Unable to understand why or what to do next, I became silent for the first time in my life. The empty feeling of wondering what I did wrong, my stomach was empty from not eating for days, I did not want to live. I regretted quitting my paralegal career which I graduated from to become the successful corporate America employee, the wonderful wife, and one day the mother of children with this man. Why, what, how and rock bottom is what I hit. Most people think that after a divorce you cannot revamp your life totally and do everything you ever could dream of. Well, I am 110% proof that anyone can do it.

Jim Rohn kept playing in the background of my mind and never stopped. It was that inner voice that made me build and create my life over from rock bottom. I recognized I was not in a good position and needed to start making money immediately. I needed to change my career again and leave the network marketing lifestyle. I couldn't think of any way to stay and make money as fast as I needed it to be able to move away and start over.

Eventually, I trusted what I knew best. I knew cleaning and organizing houses. For many years, I had cleaned houses on the side for extra money. To win the battle in my mind and in my feelings, I moved my expectations and faith to a new adventure. I would be a"maid" and clean everything I could. It was possible to start this kind of business anywhere because everyone needs cleaning.

I kept on listening to Jim Rohn for years. House after house, office after office, hour after hour, I listened to him as I cleaned each property. I allowed FAITH to carry me throughout the years.

Twelve years later, I arrived at the destination I had designed in my mind with all those Jim Rohn teachings and courses. I have proudly founded, owned, and operated five successful cleaning and service businesses. Pelican Maintenance Services, LLC is my newest service company which I still work in the office and in the field daily. They say love what you do, and I love making things in order for my customers.

I have also joined another network marketing company after 12 years away. I finally found a company with products I deeply believe in because they are healing and changing lives. I am growing quite rapidly in this business and still use the same methods I was taught years ago about networking from Jim Rohn. I like to call it net-worthing.

The lessons I learned from my experiences and hardships have also led me to venture out to do motivational speeches and coach/teach others how they can do the same as I have in any career or business. My life turned around the day I met Jim Rohn and the day I decided that I was worth everything I dreamed I could be.

I am not just a maid who cleans and organizes your home or office. I am a "made" Jim Rohn follower and believer who says you can do anything you put your heart, mind, and soul into.

WISER, BETTER, and STRONGER…. Jim Rohn

Bouncing back to a new life and knowing you can do it is the key to any success. My advice for any setback is that your success is hidden in your daily routine. You have to keep your faith by knowing you can and then go out and do it over and over. Routines make millionaires more money.

I am blessed to have had the opportunity to meet Jim Rohn at a young age and now his long-time business partner Kyle Wilson. I would have never dreamed of having mentors like both of them who have inspired me to let faith carry me.

I look forward to the journey ahead of me, and FAITH will carry me.

TWEETABLE

Faith is an extraordinary feeling. It makes your ambition, your drive, or your dream not fade. It makes you imagine things no one can see when no one believes in you. And it crushes the pain when it hurts too much to explain. So, never give up on faith.

Meredith Besse Maggio is a passionate businesswoman and founder of several service businesses in New Orleans, LA. 12 years of cleaning houses, offices, dormitories, and cruise ships landed The Queen of Clean a spot as a professional cleaner on A&E's Hoarders in 2009. When she isn't serving clients, Meredith mentors through her coaching company Merry's Choice, LLC. She is an affiliate for a new network marketing company and has changed lives with the products and opportunity.

In her copious time, she enjoys public speaking, tailgating for the Saints, family time, and being a proud Krewe of Cleopatra member in Carnival.

Contact her at meredithmaggio1980@icloud.com

CHAPTER 26

How RESILIENCE Helped a Failed Engineer Become an Entrepreneur and a Business Owner

by Alpesh Parmar

"When we tackle obstacles, we find hidden reserves of courage and resilience we did not know we had. And it is only when we are faced with failure do we realize that these resources were always there within us."

– A.P.J. Abdul Kalam

I would like to thank God for all the blessings and appreciate my family and friends for their support and guidance.

"You will have to go back to India by end of this month if we can't find a consulting gig for you. Legally, we cannot keep you here if you are not on a consulting project," said my employer in the US. I knew this was coming, I had seen my colleagues migrate back to their home countries, but I was hoping I would have a little more time. My shoulders dropped and I slumped in my chair. Lots of things started going through my mind.

I was thinking: *Have I tried my best? Have I given everything I have? Will I be considered a failure if I go back home? What will my parents, relatives, and friends think about me? Am I ready to buckle down and work towards my goal at any cost?*

I grew up in a tightly-knit working class family in the western part of India. I was a good student, and I was trained to work hard in school so I could get a well-paying job. I got into an Indian undergraduate school for computer engineering and failed during my first year. Before this, I had never experienced a failure. My relatives said, "This is a tough college to graduate from. Find a college which is less reputed and has an easier curriculum."

Despite their good intentions, I didn't listen. I went back to the same engineering college and finished undergrad easily. I did not want to prove anyone wrong, but I wasn't prepared to give up. We humans have the ability to bounce back from any kind of setback, and I was able to test that theory myself.

Why do I mention my engineering days? At the age of 18, I was unknowingly developing a character trait which was going to be very important in shaping my career and my life. And that was RESILIENCE.

I started working as soon as I graduated, but I was always looking for a better opportunity. I was hired by an US-based IT consulting firm and ended up moving to the US on a work visa in February 2001. As soon as I arrived, I saw that the dot com bubble had burst and there was no work in IT.

I kept looking for work and something terrible happened. The World Trade Center was attacked by terrorists on September 11th, and that crashed the financial market. This event took many lives and took down the US economy. Now, it was almost impossible to find work. On top of that, attacks on Indian migrants and non-immigrants increased in New York and New Jersey, making safety a concern. Non-immigrants are visitors, people with permanent residence outside the United States who are in the US temporarily for a specific purpose. The land of opportunities had turned into the land of nightmares for migrants because of the lack of jobs and the safety issues. Some of my colleagues and friends started moving back to their home countries or started working odd jobs. I was depressed, confused, and feeling homesick and I had almost no money. This was exactly when my employer asked me to move back to India.

I wasn't ready to concede defeat for something which was not in my control. Throughout this series of events, I always kept a positive attitude and I was confident in my abilities. To build resilience, one must keep calm, rely on his or her strengths and effectively manage feelings and impulses.

I was asking for advice from everyone I met, and one of my friends said "Alpesh, you have a great sense of humor and you possess good problem-solving skills. Use this failure as a stepping stone in the journey you have embarked upon and keep going."

I decided to meet my friends from engineering school who were pursuing graduate degrees in New York and New Jersey. They suggested that I also start working towards earning a master's degree. I had $2000 left when I decided that I should pursue my master's to ride the downturn and make myself marketable in the ultra-competitive job market. I knew starting to work towards a graduate degree wouldn't be easy, but I underestimated the struggle I would go through. I have heard people say that the tough times define you as a person. This was the start of the toughest time in my life, and I didn't know if or when it would end.

I realized that I would have to work odd jobs to take care of my expenses and pay the fees for the graduate degree. I worked at a restaurant, juice store, and liquor store and did everything: mopping the floor, washing utensils, making coffees and juices, selling liquor, managing inventory, and making deli sandwiches. In the meantime, I was accepted into three universities. I chose the university which offered me a scholarship and had a graduate assistantship program as well. I started working a night shift at a 7-Eleven store. This was a 12-hour grind every day until the start of the spring semester. When my first semester arrived, I still didn't have money to pay tuition for the first semester. I ended up borrowing money from friends to cover the remaining tuition.

To build resilience, you need to have supportive relationships with your family and friends. I was blessed to have a supportive family, but no one was in the US with me. Fortunately, I was surrounded by some of the most helpful and generous people as my friends. One thing I learned is, having a strong network of friends (and not just "Facebook friends") is a valuable component of building better resilience.

My classes were in the evening, so I kept working the night shift. I would go to 7-Eleven right after college. I was tired, starved, and sleep-deprived. My lunch used to be a bag of chips and a can of soda from a vending machine. I moved close to the university and started sharing a one bedroom apartment with five other students. Only one of us had a car, so there were numerous days when I had to walk in a foot of snow with regular sneakers and a couple layers of clothing. One night, I saw there was a big fight in the parking lot of 7-Eleven, and someone was shot. I was so scared that I quit my job.

"Resilience originates from hardship but has its roots in a desire to continue to survive, even thrive, and it is even better when that survival is nurtured by the collective support of others." – John Baldoni

I kept looking for another job and landed a job at another grocery store which was in a good neighborhood. This grocery store was about five miles away from college and my apartment, so I needed a car. I bought a clunker from a classmate for $1000. Finally, everything seems to be getting in order.

Until I felt really bad again during the spring of 2003. My youngest sister was getting married, and I didn't have enough money to visit India. Besides, my work visa was getting converted to a student visa, so I was asked not to travel outside the USA until that was cleared. I was forced to give precedence to my career over my family. I will never forget this.

My life started turning a corner in the summer of 2003. I found work at a local vitamin store where I didn't have to stand on my feet the whole day and I was able to study during off-peak hours. I was also able to pay back the debt I owed my friends. In fact, I worked so hard during that summer that I had enough money saved to make a trip back home in December. It had been almost three years since I had seen my family, my relatives, and my hometown. So much had changed in three years, but my family members were the same. I met the woman of my dreams during this trip and got engaged.

I finished my master's in May 2004 and landed a job as a software engineer. I kept working at the vitamin store over the weekends so I could have enough money saved for my wedding. I got married in December, and my wife moved to the US with me. After the marriage, I was privileged to work for companies like SAP and PricewaterhouseCoopers.

In 2009, I moved from the E (Employee) quadrant to S (self-employed) quadrant. I started a software consulting business by partnering with my colleague who I consider my mentor and close friend.

My dad asked me, "Would you continue to work as a full-time employee so you have something to fall back on if the business doesn't work out?" Guess what my answer was. Being an employee was over for me.

My partner and I became pretty famous and built our name in a niche industry. I became a well-known name in IT compliance world and an internationally recognized speaker. I just couldn't believe that in the past I was earning $2000 a month after 80 grueling hours every week and now I was making over $20,000 a month after starting my own business.

I may not be as smart as others around me. I may not have had connections, but I was resilient.
> RE-S-I-LI-EN-T
> RE – Responsible

S – Spontaneous
I – Innovative
LI – Liked
EN – Enthusiastic
T – Tenacious

I read *Rich Dad Poor Dad* in 2015, and I decided to start investing in real estate. I started buying single-family houses and acquired four of them in 2015 and 2016. I wanted to get out of the rat race, but it's hard to scale up quickly using single-family houses, so I started learning about multifamily buildings. I attended tons of meetups, webinars, conferences, and boot camps. With the newly acquired knowledge, I was able to acquire a couple of small apartment buildings in 2017. I have also invested in a coffee farm, a resort facility, storage facilities and in other niches so I can get enough diversification.

I consider resilience to be the catalyst behind my success. I was able to bounce back from each setback in my career and come out stronger.

After going through the process of acquiring real estate and diversifying myself, I wanted to show my friends what I learned. This is how the idea for my next business was born. I started Wealth Matters where I guide people on how to invest in alternative investments like single-family houses, multi-family buildings, mortgage notes, and syndications.

I read *The Go-Giver* this year and concluded that to reach a lot of people, I need to share my story through podcasts, books, webinars, etc.

Yes, it's been a journey, but the challenges are what helped me not only grow but also prepare me for this new opportunity to impact so many others with financial freedom. I hope I can guide others towards getting freedom from the day to day grind too.

TWEETABLE

When life closes a door, it always opens another door. We are so focused on the closed door that we forget to see the opportunity waiting for us on the other side of the open door. Don't be a QUITTER and give up.

Alpesh Parmar is an entrepreneur who owns over 100 rental units, runs a successful software consulting business, and provides wealth building services through his business—Wealth Matters (www. wealthmatrs.com). He also runs a local investment meetup and recently started Wealth Matters podcast.

Alpesh has been happily married to Kinjal for 13 years. They have two beautiful daughters. Alpesh believes wealth, fitness and mental health are the keys to living a successful and stress-free life. Contact Alpesh to discuss investments in tangible assets, syndications or anything wealth, life, or fitness at alpesh@wealthmatrs.com

CHAPTER 27

From Being Cursed to Being Blessed

by Doug Kelley

t was my high school graduation, and I was excited to close this chapter of my life and move on to what was next. I was waiting patiently for my name to be called.

The superintendent of North Toole County High School in Sunburst, Montana always shared a few kind words about the graduate before handing out the diploma. With only 32 graduates, each senior was given a few carefully chosen words to facilitate their transfer from high school to whatever was next in their life.

High school had been a blur of activity and various accomplishments. I had lettered nine times in three different sports, been co-editor of the school paper, president of the Lettermen's Club, and winner of the local oratory contest.

On the negative side, I managed to scrape by with barely passable grades in Latin, algebra, and geometry. I ranked a solid 15 out of 32 in my class, as girls, sports, and friends were far more important than good grades.

Now was my moment to leave the nest and get on with my dream to become the next Perry Mason—the master of the courtroom. Perry Mason might have been just a television rendition of the perfect lawyer, but I knew I could reach for the stars and actually become that lawyer. My dad had taught me to dream big. He preached to his family the "can do anything" gospel of work and sacrifice. A modest scholarship had induced me to commit to a small Catholic college two hours from home. I could hardly wait to make new friends and meet new challenges.

As my name, Douglas B. Kelley, was announced, I eagerly moved forward to receive my diploma. As I approached the podium, the superintendent appeared to be at a loss for words.

Finally, he said, "I don't really know what to say about this next student, except that Doug has been the MOST CONTROVERSIAL STUDENT who has ever come through the doors of our high school."

I was not sure if the superintendent had pronounced a blessing or a curse. I took my diploma, waved at my family, and joined the rest of my class.

The superintendent was not oblivious to my tenure as the head of the Lettermen's Club that went overboard in initiating new members, or the editorials I had written critical of the school administration, or my effort to change the name of the school mascot.

Graduating was a small step that would ultimately lead me to seven years of college, marriage to Cathy Dean, and multiple occupations—lawyer, pastor, personnel business owner, travel agency owner, restaurant and marina owner, real estate investor, international conference speaker, and author.

Little did I know, my life both personal and professional would be full of zigs and zags—from altar boy to born-again Christian, from doubting Doug to Pastor Doug, from prosecuting attorney to pastor of broken-hearted drug addicts, alcoholics, prostitutes, and criminals, from 50 years in majestic Montana to the chaos and confusion of the streets of South Central Los Angeles.

As my superintendent predicted, through all the changes and challenges, controversies have followed me like a barking dog. But, this is a story about more than a barking dog named controversy. It's a story about God's blessing in spite of controversy.

Lawyers are quick to ask a judge to take notice of indisputable facts. There are three facts concerning blessing of which we should take judicial notice. These apply to everybody regardless of ethnicity, economics, religion, or gender.

First, everybody wants to be blessed. We wake up hoping and praying that today will be our lucky day. We hope we will meet the person of our dreams, get the promotion that we desperately want, win the lottery, or be more loved and appreciated than anybody, anywhere.

Second, everybody is not blessed. Not everybody gets the blessing, the girl, the job, the lottery, or whatever else that represents blessing. Many of us grab for the gold and catch a handful of dust. We are all yearning for something more.

Third, God wants to bless us. The Bible says that the eye of the Lord goes looking for somebody to bless. Many of us are like the little boy waving his arm vigorously in the air while hollering as loud as he can, "Choose me, choose me!"

I recently finished a year that was more of a curse than a blessing. I like to label years in advance and then try to fulfill the lofty label. Often, advance labeling proves false and fruitless and must yield to historical reality. Honesty demands looking back and judging each year on the basis of what actually happened.

In the 1990s, when I had completed a very bad year (due to a church split, my brother leaving me, etc.), I joyfully announced to the church, "Happy days are here again." Wrong! Instead of happy days, we had more painful days to endure.

As 2010 was coming to a close, I was visiting with Kert Evans, my church administrator. Knowing how he also liked to label the years (the year of the building, the year of Arms of Praise, etc.), I told him that I had a label for 2010.

"What do you think 2010 was?" asked Kert.

"It was the year from HELL. With four lawsuits, a broken relationship, and $20,000 spent on lawyers and buildings, I am lucky to be alive," I exclaimed. "Building inspectors, bills, and bureaucrats have made my life a living hell on earth."

"I don't agree," Kert stated. "I think 2010 was the year of the House of Hope (our residential substance abuse recovery ministry begun in April 2010). Look what we were able to get done this past year."

"I can't believe you, the man my wife calls the 'most negative man who ever lived,' are more positive than me. You are right," I conceded. "We had some great accomplishments that were birthed in the midst of tribulation this year."

Was it possible that we were both right? It had been a year filled with both hell and heaven. The truth is that we all experience heaven and hell every year (sometimes every day). Even in a time that appears to be hell, you can find the blessing within. I have learned that when you are going through hell, don't stop.

Over the years, I have concluded that I am a non-conformist. I am a lawyer, pastor, author, and businessman. But more importantly, I am a husband, father, and grandfather. I want to be known as a man of compassion and passion—a man of God, a man of integrity.

Robert Frost wrote a poem about a man coming to a fork in the road. Like many before me, I chose the road less traveled. As a young man growing up in a small Montana town of 500, I was ambitious. I wanted to be rich and powerful.

I looked at graduating from law school as the first rung on the ladder of success. I was in charge of my own destiny. I committed myself to be a risk taker—buying and selling real estate, taking cases on contingency, doing what nobody else wanted to do.

My dad had prepared me to be more than a mediocre man living a modest life of obscurity. I remember coming home one night after spending time with a girlfriend. My dad met me at the door and asked me, "What time is it?"

I quickly looked at my watch and said, "It's 10:10 pm."

"And what time are you supposed to be home according to your basketball team's curfew?"

"10 pm," I answered.

"So, what are you going to do tomorrow?"

"I don't know," I confessed.

"I'm going to tell you what you are going to do," Dad said. "You are going to go to your coach and report your curfew violation. If you don't, I will call the coach and your basketball days are over."

The next day I found the coach and confessed that I had broken curfew by ten minutes. He looked shocked that I would confess such a minor infraction. He made me run a few laps as punishment.

The lesson was not having a hard-nosed dad. It was learning a life lesson of integrity. The blessing is always on the side of the truth-teller.

During my life, I have had the joy of being a candidate for lieutenant governor, attorney general, and other political offices. I met and introduced a future president, ran political campaigns, and raised my voice for the people and causes that I believed in.

I have been blessed to buy and sell a hundred properties and own numerous businesses on my way to becoming a multi-millionaire.

There are many keys to finding and receiving the blessing that we all want. I have written a book on how to position yourself for blessing. For me, one of the keys to blessing is taking risks. You must ignore the dream stealers and those who attempt to curse you with limitations.

We are responsible for our ultimate destiny. We can be a victim or a victor, a success or a failure, blessed or cursed. Thank God that He created us in His image and likeness with the ability to choose.

Over the years, I have been criticized by those who disagreed with me politically or spiritually. I have learned to eat the meat and spit out the bones. Oftentimes, criticism is nothing but a poor man's counsel. I have grown more from the criticism of enemies than the flattery of friends.

If I had accepted the label "most controversial student" as a curse, none of these accomplishments would have happened. My future would have been limited to fulfilling an arbitrary assessment. The greatest blessings are not material but spiritual and relational. By simply following the Word of God, I have been able to embrace blessing as a way of life.

Many years ago, as I was preparing to speak at a convention, I felt God say, "Tell them you are a millionaire." I argued with the Lord as I could only see misunderstanding, jealousy, and other negatives coming with such a pronouncement.

Nevertheless, I could not get this insistent impression out of my mind.

"I want to tell you something that I have never said before in public," I stated. "I heard God speak to me this morning as I was finishing my preparation for this message. He told me to tell you that I am a millionaire."

It was very quiet, and everybody's attention was glued to the podium, waiting for what was next. I told the people that God was no respecter of persons and that He did not love me more than them. Many of them were secret millionaires, as their farms were worth well over a million dollars.

I explained that I was an accidental millionaire. It was never my passion or purpose to become a millionaire but simply to serve the Lord. Many of us were "paper millionaires" because of the value of our acquisitions.

Oftentimes risk takers have to overcome their initial reluctance and battle through their fear of people, failure, or unseen consequences. The risk taker thinks and acts differently than others.

The risk taker says, "It's only money," while others say, "You could lose everything." The risk taker says, "What have you got to lose?" while most say, "Better safe than sorry." The risk taker says, "You can always start over," while others say, "I'm too old to start over."

Risk taking is more than buying and selling. Ultimately, risk taking is all about believing that God is the provider who covers us when our banker says no. He is the Peace Giver when our risk-taking raises fears within us. Blessing and success come to those willing to take risks.

Being labeled as "most controversial student" was not a setback but a motivational prod to live life without a safety net or need to conform. We choose our destiny by how we respond to accusations and circumstances.

TWEETABLE

Being labeled as "most controversial student" was not a setback but a motivational prod to live life without a safety net.

Doug Kelley has lived a life of meaning and purpose as a lawyer, pastor, politician, entrepreneur, writer, and motivational speaker. He travels to speak at leadership conferences in the Philippines, Malaysia, Mexico, India, and other places. Doug is known for his humor, directness, and transparency as he shares his faith and success in his journey to becoming a multi-millionaire. His "can do" approach comes with practical steps to lead from unbelief to faith and poverty to wealth. Doug has written a book on positioning yourself for blessing as well as many other helpful books such as Increasing Your Capacity, No Excuses/No Limitations *and* Finishing Well. *To schedule Doug, contact him at dougkelley.us or pastordougkelley@aim.com*

CHAPTER 28

Getting Fired From My Dream Job Was the Best Thing That Ever Happened to Me

by EJ Sansone

My childhood was far from picture-perfect. I was the only boy with three sisters and a single mother until I was 10 years old. Aside from being a role model of what not to be, my biological father played a very little role in my life. I haven't had any meaningful contact with him since before I can remember. Around the age of 11, my mother married my stepfather, and shortly after, gave birth to my half-sister and half-brother. I was lucky to gain a couple more siblings, but that was essentially where the luck ran out. My stepfather's hostile presence was probably more damaging than my biological father's lack of presence. My mother did her best, but despite her effort, my childhood was extremely unstable. There were times when we didn't know where our next meal would come from. I can still feel the eyes of judgmental bystanders fixed on my mother in the checkout line as she paid for groceries using food stamps. We also had to move frequently to keep a roof over our head. In fact, we moved nine times before I started high school. As a result, feelings of loneliness from having to leave friends behind and the awkwardness of being the "new kid" in school were pervasive throughout my childhood.

The "homelife" that I grew accustomed to as a child was more akin to a war zone than the stereotypical portrayal of homelife that we all dream of. Any given moment in our house held the potential of being the next knock-down, drag-out fight between my mother and father/stepfather. My siblings and I would often hide together from the loud yelling and crashing noises. When a fight started to break out, we would gather together and huddle under a blanket or in a closet and comfort one another as our parents had it out. Eventually, as I grew older, I became bold enough to step out of hiding and tried to intervene to make it stop. Unfortunately, my interventions did little to help the situation and only brought me more pain and anger. I slowly learned that there was nothing I could do to make the fighting stop, so instead, I tried to be absent from home whenever possible.

It was easy to get lost in the chaos, and I took full advantage by running wild during my high school years. This led me down a path that I did not envision for myself, but after losing my way for several years as a teenager, God steered me back to a path that was more in line with the life I wanted for myself. With the cut-off date for college applications looming during my senior year of high school, I filled out a college application and got accepted to a small liberal arts college in the middle-of-nowhere, Missouri. I spent another year discovering myself during my freshman year of college before transferring to a larger state university where I would go on to graduate with a bachelor's degree in business administration and a Juris doctor degree. After countless interviews and receiving rejection letter after rejection letter, I finally locked in my dream job with a large real estate development and investment firm.

My first few months on the job were a whirlwind. It was very much sink or swim, and sinking was not an option for me. I had worked too hard to get to this point. So, I worked overtime and did everything I could to excel at my job. After about a year of on-the-job training, I felt like I was firing on all cylinders, and I was being recognized for all my hard work. I received raises and bonuses every year until my salary pushed into the six-figure range. It was a great job that was providing me with many luxuries—my employer provided a generous six percent match to my 401k contributions to help me save for retirement, I had two weeks of paid time off per year, I was living in a downtown loft, I drove a nice car, and I had discretionary income for nights out on the town and a few vacations a year.

I had followed "the playbook" to an absolute tee—get an education, get a job, work hard, climb the ladder, make money, be happy. But something was missing. I was about four years into my job, and I was getting a bit restless. Maybe it was time to make a move and try something new? Maybe a promotion at work would make me feel better? Around this time my boss told me one of the vice presidents of our company wanted to talk with me. I was very excited because I thought this could very well be the break that would help to settle the restlessness that I had been experiencing. I was on vacation in Colorado at the time, but I gladly set aside some time to receive the call. I took the call and was identified as a key person within the organization and was informed that I would be eligible to receive multiple six-figure bonuses. Here is how it would work: all I would need to do is continue working for the company for the next ten years to collect all the bonus payments, the first of four bonus payments would occur in three years, then several more after that until I hit year ten. Pretty straightforward. I got off the phone and told my wife about the call. She could sense how I really felt and questioned why I seemed disappointed after receiving such exciting news. I was disappointed because this was not the type of incentive package that incentivizes people like me. There was absolutely no upside based on performance—just ride out the next ten years of my life while working for them and I would get paid lump sums (fully taxed as bonus compensation). I had just received a snapshot of the next ten years of my professional life, and the next ten years looked roughly the same as the last four years. Sure, I would have more money, but I would still be punching the clock for someone else, and my destiny would be in their hands.

I was feeling more uneasy than ever, so I started to look at my options. Lucky for me, I had acquired a great skill set in the past four years with my employer. I had learned how to harness the power of real estate syndication. Real estate syndication is basically the pooling of funds from investors and channeling them into real estate projects to complete them using very little of your own money. Maybe I too could benefit from syndication by raising money from investors to complete my own deals? I stewed on this idea for a while and then began to put together a small deal where I would be the deal sponsor and one of my family members would be the investor. I wasn't ready to go "all in," so I was careful to put together a deal that could be viewed as a personal investment and that would not compete with my current employer's deals. There were plenty of people that worked for the same company who had real estate holdings, so I didn't think that having an investment of my own would ruffle any feathers.

To keep everything on the up-and-up, after the deal began to materialize, I planned to inform them of my plans to ensure that there would not be a conflict. I never got that opportunity. While I was vetting the deal, I presented it to a lender to get a feel for the financing terms that would be available for such a deal. Unbeknownst to me, the lender had a tie to my employer and threw me under the bus. I got called onto the carpet and fired on the spot, no questions asked. I had gone from the "key," six-figure salary guy to totally expendable and fired. I left work that day without a cell phone to call my wife to tell her the news (my cell phone was company property and was confiscated). I arrived home that evening scared to tell my wife what had happened. I was the primary provider for our family, and I was sure she was going to panic. It felt like everything that I had worked so hard for evaporated into thin air. Life was over as we knew it.

Now, it's only fair to stop here and say that I don't necessarily blame anyone for my getting fired. Was the lender wrong for breaching confidentiality and ultimately getting me fired? Yes! Could my employer have responded differently and asked more about the opportunity that I was exploring? Yes! Was I looking at an opportunity that may have led to me leaving my job anyway? Yes! However, I ended up walking away from the deal, and it never came to be. So, it is more than likely that I probably would've continued working at that job until the time was "right" to leave, and who knows when that would have been, if ever. Instead, I got a universal kick in the ass that set me on the path to pursue my passions—real estate development, investing, and syndication. Sometimes we ask God for things and he delivers in unexpected ways and at unexpected times. These are often life-defining moments.

After arriving home, sharing the news with my wife, and wallowing in self-pity for about 24 hours, it was time to refocus and get back to work. What was I going to do? We needed my income to survive. We discussed the possibilities of me getting another job or me trying to make it on my own. We knew that it wouldn't be easy if I tried to start my own company because we had not prepared, and I was starting from nothing. My only option to fund a new company was to dip into my retirement fund. For me, the decision was obvious, this had happened through divine intervention and my path was unfolding just as I had asked for in my prayers. I had to go for it! Lucky for me, I have a wife who believes in me just as much as I believe in myself, and above all else, we both have faith in God to see us through any worthy mission.

So just like that, I cashed out my 401k account and founded Edgewater Real Estate Co. in February of 2017. I was betting big on myself because I knew it was a sure bet. Edgewater was founded with a rebellious spirit and abundance mentality—to create and share lucrative private investment opportunities that are outside of the high-volatility Wall Street machine. It has been an absolute grind, but I wouldn't trade it for the world. I have officially escaped the rat race, and I am building wealth through real estate investing. My destiny is no longer in someone else's hands, and I don't have to trade my time for money. My success is a product of how hard I work and is only limited by the strength of my desire.

In just 18 short months, I have assembled a real estate portfolio worth over $5,000,000. The most amazing part of this is that I have done it with very little of my own money. It was all done through the power of real estate syndication.

I now live a life by my own design. I have more time to spend with the people I love and doing the things that I enjoy. I can honestly look back and say that getting fired from my dream job was the best thing that ever happened to me. Often, when it feels like everything is falling apart, it is actually everything falling together. Trust the divine unfolding and seize your life-defining moment.

TWEETABLE

Often, when it feels like everything is falling apart, it is actually everything falling together. Trust the divine unfolding and seize your life-defining moment.

EJ Sansone is an attorney-at-law, real estate broker, real estate developer, investor, and syndicator. He has vast experience acquiring, developing, constructing, syndicating, and managing complex real estate projects in multiple asset classes. EJ founded Edgewater Real Estate Co. to create income and wealth for his family and his investors and their families that will endure for generations. Contact EJ for investment insights, speaking engagements, or to partner with the Edgewater Real Estate Co. esansone@edgewaterreco.com, www.edgewaterreco.com

CHAPTER 29

Resilience and My Tribute to Those Who Serve

by Ron White

I started speaking on the topic of memory in 1991. At the same time, I was a telemarketer for a company that cleaned chimneys.

One day I called up a guy and I offered to clean his chimney, and he said, "We don't want our chimney cleaned. We're trying to sell our house."

So I said, "Well, if you're trying to sell your house you need a clean chimney."

He laughed and said, "I don't know about that, but I need a good telemarketer." He taught memory seminars, and not long after, he hired me as a telemarketer.

It was hard. The first year in business I made $7,500 for the entire year. That was 1992.

In 1998, things were going decent. I was making $25,000 a year, but I was still only 24 years old. I was dating a girl, and she ripped my heart out and stepped on it. I had to get out of Texas. So, I looked at a map and picked the farthest city away from Fort Worth I could find but still be in the United States: Seattle.

I got in my car and drove to Seattle. The first six weeks in Seattle, I made $20,000. I hadn't made $20,000 in a year, and I had just made it in six weeks. I was succeeding, and I was focused, but then I started being a big mouth and talking. I often played pool with my buddy at a bar, and there was a guy there who I never saw playing pool with anybody. I kept seeing him night after night. And so, one night I said, "Hey man, I see you here every night. Why don't you come play pool with us?" From there, he listened to me talk for two or three days. He just listened and asked me questions. I kept saying "Oh man, I just made $20,000. You know I'm gonna make $10,000 next week."

Then he told me his story. He told me that he owned all these restaurants, that his best friend was the manager at Microsoft, and that his other best friend was the basketball player for the Seattle Supersonics. The next thing I knew, he wanted to be my business partner.

He moved me into a $4,000 a month apartment in downtown Seattle on 1st Ave. I was 25 years old, I was making $20,000 a month, and this guy was my new business partner who was a multi-millionaire, supposedly.

Then one night at dinner, it was me and him and his date. He turned to his date and said, "Did I ever tell you what happens when the person with money meets the person with experience?"

She was like, "No what happens?"

He said, "The person with the experience gets the money, and the person with the money gets the experience."

It immediately sent chills up my back, 'cause I knew he was talking to me, but I didn't know why. I really couldn't put it together.

A couple days later, at 2 am, my phone rang. He said, "Ron, the IRS. I just got a letter from the IRS. They're seizing your bank account. You're making so much money—they just drained it." What?!

The next morning when I woke up, my account was empty, and I believed his story. This was the beginning of a series of events that would follow where this guy took money from me.

Then, the landlord of my condo he moved me into called me and said, "Ron, you need to get your stuff out. Thomas hasn't paid the rent for this month, and it's two weeks late."

I said, "What do you mean? He owns this condo."

And they said, "There is no restaurants. He's a con man. Google his name." I should have done it three months earlier. He was a con man.

Now I was broke. I didn't have one dime to my name, and I was getting evicted, had to be out by the end of the day. So, I woke up that morning in a $4,000 a month apartment, and at the end of the day all my stuff was in my vehicle, and I was homeless, and I had no money.

I went to his condo. He was evicted and wasn't there. I called one of our common business associates. I said, "Tell me where he's at."

And they said, "Ron, he's in a hotel. I just loaned him money to check in." So, I went to this hotel, and I sat outside for eight hours waiting for him to walk in or out.

When he did walk out, I started following him. I followed him for about eight blocks, and then I grabbed him from behind. I pushed him up against the wall, and I said, "Thomas, did I ever tell you what happens when the person with experience meets the person with muscles?" And it was just as if he had taken a laxative. I threw him as hard I could. He hit the ground, and when he came back, I lifted up my hands. He lifted up his hands, but then he put his hands down, and he wouldn't fight me. I couldn't fight someone who wasn't going to fight me.

I let him go.

I was broke. My business partner took my money and was a con artist. I didn't have a house. I didn't have money. I didn't have anything.

I took a job as a waiter at a Red Robin restaurant. I lived in my car, and I would go to work at the Red Robin. People would ask, "Ron, you wanna pick up my shift tonight?"

Always, I said, "Yeah, I'll pick up your shift. I don't have anywhere to go." I would take food from the restaurant to eat.

I lived in that car for six weeks. I paid $30 a month for the gym. I would wake up every morning go to the gym, shower, and leave. The people at the front desk were like "Hey Ron hey, why do you leave 10 minutes later in a suit?!"

During that time, my friend Frank Massine called me and said, "Ron, there is a speech in Lake Tahoe this other speaker Brian can't do. They only want to pay $2,000."

I'm like, "$2,000? Are you kidding me? Yes, I will do it." Well, Lake Tahoe to Seattle was at least a 12-hour drive. I had to buy my plane ticket up front, but I didn't have $300 for a plane ticket. I started looking at my tires the week before the event. The metal was coming through and sticking out. I was thinking "I don't know if I have enough gas, but if I do have enough gas, the metal is showing on these tires. The wires are sticking out. But I gotta go. I gotta make it." I remember walking into the Red Robin that day to work a double and telling myself, "I have got to make $250 today, or I can't make this trip. I won't have the gas." I'd never made $250 in a shift before.

I walked out with the $250 almost exactly. I almost wanted to cry.

When I got into the parking lot, I saw my car was gone. It had been towed. I had all these unpaid parking tickets. It was 80 bucks to get it out. It wasn't a cost like there would be today, but with that 80 bucks, now I had $170—not enough gas to get there and back, but enough gas to get there. I'd figure out the rest.

I drove the 12 hours to Lake Tahoe, I gave the speech, and they gave me the $2,000 check. I cashed it and made it back to Seattle. Through a series of lucky trials like that, I was able to build my business back up. Eventually, I moved into a hotel where I lived for a year, and then I moved back to Texas.

After I moved back to Texas, September 11th happened. I was 28 years old, and I joined the Military as a Navy Reserve.

My business was still up and down. I had money, but it wasn't going really well. I had a top-secret Naval clearance because I was an intelligence analyst. At the same time, I was a security risk to the Navy because I was $40,000 in debt to the IRS, so I was going to lose my security clearance. I was trying to be in the Navy, but I was also trying to build my business up while trying to pay off $40,000. It was a big, really stressful time.

One day, my friend Chris Widener said, "Ron, do you realize Kyle Wilson, the founder of Jim Rohn International, lives 10 minutes from you?"

I said, "Yeah, I know that, but what am I supposed to say to him?"

He said, "Take your CD series over there, and he'll sell it. I'll tell him you're coming." I was sure Kyle would have no interest in selling my CD series, but Chris said, "Just do it."

I walked into Kyle's office, stuck one leg in the door, handed the CD series to Crystal, and asked her to please give it to Kyle. She said, "Oh, he's here. Do you want to talk to him?" No, I did not want to talk to him! I was scared.

Two or three days later, Kyle called me and said, "Ron, I wanna buy 1,000 sets of your Memory in a Month CD program." I hadn't sold 1,000 sets in my life! This was the biggest day of my life income-wise. Two weeks later, Kyle had sold them. He called and said, "Ron, I need 2,000 more."

A couple weeks after that, I was at a restaurant with my friend Brian when Kyle called again. He said, "Hey Ron, I'm going out to Shreveport this weekend to a casino and wanted to see if you want to go. I don't know you really well, but this would be a chance to spend some time together." I was all in.

We drove out there and became friends on the way. We ended up making that three-hour drive each way three or four times over the next several months.

I remember it very specifically, on one drive back, Kyle said, "Ron, what's wrong? What's on your mind? Is everything going okay?"

I said, "Kyle, look. I have a security clearance. I'm in the Navy. And if I don't pay my $40,000 IRS debt, I'm going to get kicked out of the Navy." Kyle listened to me, and I could see the wheels turning in his head. I was certainly not asking for a loan. $40,000 was out of my realm of possibility for a loan. When we got back to Dallas, we pulled up to Jim Rohn International, went into the office, and Kyle had Hilary write me a check for $36,000 (the amount we decided I needed). We made a deal that day that Kyle would sell my program, Memory in a Month, and instead of paying me the commission, he would just deduct it out of the money I owed him. Within six months it all was paid back. We have had a great friendship and ongoing business relationship to this day.

For me, that several years of no money, living in my car, waiting tables, and showering at the gym was a time of resilience. The day I drove back from Lake Tahoe on bald tires, having not been sure I had enough money to get there, let alone back, I saw the skyline of Seattle pop into view, and I just started laughing. I couldn't believe I pulled it off. And then, when I met Kyle, that was another really hard time. With his help and guidance, I was able to get through that.

A lot of times, people will tell me, "Ron, I want to do what you do. I want to be a speaker. I want to get paid 10 or $15,000 to give a speech, and I want to travel the world and speak. I tell them everything I've done. I start laying it all out, and they cut in, "No, I don't want to do any of that. I want to do what you do now." If you don't want to go through the hard stuff, forget about it. The hard stuff of building your business and coming up with solutions and the character that's built in that is the only way you can handle success.

In 2007, still in the Navy, I was deployed to Afghanistan. When I got back, I decided I wanted to do the US Memory Championships, and I hired a coach, United States Navy Seal TC Cummings. He taught me a lot about discipline. He had me memorizing cards underwater. He had me memorizing cards at bars. He had me changing my diet, getting up early, and training like a Navy Seal would train for war, but I was training for a memory tournament.

I won back to back years and became the two-time USA Memory Champion. And in the process, I set the record for the fastest to memorize a deck of cards in the United States. Later, that record was broken in 2011.

Afterward, I wanted to do something more special with my memory, something I was passionate about.

Having been a veteran and served in Afghanistan, I decided to create a tribute for everyone who died in Afghanistan, so they would not be forgotten.

There are 2,300 fallen soldiers. I memorized their rank, their first name, and their last name in the order of their death. It took me 10 months to memorize and be able to write out and spell each correctly (there are multiple spellings of so many people's names).

With this list, I created The Afghanistan Memory Wall, a project where I travel the United States, writing out these 7,000 words from memory on a wall. It takes about 10 hours to physically do it.

The core message of the tribute is that *you are not forgotten*. I'm humbled by all the friends and family that come to witness while I'm doing this in different cities and at some major events like NFL games, Nascar races, MLB games, Independence Day at the National Mall in Washington DC, and on Veteran's Day. I have countless stories that shake me to my core of how The Afghanistan Memory Wall has made an impact on friends and family of fallen soldiers.

The wall is also a testament to discipline, which is another word for resilience in some ways. When I was memorizing that wall for a year, I lived in solitude. I took a book filled with each soldier's name with me everywhere I went. When I was sick, I was memorizing. When I was tired or on trains or airplanes, I was memorizing.

Living in my car, being close to going out of business, almost getting kicked out of the Navy, serving in Afghanistan, and then the climactic moment of The Afghanistan Memory Wall are all a story in resilience. I'm thankful for the journey.

TWEETABLE

If you don't want to go through the hard stuff, forget about it. The hard stuff of building your business and coming up with solutions and the character that's built within that is the only way you can handle success.

Ron White is a veteran of the United States Navy who served in Afghanistan in 2007. He is also a two-time USA Memory Champion who held the USA record for the fastest to memorize a deck of cards for two years. He travels the United States with a 52-foot long wall where he writes out the names of the fallen from the war in Afghanistan from memory to honor them and to say you are not forgotten. To listen to the podcast that tells these amazing stories, please visit www.americasmemory.com

CHAPTER 30

From Girl in the Projects to Real Estate Millionaire Mom

by Anna Kelley

Statistically speaking, you would not expect a girl growing up in "the projects" to escape poverty. By the grace of God, I beat the odds. And by the grace of God, I was allowed to experience the difficulties, challenges, and pain that would mold me into a wiser, more resilient, and more compassionate person than I would have been without having gone through such deep waters.

Like many children, I am a product of divorce. When I was six, we moved in the middle of the night to another town to escape another night of abuse at the hands of my stepfather. My pregnant mom, sister, and I moved in with my grandparents until she found a job as a leasing agent in a Section 8 apartment complex in an upper middle class neighborhood in San Antonio, Texas.

We were given a free apartment, but that was not enough for us to survive. My mom began waitressing at night, and the rest of our needs were covered by food stamps. She could not afford a babysitter, so at nine years old, I began watching my siblings overnight. I was aware that bad things sometimes happened in apartments like ours, and I was scared. The free-spirited little girl, who just wanted to have fun, learned she had to be much more responsible than other kids. I grew up fast!

My mother loved us and did her best to provide for our needs. But I figured out that if I wanted something, I would have to make my own money to buy it. I sold candy at school, made things and went door to door to sell them, and got a job in 8th grade to buy a flute and name brand clothing.

My mom remarried and had more children, and the cycle of alcohol, drugs, and abuse continued. We found ourselves in battered women shelters and on the couches of family members multiple times. My only escape was school and music, where I worked hard to be the best at everything I did so that I could have a better life "one day." While I tried to fit in, the whispers from kids about how poor I was and how I was not like them pierced my heart with shame and shook my confidence and my hope that I could ever escape the kind of life I was given for one more like theirs. The lens through which I saw life, work, and money was not rose-colored.

At 15, I called my father and step-mother and asked to move in with them. Leaving my mother and siblings was one of the hardest decisions I have ever made. I feared that if I did not stay to protect them, they would end up dead. Yet, I also knew I had to get out and think about my own future. The guilt, responsibility, sadness, and fear for what I was leaving behind were at war with the relief, freedom, joy, and hope for what lay ahead. I longed for a better life and had a profound sense that God would lead me to better shores.

Settled in a new school, new town, and new family dynamic, I saw things through a new set of glasses. I saw that people with higher-paying jobs could afford good food and nicer things, that life without drugs and alcohol was peaceful, and that keeping Jesus at the center of every action and relationship was the key to an abundant life. My experiences made me determined that I would never rely on a man to take care of me financially and that I would do whatever it took to forge a better future.

This determination led me to become an overachiever. I graduated high school early with honors and finished my bachelor's degree in three years while working full-time and living on my own. I was hired for a degree-required job while still in college and won employee of the year two years in a row. I became a financial relationship manager in a large bank, another position for which I was underqualified, and won the award for #1 relationship manager in Texas the first year. Finally, I landed a high-paying job at an insurance company. I was thriving in the corporate world and convinced my problems were behind me.

At 25, I married my husband, and three years later we had our first child. While I was driven to succeed in corporate America, I had a deep desire to stay home with my child. My husband had a $120,000 college debt, and there was no way for us to live on one income. It broke my heart to put my baby in daycare, and as a latchkey child myself, I did not want to be an absent mom. I prayed every day for a way for me to stay home, and HGTV convinced me that flipping houses was the way for me to do it!

With new baby in tow, we bought a Victorian house with the intent to bring it back to its former glory. We bought in a terrible location, over-improved it, and lost money due to the year of holding costs before it sold. During the remodel, my husband lost his job. With two mortgages, a school loan, a car payment, and one job, we were barely scraping by. I was deflated and depressed and began to hate my job. How could this happen? How was I ever going to get to stay home? I wrestled with God through many tears and just could not understand His plan.

I decided I needed to leave my company for more money and was offered a job at a large subprime mortgage company. Salary negotiations broke down, and I wasn't able to take it. I was then offered another job at a large bank, only to have a hiring freeze eliminate the position the next day. I was angry, confused, tired, and discouraged.

A year later, we moved to Pennsylvania with our son and new baby. We bought a commercial building for my husband's business, which had three apartments that would help cover the mortgage. My company allowed me to work from home, and we moved in with my in-laws while we built his practice. We later bought a four-unit apartment building so we could live in one unit with our mortgage paid by the others. It was cramped, and a far cry from our large home in Houston.

Just when I thought we might get ahead, the housing market collapsed and my company was on the verge of bankruptcy. I lost thousands of dollars in my 401k and thought I was losing my job. So, I borrowed money from my 401k to buy another four-unit apartment building. If I lost my job, at least we would have income from another apartment. The two companies I almost left my job for two years before went under, while my company survived. For the first time, I could clearly see God's protection and provision through my job. I was so grateful. Yet, I still longed for a way to stay home with my babies.

After having a few tenants, remodeling, and raising our property values, I thought it would be great to get into larger apartment buildings. I was excited to find a webinar that claimed I could buy large apartments with none of my own money, and I flew to a conference to learn to do just that! The conference rocked my world, and I just KNEW buying apartments was the answer. I signed up for coaching, and the woman who owned the company offered me the job of a lifetime! I would work for her from home as a coach, and she would help me buy a large apartment building that would allow me to retire. My prayers had been answered…I thought.

Just before I left my job, I discovered she was dishonest. I confronted her, and she made life very difficult for me. She threatened our livelihood, destroyed my confidence in my discernment, and completely jaded me from the world of real estate. She later ended up in prison for fraud. I was clearly protected from unknowingly becoming entangled in her world of deceit. Still, my dreams of becoming a real estate millionaire were crushed, and I did not buy another property for four years.

In that time, I had two more children and continued to help my husband with his practice. The changes in the economy and healthcare took a toll on his chiropractic business, and I had no choice but to continue to work. Though I knew I was a good mom, I was with my kids every night and weekend and they were safe with Grandma during the day, I was afraid that my working in their younger years would make them suffer emotionally, intellectually, and spiritually.

Determined to figure out a way to stay home, in 2014 I decided to give real estate another try. The first two months, I bought two apartment buildings from retiring landlords willing to finance me without a bank. I continued to buy properties to renovate, rent, and refinance; using the equity to buy more. I worked my real estate business almost every morning, lunch break, evening, and weekend for over four years while working full-time and juggling my children's wellbeing, homework, and sporting events.

Last year, I hit my goal of acquiring $5,000,000 in rental real estate, and I have a $6,500,000 apartment complex under contract today. Our rental income has significantly exceeded the six-figure income from my job, and after many years of hard work and determination, I can finally retire! I am now focused on growing our real estate business with larger multifamily properties and helping others to do the same.

While I have not given my children a "stay at home mom," I'm proud that I am leaving them with a legacy of a mom willing to do whatever it takes to provide for them. Through our journey, they have seen that we can accomplish anything through hard work, integrity, determination, perseverance, grit, resilience, hope, faith, and a refusal to give up. They know what it looks like to work together to build something and the importance of giving and investing instead of wasting money. Finally, they have been taught to treat people from every walk of life with compassion, kindness, and respect, as we strive to provide nicer, safer housing to tenants than I had growing up.

Looking back, God has used all of the difficult experiences, and what seemed like unanswered prayers, to build me brick-by-brick, day by day, year by year into a better, stronger person. I realize now that all my years in the corporate world have given me the skills, wisdom, and confidence I need to run my real estate business today. I've learned that perceived failures and setbacks are actually lessons and stepping stones for you to walk on, as you climb the stairway to where God is taking you! Finally, I've discovered that it matters far more who we become through our actions than it does the cards we are dealt. Dave Ramsey said that if you don't like where you are, you can make better financial decisions that can "change your family tree." Thankfully, I have.

This journey into real estate has allowed me to speak for local REIAs and real estate podcasts and to help others all over the US toward reaching their real estate investment goals. I have learned from my mother, step-mother, and three grandmothers to be a strong woman, to do whatever it takes to keep going, and to trust God's plan. I am passionate about helping other girls and moms to do just that, by building a legacy for themselves and their families, through the wise handling of money and investing in real estate. My motto in life is this: Love God, love people, use money, and NEVER give up!

TWEETABLE

I've learned that perceived failures and setbacks are actually lessons and stepping stones for you to walk on, as you climb the stairway to where God is taking you!

Anna Kelley is a seasoned real estate investor, having bought, rehabbed, and managed over $6 Million in real estate, from single-family to multifamily. She and her husband have four beautiful children. Anna is a sought-after speaker for numerous podcasts and real estate investment groups. She mentors investors entering the rehabbing, multifamily, and vacation rental space, and educates others on how to realize strong returns through passive real estate investments.

Contact Anna about speaking, coaching, or investment opportunities at info@reimom.com.

ReiMom.com & MomBuysHousesNow.com
ZenithCapitalInvestments.com
On Facebook at Anna ReiMom

CHAPTER 31

There Is Always a Solution to a Setback, If You Listen

by Howard Pierpont

My mother and father came from very different backgrounds, both with large families. My mother became a school teacher after she finished college. My dad went to school to be a weather observer after he came home from World War II. Both had careers that involved the need for agility due to setbacks.

My dad and my mother were influencers in the community. Neither ever ran for office, but they worked in the background to assist people with making decisions. My dad would forecast the weather only to have some system stall or advance and requiring him to redo the entire forecast. My dad went on to work full time at one job after another. My mother returned to substitute teaching when I went to school and taught full time during my later high school days. Some days when lesson plans would not go as anticipated, my mother would adjust the plans to meet the current needs and advance the learning.

I was never pushed in a direction for a career but was encouraged to explore the possibilities. I learned from my parents that striving to a predetermined goal often does not yield the desired result.

As I worked through my career, I found that people only wanted me to work on outcomes, even if the outcome would not be effective. I held a series of jobs where I would be given an assignment to deliver a particular product or process. Often the product or process did not meet the need of the end user or was outdated before it was delivered. Often the end user and I were not pleased with the final product. Although I tried hard, the lack of successful fulfillment continued to cause me setbacks.

As part of a new job, I had to work with the dreaded corporate audit team. No one had ever had any success dealing with them and they were seen as work drivers, not solutions creators. I was sent in to change things. Rather than work toward a specific result, I looked around the entire landscape to see all sides of the issues. I removed the predetermined outcome and the idea of the adversarial relationship between their department and the others. When one takes out the melodrama and the "I must be right and win," a reasonable solution can be found. Eventually, with my background in corporate knowledge, persuasion, and consensus building, I was asked to join the audit team. I had never been an auditor, but that wouldn't hold me back, and I soon became the subject matter expert on business continuity.

In the spring of 2002, I assumed a position in the corporate business continuity office. I had been enjoying the audit job and had traveled to Russia, Malaysia, China, Mexico, Ireland, and across the states. I worked to hone my listening and solution skills. Over the next 18 months, I had to take my business background, my personal corporate knowledge, and my business continuity background to coach a third of the 254 business units to creatively do business risk assessments, create business continuity plans, and incorporate methods into day to day operations. In layman's terms, I was making a huge impact on the individuals in the company and making the business run more smoothly as a whole.

Every situation needed to be handled differently, but I was always working for a positive outcome. Sometimes those outcomes would be nothing that I expected.

Some situations were caused by people who were hard to work with. My biggest obstructionist went to Miami on vacation. While there, she had encountered the remnants of a hurricane. There was no electricity or air conditioning in a hot humid environment. When she returned at the end of the week, she asked how she could move the continuity plans forward because she never wanted anyone to go through anything like her past week again. With some discussion, she came up with a mutually agreeable solution to her organization's needs. I was struck by the impact the hazardous conditions had on her, and I felt pulled to become more involved. I had a feeling my adaptability and creativity could be put to positive use.

I decided to join FEMA as a reservist in the long-term recovery group. Disasters are real, and disasters are personal. Many people think a disaster will never happen to them. My job involved going to work with survivors, small businesses, not-for-profits, and governments on how to recover toward a sense of new normal.

While it is satisfying to assist people, they need to make their own decisions. They are ultimately in control of their recovery.

I was assigned to support Waterbury, Vermont as part of the long-term recovery team. To give you the lay of the land, the following is from the final recovery plan, May 2012 that I co-authored:

> "The 2011 spring flooding in Vermont was exacerbated on August 28, when Tropical Storm Irene dumped eight inches of rain on an already saturated terrain in a 12-hour time period, damaging hundreds of roads and bridges across the state. Thousands of homes and businesses statewide suffered long-term power outages, substantial damage, or destruction from the massive flooding. The Village of Waterbury, in Washington county, was uniquely impacted. Home to Green Mountain Coffee Roasters and Ben & Jerry's Ice Cream, Waterbury is also the site of a large state office complex and the Vermont State Hospital. Flooding at the Waterbury State Office Complex displaced approximately 1,500 state employees, seriously jeopardizing the community's economic sustainability.

> "In the aftermath of the disaster, Waterbury community leaders recognized the need for the community to come together and create a path forward for recovery. The Waterbury community began the process of developing a long-term recovery plan in November 2011 with support from the Federal Emergency Management Agency (FEMA) Long-Term Community Recovery (LTCR) team. A series of public meetings and workshops were held to facilitate the development of a community vision and a plan for long-term recovery. Community members developed specific projects to address recovery efforts in the following six sectors: 1) Community Planning and Capacity Building; 2) Economic Development; 3) Energy, Efficiency, and Transportation; 4) Housing and Human Services; 5) Infrastructure and Hazard Mitigation; and 6) Parks and Recreation."

At the start of January, I was assigned to lead the Economic Development portion of the long-term recovery. In the next few weeks, the community committee members had to decide what projects they wanted to propose to the committee-selected project champions and take forward to the community.

All Project Champions understood from the beginning that FEMA and the supporting staff would not be on the ground forever. They could choose or reject any of the project ideas. The decision was theirs, and they would own their success.

In the Economic Development space, a project champion made a request to create a performing arts center. There was already a visual art center in place that had not been disrupted by the flooding. A significant amount of disagreement arose between the two factions in the project on whether there was a need for a separate center.

Monica Callan, a local resident and national stage and television performer, put together a proposal for the performance center, but there was a price tag of over $5 million. As a solutionist, I assisted the project by suggesting multiple alternatives and possibilities for success. The group came to their own consensus, and they agreed that this project would move forward.

With agreements on several projects to move forward, the committees further developed their projects for presentation. There were 21 projects proposed and presented at the Community Recovery Fair. Voting for which project would actually be pursued was done by ballot with the community selecting "Most Important," "Important," and "Less Important." Two of the four economic development projects were voted "Most Important" and the other two were "Important."

A week later, all projects were ratified in a joint meeting of the Waterbury Select Board and Trustees in a slightly different priority order. At the annual town meeting, the town voted to go forward with all the projects' potential funding requests.

The performing arts center was still a dream, but Monica Callan moved forward after she and I discussed and exchanged ideas around the creation of a not-for-profit. The Across Roads Center for the Arts was formed. In celebration and preparation, the center sponsored events and performances at the National Grange of the Order of Patrons of Husbandry facility. The Grange had been around for years and the building was showing its' age.

What the community perceived as an even bigger issue was the cost of potential construction of a performance location. Where would the money come from?

One phone call would change the direction and velocity of things. The members of the Grange were getting older and the membership was shrinking. The call led to a meeting where, ultimately, the Grange members agreed to sell the hall to a new not-for-profit (our Across Roads Center for the Arts) for an amount that would never be disclosed. A rebrand was needed. Grange Hall Cultural Center came into being. Because all parties, with my minor contributions, remained flexible throughout the solution-creation process, Waterbury has a wonderful new landmark. Grange Hall Cultural Center has become the second most popular family-friendly destination in the area behind Ben & Jerry's.

Were this merger and subsequent success part of the original proposal? No. Could this be an even better, more flexible space than originally envisioned? Yes. There were and still are upgrades and updates that need to be done. To date, projects have replaced the furnace, aging plumbing and wiring, stairs, flooring, lighting, and landscaping, and have significantly improved the function of the building. A complete kitchen renovation is almost finished and will enhance the overall experience. Using a solutionist method allows for the flexibility necessary to achieve these positive ends that bring everyone into a happy agreement.

I left FEMA to go on invitational speaking sessions with a small group of development subject matter experts. I was required to have a group of set slides to cover, but I was able to turn the sessions into discussions. In each session, the audience had issues that they wanted guidance on. There were multiple two-day sessions in each of the states on either side of the Mississippi River. Intentionally, I learned as much about their issues and possible solutions as they did about my ideas.

Here, again, I was able to listen to their setbacks and have an open dialog on potential courses of action. Others in the group just read their slides and had little interaction with the attendees. My results were spectacular. A solutionist method allowed space for several creative solutions that I didn't even expect.

I spend most of my time now listening to people talk about what they think are their issues. Then we have a discussion on what are the real issues and potential solutions. Finally, I assist with creating a roadmap and by checking in to see the progress they have made.

I have found that too many groups have had someone come in, think they know the organization's problem, and then create a final action plan. These groups feel that their investment was not optimized with a predetermined consultant output.

Look at each setback and see how there can be a comeback. Look at what you have done before, even if it wasn't the right solution then, look around and see what has worked or not worked for others. Build on the best of everything and be willing to be flexible.

TWEETABLE

Explore the possibilities. Striving to a predetermined goal often does not yield the desired result.

Howard Pierpont is a solutionist for the Institute for Preparedness and Resilience. The Institute is the educational preparedness arm of the International Association for Disaster Preparedness and Response (DERA). DERA is a membership not-for-profit 501(C)3 organization.

Mr. Pierpont retired from Intel Corporation where he assumed responsibility for business continuity and preparedness for Worldwide Engineering. He later worked in the FEMA Disaster Field Training Office. He then spent three years speaking about resiliency, social media, and dealing with the government during times of disaster.

www.Preparedness.org

Howard_Pierpont@Preparedness.Org

www.Howard.Solutions

Twitter: solution_howard

970-397-5526

CHAPTER 32

Who Needs A Comfort Zone

by Justin Richards

N o matter what others say or what they think, follow your **why**. Most (especially loved ones) speak from fear not experience. So, choose who you follow wisely! As the famous philosopher Friedrich Nietzsche, once said, "*He who has a why to live for can bear almost any how.*"

I was one of those kids who thought he had it all figured out by high school. I knew I wanted to be an entrepreneur and not an employee, but was still lost as to how I would do this or what business I would build. I spent a tremendous amount of time helping others perfect their resumes, and start their startups, but never focused on my resume. I had reasoned I didn't really need one.

After winning an award for my first business plan in an entrepreneurship competition at Michigan State University, I was excited to create a graphics company allowing people to add their personal style to their phones and laptops through our licensing of popular logos. My buddy and I had fun with it, licensing from the NFL and Disney, but I struggled with funding. I didn't realize the difficulties of capital raise and, failing miserably at this part, my graphics company became a hobby.

A year later, working with a friend to expand his service company, I had my next business idea. It came midway through another 100-hour week. I was servicing a dental client's office when I noticed a stack of checks on a desk next to a computer. It was surprising to see that much money sitting around. I later asked the client about it and was told the checks are manually inputted into their computer for processing. It seemed to me to be an antiquated way for him to manage that part of his business. And a light bulb came on: automation!

Rather quickly, I connected with my mom, a high-level executive for Fortune software companies. Seeing my vision, she met with her friend who had the knowledge to develop B2C2 compliant platforms, which is one of the highest software applications upon which government documents can be transferred between users. I then put a team together, and we built a beta version and began marketing it to key executives in the dental market with the original dental client as our first call. The software product was well-received, and our prospective clients were very excited!

Having initial success, we created a full-scale presentation model for the governing body of dentists in Michigan. Our goal was to have our software product used across all dental offices in Michigan, then organize a national product roll-out campaign based upon success in Michigan. This was a fair amount of work, taking weeks to pull together, but we were well-prepared with a professional support team and a proven model. My team and I also located a building where we would operate the business and began remodeling efforts to equip the space for our requirements. This would become part of our presentation.

As a part of their procedures, the governing dental board used a voting process to make large and important decisions. Sadly, our business model was voted down, narrowly missing approval by a single vote! I was devastated, and this failure happened at one of the most stressful times of my life. My parents were experiencing financial challenges as the economy was sliding, and they were going through a divorce. Most of the prized assets my parents owned had to be sacrificed, including our primary home. At the same time, my girlfriend had just agreed to move from Tennessee to join me in Michigan. Prior to my girlfriend agreeing to move, I painted visions of success for her and me. But, now, those visions were gone. Having no money and being unable to afford housing in my hometown, we moved into a small rental cabin I owned in Northern Michigan. Up there, well-paying jobs were scarce and access to career-grade employment options even more so. I told her this would be temporary, but it actually seemed impossible.

For the next few years, I worked a variety of odd jobs to generate income while I searched for a mentor. I was a server at two different restaurants, and—ironically—I lost my job at one for talking too long with some customers who owned successful corporations. Those talks with successful customers helped point me towards a new goal: real estate. It was already a passion of mine, and my confidence was building to start taking definitive directions in my passion. Moving forward, I got my real estate license and sold timeshares for a large vacation brand company. My first step to reaching my goal as a real estate investor was getting into real estate this way. I also worked with a contractor on the side, doing exterior renovations on apartment communities. But, I just felt lost...displaced. I knew I wanted to be in real estate, but from where I lived and worked, the process was slow. Yet, I continued to read and study as many books and videos on real estate I could find from the library and online. I was fascinated with people like Rockefeller and Trump and the journeys they went through to become billionaires.

Before long, my wife Shea became frustrated with her job and with living in the remote Michigan country. We had many discussions and agreed it was time to move, but we differed on where we wanted to move. I wanted to return to my beloved eastern Michigan, and she wanted to move to western Michigan. So we made a bet. Whoever got a new job first would decide on where we moved. The race was on! Little did I know, Shea had long-standing relationships with business colleagues in Grand Haven in western Michigan, and—with a single phone call—she had a new job.

The move was exciting, but it set us back financially. We had fought hard over the past few years to keep my investment property we called home and almost lost the battle a few times. I purchased this property upon graduating college on a 15-year land contract. Long-term, this was a great decision since it builds equity fast. The downside is high monthly payments. Because of these high payments, we had no idea how we would also be able to afford an apartment. To start her new job, Shea moved immediately into her aunt's home as a short-term solution.

While visiting her one weekend, I was walking down the road where her aunt lives thinking how we were going to make this all work. I came across a ranch home on two acres that had stickers in the windows and looked vacant. I asked Shea if she could find the owner online, because she has a talent for research and finding almost anyone. Success. We called the owner and said, "*This house looks like it's been vacant for a while and in rough condition. If you are willing to let us move in, I will renovate all the rooms for you...And, after I renovate it, we would be willing to stay, if we can negotiate a reduced rent for my labor.*" He would have to pay for the renovations...of course. He told me he would meet us on the property the next day.

After he met Shea and I and we talked for several hours, he went home to his wife, then came back and handed us $1000 cash to start immediately. He said, "*Let's see what you can do. Keep all the receipts and let me look at your progress.*" This was music to my ears! I was blessed with a family of contractors from whom I could get the information needed and designers to create the new look and feel which would help me make this a beautiful home. After four months of working 10 hour days on the house and working 8 hours at my new job in sales at Verizon, we had a new and safe place to call home again. Post construction, the landlord was very fair and charged just $300 a month for the next year, which fit the budget, and was a blessing.

My stint at Verizon was short-lived. I did not like that type of high pressure sales on customers. So, I began circulating my resume to property management companies because I still dreamed I would own multifamily properties one day. Verizon gave me one great thing, and that was Aaron Lenartz, today my business partner. We talked on breaks and lunch about our similar upbringing and dreams of our own business. I shared my goals for real estate investment and a multifamily empire. After a couple months of looking for a new position, I was accepted to work at a 328-unit community in Grand Rapids, MI as an assistant manager. I was so excited about the opportunity because it meant learning everything I needed to know about the operations behind a multifamily community, including the financials. I loved all aspects of this job and was learning a ton.

My partner Aaron Lenartz and I decided that if we were one day going to own multifamily properties, we needed money. And we had none. So, we thought flipping houses would be an excellent way to build up capital to invest in larger deals. From this desire came our next venture: Greyson Investments.

We spent the next 18 months flipping three homes and investing in two four-unit buildings. I was the contractor on site for all these, and Aaron was responsible for raising capital amongst family and friends. We were growing our portfolio and cash flow slowly, yet it was very labor intensive and would take years to get to where we could financially buy apartment buildings. This plan was not scaling the way we envisioned. We decided to use the proceeds from the flips to start traveling the US and meeting people who were successful in doing what we wanted to do.

We spent a lot of time over the next few years listening to podcasts from The Real Estate Guys (Robert Helms and Russell Gray), and attended a few conferences as well. At one of these conferences we met Mark and Tamiel Kenney at breakfast. They were fellow Michiganders now living in Texas and building an education company around their multifamily investment company. Despite many conversations, I was not ready see how the Kenneys would fit into our business model. So, we continued flipping and seeking larger, local multifamily deals.

Over the next 15 months or so, we floundered around without making inroads in any new direction. We uncovered a large development opportunity that was way over our heads. Getting frustrated on how to go about vetting and securing outside capital, we decided to reach out to Mark Kenney. He not only picked up the phone after so much time had passed, he was excited to hear from us! After we clued him in, he immediately referred us to someone who knew a lot about developments, his friend Victor Menasce. After one look at the deal, with his years of experience, Victor was able to show, definitively, why this deal did not make sense.

Exiting that, we decided to look at self-storage businesses, and later, car wash businesses. We chased any business we thought we could get into "easy" to make more money now.

During the business chase, my partner Aaron decided that if we were going to make it, we both needed to be full-time, heads down on business! This was a hard decision for Aaron because he had a comfortable job at Verizon where he made good money and he had a wife and two small children. Yet, if he wanted to make great money, it meant burning the boat. Ironically, Aaron made his decision as Verizon forced his departure because they were folding his department. The timing was perfect! But this meant he had to pull all of his 401K funds out to live on for the next 24-months so we could build-out our company. Shea and I had also gotten married and had a new baby girl. We were burning the candle at both ends and risking it all for the future. My wife was holding down the fort financially, and my contributions from our portfolio cash flow and flips were minimal. Pretty much everything I earned was going back into our efforts.

Greyson Capital was born. We went through four attorneys (and law firms) before we stumbled upon one who understood what we wanted to do regarding fine-tuning the details of our corporation and our company. Greyson Investments became Greyson Capital and all assets were wholly owned LLCs but, we still felt we had no concrete direction. Aaron and I were sitting in our office (my spare bedroom) one night when we got a call from Mark saying, "Hey guys, I have an educational event tonight if you want to join us on the web."

Like kids going to a candy store, we readily agreed to join! On the call, we learned Mark had a mastermind group. We were impressed and immediately signed up to gain the much-needed guidance we needed! Reading more on Mark's website, we noticed there was an Inner Circle group. We called Mark to inquire about it. We were surprised that Mark had never shared this earlier with us, but later learned he was only looking to give us the specific help we were seeking. Mark's Inner Circle was expensive, but we desperately wanted to be a part of his team and this group. We knew having that level of access to such successful people and the knowledge they had was exactly the key we needed to jumpstart the big growth. We reasoned this expense, albeit very high for us, was critical now to succeed in the next step for our company. We needed the expertise from these professionals in this multifamily arena. We decided—just jump and don't look back!

WOW. To begin, there was a course we had to take. This course provided the background and necessities to become familiar with the multifamily business environment, legalities, terminologies, and related content we would be soon exposed to as we progressed. It was nearing the Christmas holidays and 2017 was rapidly coming to a close. We wanted to be aggressive out of the gate by completing the course and to be able to hit the ground running at the top of 2018. We had a few scheduled business calls starting in January, followed by upcoming interaction with many brokers. We wanted to have great questions ready and most of the coursework completed by year end.

Mission accomplished! Prior to our first call with these new knowledgeable contacts, we asked several questions and bounced many ideas off Mark. Suddenly, everything accelerated, and we were moving faster than any other time since pulling together Greyson. Within two short months, Mark was able to help us gain visibility and business relationships with brokers in multiple states. We started to get deal flow for the first time, and it was very exciting! We were traveling and visiting potential opportunities. Quickly, we learned that in addition to relationships, the multifamily business is a numbers game. You play the odds to win. We learned rapidly how to vet deals quickly and assess as many deals as we could stare at in a day. Within the first three months after joining with Mark and his mentorship model, we were vetting 10 deals a week and working hard to submit at least one letter of interest (LOI) a week. This led to tremendous exposure to a large portfolio of prospective deals and many opportunities to organize bids to win the real estate deal.

BAM! The effort finally paid off, and in April of 2018 we were awarded our first accepted deal for 144 units in Memphis, TN!

With the Memphis deal under our belts and all the lessons learned in going through the whole process, we continue to press on the gas even harder! We push ourselves to exceed the norm and push ourselves further than most feel is wise. The growth we've experienced in such a short period is exhilarating. As we move forward, our vision is to develop and acquire beautiful and unique income-producing properties around the globe. We will continue to strive to create a lifestyle-based investment company that helps our employees, our investors, and our residents achieve "the good life." We define the good life as financial security, having futuristic vision, and being prepared for what comes next while making smart investment choices to get there.

We realized early on that if we are going to be achievers, we needed to push harder and smarter. Like most new companies, we struggled and will continue to have challenges while driving Greyson forward. But having access to talented teams of people, along with Mark's incredible leadership, we can see our way through, and reaching our goals has become feasible and, most importantly, visible!

We have succeeded with Greyson Capital Group only through tenacity. There have had many bumps in the road and many long, hard climbs, but we have continued because we knew why we wanted to achieve our goals. Because of those struggles, our company today has the grit to accomplish anything we set out to do. Get clear, know your why, and take action!

TWEETABLE

What is the difference between hitting a wall at 100 mph or 80? If you are already in motion and you fail, you are already getting hurt, so just go for it!

Justin Richards is a trailblazer, visionary, and co-founder at Greyson Capital Group where they look at building wealth differently. He is also a father, husband, and mentor with competencies that span from commercial and residential construction to portfolio management as well as physical asset and property management. If you are looking for a different way to build wealth using real estate and spend more time with family, contact me at Jrichards@greysoncapitalgroup.com, www.greysoncapitalgroup.com, https://www.facebook.com/GreysonCapitalGroup/.

CHAPTER 33

How Resilience Took Me From Trouble Maker to World's Top 50 Speaker

by Chris Widener

was raised by a single mother who loved words. I once handed her the Sunday morning *New York Times* crossword puzzle and she finished it in 11 minutes...in pen. One of the great lessons she taught me about being able to finish a crossword puzzle so fast was understanding Latin. She said Latin was the key. As a professional speaker and author, diving into words gives such a rich meaning and context to some of the things that I talk about. The word resilience is no different.

The word comes from the Latin word *resilire*, which meant *leaping back*. This is why we typically think of a resilient person as one who can bounce back from negative circumstances that affect them.

Definition of resilience:

1. the capacity to recover quickly from difficulties; toughness
   "the often remarkable resilience of so many British institutions"

2. the ability of a substance or object to spring back into shape; elasticity
   "nylon is excellent in wearability and resilience"

Looking at these definitions, I realized that resilience has been a major part of my life from a very young age. When I was just four years old, my father passed away. My brothers and sisters were all much older than me. They were out of the house shortly, and then it was just my mother and I. I was essentially raised by a single mother as an only child. She did everything that she could to lead our little family, and she hustled in her real estate business to do so, but it was hard.

One of the things that my mother did was flip houses. This was long before it was popular or made famous on television shows on HGTV. Because of her flipping houses, we moved continuously, and I ended up going to a lot of different schools. Over the course of my schooling, I went to 11 different schools and I moved 28 times.

Life was tough for me because of how I responded to my dad's death. I became angry and bitter as a young man. I began to act out in school and cause problems. My mother shipped me off to live with relatives twice, once in the fourth grade to my aunt and uncle's, and once in the ninth grade. I began drugs and alcohol in the sixth grade. I made most of my money while growing up by scalping sports tickets to the professional sports team's games in Seattle and betting the horses at Longacres horse track. You get the point. I was going in the wrong direction!

Eventually, I got my life together and ended up going to college and getting a degree in youth and family work. After graduating from college, while working, I was also speaking professionally, mostly to youth groups, high schools, summer camps, and colleges. Eventually, that became a speaking business that focused on leadership, influence, and speaking to corporate audiences. I've written nearly 20 books and produced almost a hundred audio programs both of my own and of other professional speakers that we sold to Costco and Sam's Club. I was mentored by two of the great legends of the speaking industry, Zig Ziglar and Jim Rohn, who I met through my agent and promoter, Jim's partner Kyle Wilson. What began as a very negative life has ended up becoming a very positive life. And that's where resilience comes in.

As I think about resilience, I think of a few key lessons that I learned that enabled me to not get stuck in my negative life and to change it into a positive and fulfilling life.

My first lesson came from all the moving around that I did. Every year or two I ended up going to a new school. Now, this can be a real negative unless you operate from resilience. I would bounce back from having to leave all my old friends by becoming the gregarious person who would walk into a new school and meet new people and talk to new people and make new friends. That was a great lesson for me that still serves me well as an adult.

It could have been something that drove me deeper and deeper into a shell, but instead, the moving around caused me to bounce back from the pain of leaving old friends to the joy of meeting new friends. As I write this, well into my adult life, I'm still friends with so many of those people that I met, going all the way back to as early as the third grade.

Another lesson that I learned came out of my own bad behavior. I acted out quite a bit in school, and so the setbacks that I experienced were often my own fault. I would get teachers or other leaders such as coaches angry at me. I would be kicked out of class or benched during a game because of my bad behavior. Eventually, I realized that bad behavior leads to negative results, negative results that I would have to bounce back from. I realize that you can bounce back from negative results by living out positive actions. Positive actions produce positive results. I could create my own resilience by changing my actions. What a powerful and profound thought!

The latest and probably the greatest thing I have learned resiliency from happened later on in my life. Because of my success in the speaking world, I was able to purchase my dream home for my wife and I. I had driven past this house for 21 years. I would stop at the front gate and look beyond the circular driveway and tell myself that I would buy that house someday. Eventually, I did. It was well into the seven-figure range. Long story short, there was a problem with the property, and it began to collapse into the river that it was on. We had 30-foot sinkholes all around the house. Because the county had recently been on my property, we ended up in a lawsuit with the county. I ended up losing the lawsuit against the county which cost me hundreds and hundreds of thousands of dollars in addition to all the money I spent trying to keep the house from falling into the river. I also ended up losing my marriage and selling that home for $400,000 less than I bought it for. That was a tough time in my life.

But I wasn't the type of person to just crawl under a rock and die. I am resilient. Part of bouncing back was making sure that I was healthy emotionally, which included a couple of years of counseling and meeting with my pastors on a regular basis. It also included reading lots of books and doing lots of self-reflection to produce self-awareness.

Doing all of that internal work while praying and hoping for a second chance, I became the type of man that I wanted to be, and I began to see the kind of success that I'd had before. I had a greater appreciation for life, work, and the people in my life. Now everything is on track. My career is great, I have found a beautiful woman who I love deeply, and I continue to make a difference in the lives of people.

There are all sorts of bad things that happen in life, and they happen to everyone. They happen to rich people and poor people. They happen to young people and old people. They happen to men and to women. They happen to people of every color, race, and nationality. Life is tough. Resiliency is the antidote to that tough life. Doing everything that we can to fight back in the battle against the tough parts of life is something that every person should strive to do if they want success, because resilience leads to success.

TWEETABLE

Life is tough. Resiliency is the antidote to that tough life.

Chris Widener has been named one of the top 50 speakers in the world and one of Inc Magazine's *top 100 leadership speakers. He is the author of nearly 20 books, including* The Art of Influence, *which has taken him all over the world speaking to crowds as large as 25,000 people. Chris worked with both Zig Ziglar and Jim Rohn. He co-hosted Zig's TV show,* True Performance, *and co-wrote Jim's last book,* Twelve Pillars.

https://www.Facebook.com/ChrisWidenerSpeaker

https://www.Instagram.com/ChrisWidenerSpeaker

https://www.Twitter.com/ChrisWidener

CHAPTER 34

Give Up, Give In, or Give It All You've Got!

by Diana Hightower

"Your husband has cancer." Those words hit me like a boxer had punched me in the stomach. The diagnosis sent us on a lengthy journey that we had no desire to be on. It came out of the blue when we were involved, as all of us are, in much more important things in our life.

It was April 2013. Both our professional lives and our personal lives were moving along at a crisp pace. Richard held a key position within the largest division of a Fortune 100 company. I had recently retired from an executive position within that company and had entered the entrepreneurial world where I was blazing new trails. Business was great, our family life was great…everything was great.

Then, in an instant, our life was knocked off track. A normal, annual physical turned into a discovery of enlarged lymph nodes. We thought nothing of it—we both battled allergies that time of year. Imagine our shock when our doctor gave us the news. We received a diagnosis that everyone dreads to hear. That diagnosis was "cancer." Specifically, stage-IV chronic lymphocytic lymphoma with 98% bone marrow involvement.

My body went numb as the doctor began to discuss the details. "This form of cancer is treatable," he said. "If you are going to have cancer, this is the kind to have." He told us there was a strong chance of reducing the cell sizes and activity so that Richard's normal immune system could deal with it and keep it in check. But, it was still the "Big-C" and the disease was showing up from the top of his head to the soles of his feet. And I was powerless to do anything about it.

My personality makes me a "take charge, let's win every battle" type of person. But here I was, faced with the biggest challenge of my marriage, my business career, and my life. In my professional life, I was used to feeling as though I was in control. We were now beginning the most important battle of our lives, and I knew that I was NOT in control. There was nothing I could do. It was beyond frustrating. And it was scary.

When a crisis happens, you learn what matters in your life and in your business. The lessons you learn help you grow in all areas. Here are a few lessons we learned along the way.

1. Surround Yourself with the Best Team

There is no time for negative energy during a cancer battle, or any battle in our life. We needed to be around people who inspired us, challenged us, and made us better. In the pursuit of winning our battle, we took a step back, assessed our support network, and adjusted accordingly.

2. Challenges Force You to Be Focused!

A crisis will make you realize that life is short. As a result, we became more intentional with whom and how we spent our time. Living with the uncertainty of a cancer diagnosis meant that wasting time was no longer an option. Every day became treasured, every adventure became enjoyed, and every celebration had a new meaning. Each decision had a new filter, and this had a very positive impact on our entire lives.

3. Cling to Faith

Our foundation for staying positive and remaining hopeful is faith: an abiding faith in God and faith in our care providers. Throughout the journey, we were comforted and sustained by God and by our support system. While our faith has always been important to us, it became even more so during this time.

4. Never Stop Setting Goals

Goals are what take us forward in life. They are the oxygen of our dreams. If you stop setting goals, you open the door to doubt, fear, and defeat. Richard and I responded to our battle by setting new goals. We began setting new goals focusing first on our health journey and our spiritual journey. We designed a healthy lifestyle routine for ourselves. We changed our diet, our exercise routines, and our spiritual awareness. We purposefully scheduled additional fun into our lives. And interestingly enough, our professional lives took a dramatic swing upwards! We did not want cancer to stop us from achieving our dreams. For us, our goals fueled our hope and kept us focused on our future.

5. **Stay Positive in the Face of Opposition**
   We knew it was critical to stay positive as we faced our battle.
   But how do you accomplish this during the days that the battle is
   overwhelming? We made a conscious decision to feed our minds.
   We read motivational and inspirational material each day. We
   needed to condition our minds day by day in order to stay positive.
   We made this a daily ritual. We read stories and autobiographies
   of people who had overcome adversity. Know that the human spirit
   is strong, and if others can survive and thrive in tough times, you
   can too.

6. **When in Doubt, Just Take the Next Small Step**
   There were days in our journey that felt overwhelming and
   paralyzing. It was during these times that we realized we did not
   have to be perfect or know every answer. But we must still move
   forward. The small steps became a big part of our success.

When facing a crisis, you have three choices: Give up, give in, or give it all
you've got.

One of the biggest lessons we have learned during this journey is that we
cannot wait to be perfect to say yes to our lifelong dreams. We must learn
to replace fear with faith. Fear is a dream killer. Fear is a destiny killer. Why
do we wait for the "perfect opportunity" or for "perfect timing?" We wait
because we are doubtful in our own ability to succeed. The truth is that most
opportunities don't wait around, so act now. Exercise your faith. Jump in and
learn from new opportunities that present themselves. Don't wait so long that
you cannot take a risk only to be consumed with remorse for what "could
have been."

We live in the greatest of times. The opportunities abound. Saying yes
can make life far more interesting than saying no. Fear can be the primary
barrier holding you back. People are afraid. They are afraid to try, afraid
to fail, afraid to succeed, afraid to change, and afraid in general. Business
leaders will often choose the status quo, all because they are afraid of the
"what if." What if it does not work? In our experience, the "what if we don't
try" is a more serious consequence to consider. Don't let fear overcome
your life. This health scare has reminded us that life is short. Live, learn, and
love throughout the process.

After six months of chemotherapy, the doctors were able to reduce
Richard's cancer from 98% coverage to less than 1%. We have remained
cancer free five years and counting! Both Richard and I have used this as

an inspiration to improve our health and to make better choices throughout our lives. And we are living a victorious and purposeful life together.

We all face challenges in life. The great news is that you get to live a better life because of your experiences. Wisdom comes from experience. The journey will make you stronger. We are surrounded by examples of people who made it when they didn't think they could. They pushed, pulled, and persevered. They changed for the better and started winning again. You can too. It is your turn to transform fear into faith and to step into your destiny.

TWEETABLE

We all face challenges in life. The great news is that you get to live a better life because of your experiences. Wisdom comes from experience. The journey will make you stronger.

Diana Hightower has blazed a career trail that many would envy. From successful corporate executive to entrepreneur extraordinaire, this woman of power is a passionate leader. Training others to achieve their own success motivates Diana daily. With a background in a Fortune 100 company and with a drive for excellence, she is in high demand as a speaker, teaching others to work without limits, become servant leaders, and reach the next level. With questions or to request a booking, contact Diana at:

Facebook: www.facebook.com/EmpoweringYourFuture

LinkedIn: www.linkedin.com/in/dianahightower/

Instagram: dihightower

Twitter: @DiHightower

Email: Diana@DianaHightower.com

CHAPTER 35

How Following Your Gut Will Lead to a Purpose-Driven Life

by Jared J. Christian

I had never, ever felt so alone in my life. Some days, all I could do was focus on the next breath, trusting that it would come. Why was I suffering so much if I was doing everything right? Was there more I needed to do? Or was this just part of the entrepreneurial process, trekking through the emotional and spiritual pain in hopes that one day soon I'll find relief? If I had followed my gut right away, would the utter helplessness have been dampened, even just a little? These thoughts swirled around my head constantly, often to the point of paralyzing me from taking another step.

I was 16, maybe 17, years old when I thought, "I want to be a businessman." I remember thinking shortly afterward that instead of starting a business, I was going to attend university, get a well-paying job, provide for my family with the steady income, and then start a side hustle. The plan was then to, after a few years working on this side hustle, leave the cushy, well-paying job and venture off on my own. Little did I know, following my gut as I pursued this dream throughout my life would serve as the springboard to launch me into a rewarding journey of self-identity and purpose.

Fast forward 10 years. My plans laid out as a teenager were thus far a success. I attended a great university where I got a solid education in finance. I met and married the woman of my dreams, and we promptly started our family and were blessed with three active little boys in three years. I started that well-paying job right out of university where I worked hard to add value.

Alongside my new job, I started my side hustle in an industry that I have been fascinated by since I was a teenager: real estate. My path into this world came by way of flipping purchase agreements and houses. I began mastering the skill of marketing for off-market, distressed properties. The goal was to build up that side business and get it to a point where my family and I felt comfortable with me leaving my job. To help me accelerate this process, I joined an exclusive real estate mastermind group.

After about a year of leveraging the knowledge of the mastermind group, which aided me in setting up a real estate business that I could run online in a market an hour and a half north of my local market, I got the business to a point, and had saved what we felt would be plenty of money, for us to feel ready to take the leap of faith and dive all in on the side hustle.

This tipping point occurred at a time when I was in early talks with the partners of the firm where I worked about potentially opening a division in another part of the country. This was the first opposition I faced in pursuing my dream. The temptation to stay, add more value, make more immediate money, and continue feeling secure was high. It wasn't until after I exercised faith in the face of opposition, followed my gut, and told the partners that it was time for me to move on to the next phase of life, that the stress I felt around whether it was the correct decision was lifted.

One day, a few weeks after leaving my job, I was listening to a podcast from The Real Estate Guys, and they were talking about a specific niche in real estate that caught my attention. So, I decided to attend a conference that would be discussing this niche in greater detail.

It just so happened that one of the hosts of the podcast that recommended the conference, Russell Gray, was also attending this same conference. I made it a point to sit next to him at dinner, so I could ask him questions. My life has not been the same since. Russ taught me about real estate syndication, the power of partnering with and helping others pool their money and resources together to invest in larger real estate projects than they could on their own. He also taught me that I would need to know how to speak with people to learn their needs, wants, desires, goals, and objectives.

He invited me to attend their sales training, How to Win Funds and Influence People, which was just five days away. My gut right away told me that I needed to go. Then, logic set in, "Money is super tight. I'm sure you can go to the next one." But then I remembered why I had quit my job, and that it was incumbent upon me to surround myself with people that were master's of the craft that I was looking to learn.

So, I listened to my gut and attended the training. Upon completion of these conferences and trainings, my wife and I felt that we should pursue this real estate niche for our long-term investing strategy. And we felt we could make a greater impact and grow more quickly by taking on the role of the operator and partnering with other investors through syndicating deals.

Three months later, I had already let go my two employees due to poor performance and had spent some of our savings on marketing and other ancillary expenses without receiving a dime of revenue. This was an incredibly trying and confusing moment. It was here where I started to feel more lost than I had ever felt before in my life. Feeling lost was something new to me. Up to this point, my life had run relatively according to plan. And, although I never fully knew the exact how and had many moments in my life where I had to move forward in faith, the how would usually manifest itself fairly quickly.

This was the longest gap of not knowing how the plan was going to fall into place. I found myself questioning if this was even what I wanted to do. Flipping purchase agreements and houses was always the short-term plan and was meant to serve as a feeder into my long-term plan of syndicating real estate. I had tried the short-term long enough, right? Was my gut telling me to just jump right into syndication? I wasn't exactly sure what it was saying. I had just barely started full time as an entrepreneur, so I suppressed those feelings.

To make matters more trying, my virtual business didn't run without someone being there. If I was going to keep the business alive, I had to shut off marketing to conserve funds until I found a new salesperson. After almost two months of searching and sifting through a mound of applicants, I found one. Finally, there was a moment of relief, or so I thought.

I didn't think it was possible, but things got worse. We worked with this new salesperson for over three months into the new year, giving him all kinds of training and opportunity but to no avail. Not one deal was closed. As each dollar left our bank account and each week passed by, the feelings of despair and being utterly lost and confused increased. I desperately wanted to blaze my own entrepreneurial path. What scared me most was the thought of potentially having to return to work for someone else as an employee instead of partnering with others to build businesses and ultimately my legacy.

The feelings of wanting to pull out of house and purchase agreement flipping all together simmered at the surface during these three months, but I continued suppressing them, as I was confused on how they were trying to direct me. Even so, the feelings did get us thinking more broadly. My wife and I found ourselves asking the age-old questions: Who am I? What is my purpose and value-add to the world? We decided to do a deep dive into all sorts of books: mindset, business biographies, strategy, sales, etc. It was an absolutely amazing experience. They gave us the tools and confidence to do whatever we felt we were being guided to do, to live untethered from fear and move full steam ahead in faith. If we felt in our hearts that we were to speak with this person, or attend that conference, or make that move, then we were going to show up.

It was at the end of these three months that we felt compelled to have me join The Real Estate Guys Syndication Mentoring Club in efforts to put me in the right room with the right people and further my education on my long-term investing strategy. I learned in this group that I had to decide what role I wanted my syndication business to take on. It evolved from what we had originally planned. I realized that all these years of working with both investors and homeowners prepared me to do the same thing in the syndication space, except instead of homeowners, I would be working with operators that knew how to find, operate, and add value to whatever hard assets in which we were investing.

By this time, we had spent all our savings, and for a month or so we were surviving on credit cards in efforts to try just one last time to keep the business alive. It wasn't until our backs were against the wall and pressed in by a couple of feet that we made a last-ditch effort. With an opportunity to test our newfound confidence, I sold all my marketing rights and leads in my virtual market to another house flipper, to burn my ship so to speak. And knowing I was a decent salesperson, I decided to do one last marketing campaign in attempts to do a deal and earn some money in my local market, a market in which I had never worked.

A lifeline was thrown. After about a month, we got the first deal we had done in more than six months. While the decision to halt everything in the virtual market was extremely difficult, given all the time, energy, and resources we invested into it, we saw an immediate blessing because we had finally understood and followed our guts. We realized that those feelings of wanting to pull out of the flipping business weren't about quitting altogether but were about putting all the hats back on me and focusing on my local market. This is what I was to do given that this business was so short-term anyway.

I wondered had I followed my gut earlier, would I not have struggled so much? It's possible, but I also don't know if whatever other struggle I may have passed through would have been potent enough to get me to ask broader questions about the life purpose of my wife and me. This question of, "What is our purpose?" occupied a lot of our daily conversation.

Building towards resilience in all areas of life was a common thread throughout all our planning. We took time one day to do a master brainstorm and get it all out on paper. From that, the seedlings of what we feel is our purpose right now began to sprout: We will become resilient through building businesses and investing in assets, and we will help millions of others become resilient as well.

While we strived to follow our guts and exercise faith, and saw the blessings when doing so, we lived in this cloud of doubt formed by not having a beautifully delineated life plan for the next five to ten years. Then one day it hit us, "Just focus on what you feel is your purpose, and God will take care of the how." We're not to know the plan, because if we did, we wouldn't have to exercise faith, which is where the power lies. We are to focus on listening to our intuition and taking the next step. Each time you exercise that muscle of listening to your gut, it becomes more toned, and your faith increases to take the next step toward fulfilling your purpose.

TWEETABLE
We're not to know the plan, because if we did, we wouldn't have to exercise faith, which is where the power lies.

It is Jared Christian's purpose to become resilient and to help millions of others become resilient as well. He educates others on the enormous benefits of investing in real estate. And he puts together real estate investments, so his investment partners can make safe, consistent returns. Prior to investing in real estate full time, he worked in business valuation, where he valued hundreds of companies ranging from startup technology companies to later stage PE-backed companies. To contact for opportunities to invest in real estate, or just to connect, email: jaredjchristian@gmail.com

CHAPTER 36
Mental Health Matters Most

by Paul M. White

There is no health without mental health.
— **World Health Organization**

“ ’d be better off dead.”

Those words struck me like a bullet to the heart almost 20 years ago. While walking home for lunch on a bright sunny day, I was in a very dark place. It was June 2010, and this junior high school teacher was in a deep, dark fog, with thoughts of self-harm close at hand. Something was wrong. It was not like me to think those thoughts, yet where did they come from, and why? And, what next? Thankfully, after many challenging years of mood swings combined with painful moments, peace of mind settled in. It can for you too. I hope this story offers hope, and helps somebody. It is a story of male depression, and resilience, for men and for the spouses that love them.

People that I have worked with and clients that I have coached and counseled often have struggled for years, and in some cases decades, with mental illness. Depression is the ugliest human medical condition. It cannot be seen like a physical illness. Depression lives within the mind, and as a mood disorder, it affects everything. That June day when I had that irrational negative thought, it shook me, and I knew I needed help. Down and out, unable to function at work, this new experience was both humbling and crumbling. A relationship breakup combined with uncertainty after leaving university left me in a space that only those who have experienced it will understand.

My main theme for 20 years as I struggled to find inner peace from depression was simple: destruction. I lost two loving romantic relationships and several other potential partners. I abandoned family and friends. I was fired from a job and reprimanded at a few others. Not only did I burn bridges, I usually blew them to oblivion. I did not care about my health nor my career. It was always survival instinct, struggling to keep the inner demon away; yet it was always there. When you run from your problems, they always follow you. Wherever you go, there you are. I was always running, trying to feel good, happy and healthy, like I once was at age 19.

While living in Ontario, my girlfriend was totally perplexed by my behavior. Unmotivated, I could not get off of the couch to go to work or even the gym. I found it very difficult being in public. I would get angry over the smallest, trivial things. Anger is one major sign of someone suffering from depression, and anger is one letter shy of danger. Further, anger also means pain, and we often take this pain out on the people we love the most. Some people who suffer depression often "fly off the handle" in a fit of rage. The struggle to be normal and to feel good is real when one is down in the depths of despair.

Trying to push through the mood challenges and eliminate the nasty self-thoughts, as a tough male who grew up in a jock culture, never worked long-term. The thoughts of suicide and self-harm never resurfaced again, yet the patterns of depression were evident…just not to me. What I portrayed was not normal behavior, and it was only years later that I recognized this while reflecting on past patterns through my journey of personal development.

Back in my home province of Newfoundland and Labrador, I met a fantastic lady. Once again though, sabotage was inevitable. It is hard to describe what it's like when feelings are present yet mental illness keeps them hidden. For me, under mental illness was chaos, insecurities, and abuse. The patterns carry over in all life areas: career, relationships, health, and finances, among others. It is in a romantic relationship, however, that we often finally come to grips with past behaviors in order to change for the better.

My beautiful girlfriend in 2011 was a blessing in disguise. Tall, fit, fun, energetic, a lover of nature, intelligent, hardworking, and from a fantastic family, she gave me hope after several failed past romances. Unfortunately, I still remained stuck in depression, and I hid it very well. She loved me dearly, yet I was a disaster. Nadine often commented, "What goes through your head?" I was not really sure. I certainly did not choose this illness, no matter what the positive thinking movement may sometimes want us to believe.

When suffering from depression and you love someone dearly, you cannot reveal or even feel your true, deep human emotions. One side of your brain tells you "everything is fine" while the other side whispers "you need help; this is not normal." Back and forth, up and down, with yo-yo moods, I could not come to grips and just be normal. Moments of happiness were scarce and stressful moments were abundant. Men often cannot put into words how we feel. Throw mental illness in that mixture, and how we feel seems impossible to comprehend. Getting through life the best and only way I knew how (day by day, one foot in front of the other) with excruciating mental pain, finally caused me to get a grip on reality. It was the loss of this romantic relationship that shook me to my core, causing me to mentally crumble to the point of needing help…immediately. When Nadine and I ended things romantically, my whole world collapsed. Rivers of tears flowed, sometimes daily, for months at a time. Four summers in a row, when I went to the Torrent River to salmon fish, I would walk the boardwalk and cry profusely like a baby. I knew what I had lost and what mental illness had taken from me. It was time for change, and I promised myself this would never happen again.

A big breakthrough came in a multitude of ways. After almost 20 years and enough suffering, I somehow got the drive to make the necessary changes. Health is wealth, so this was what I went to work on first. I made doctor appointments. I decided to adopt medication to boost my mood and level off the ups and downs. This combined with nature and fly-fishing therapy, personal development, and a healthy lifestyle helped pull me through. After all, the only way I could go was up. Rock bottom was my foundation, and it was solid. I had made just about every mistake a human could make in human interaction and behavior. Self-esteem was the next phase. We must build our self-esteem daily because it is the first thing that disappears when we are depressed. Find your passion, any activity that keeps you motivated, and do more of this passion. Doing more of what we love to do makes us feel good and helps build resilience so we bounce back from adversity.

Other resilience strategies, which I use and teach include:

1. Drive the depression into "a small corner" to take away its power. Realize it is there, but do not give it any fuel. Depression masks true talent, and this is why people who are mentally unwell often stay stuck and do not reach their full human potential.

2. Always remember: you are not alone. Many also have the same mental health challenges.

3. Having one or two good friends to talk with, vent problems with, and help you is one of the best strategies.

4. Accept the fact that if depression is in your biological family, you cannot beat genetics. You may need medical help. There is a difference between feeling better and getting better. Of course, always consult with your medical professional when in doubt.

5. Keep life simple. Extra stress and clutter are not worth the mental anguish.

6. "This too shall pass." If it does not, help is available. Push through as best you can and be good to yourself.

Everyone has a mental health story to tell, either directly or indirectly. In today's society, the prevalence of mental illness is rampant. Suicide rates are too high and appear to be growing. Lost economic productivity in the marketplace due to depression is in the billions of dollars; a current estimate is $51 billion in Canada (Canadian Mental Health Association, 2018), and Canada's population is only 37 million. Depression is not a choice. It is an illness. The only choice, when the time is right, is to decide to get help. Nobody wakes up one morning and says "I cannot wait to have clinical depression," or "I cannot wait to suffer from anxiety for the rest of my life." These are medical conditions, and anyone who has experienced such challenges understands the horrifying effects that they have on families, friends, and relationships.

There is, however, hope. Once I realized the patterns and accepted the fact that I was suffering from a medical condition, I found the power to change. Twenty years, though, is too long to suffer when help is available.

These days, due to my life experiences, I teach and counsel people how to stay mentally well and balance life. As a professional speaker, I enjoy the opportunity to offer hope to audiences and teams around the world. The mental health profession is tough, but it is my calling—to serve and help people build their own resilience. I can only do this work because of my past experiences. You can push through too and bounce back from the most destructive illnesses. Mental health matters most.

TWEETABLE
Mental health resilience is built from life experience. You are never alone, and there is always hope.

As a corporate trainer, Paul Michael White helps your business achieve zero (or near zero) absenteeism! As a professional speaker, he inspires your audience to achieve optimal mental wellness and life balance. Paul is a mental health resilience expert, consultant and counselor, author (his first book is called Fishing for Reality), and professional speaker. He holds a master's degree in counseling psychology. He is a member of the Canadian Association of Professional Speakers and a member of the Canadian Counselling and Psychotherapy Association. Paul is all about creating lasting results. Contact him today to see how he can help your team as a speaker and trainer: www.paulwhite.ca; info@paulwhite.ca

CHAPTER 37

Life and Business Lessons From a World-Class Golf Mentor

by Nick Bradley

I had a fantastic upbringing in England with two amazing parents. Both were very supportive.

One of the greatest lessons my dad ever gave my brother and I was that he really didn't mind what profession we went into. The main stipulate was, whatever we chose we would try to be the best we could be in that profession. It could have been collecting the trash at McDonald's or it could have been trying to design a space rocket. The bottom line was that we gave it our all and we tried to overachieve.

My first sport was swimming. I was a very good butterfly swimmer, and I became a county champion. Swimming took me up to the age of 16, so I was very disciplined from a young age, spending almost two hours a day looking at the bottom of a swimming pool and just training and training. It's remarkable when you have that much time to yourself how you can cultivate a unique awareness of what you are thinking and how you can control your thoughts.

At age 15, I took up golf after we went on a family vacation to an island just south of England. We were going there really to do some windsurfing and waterskiing, but the weather was poor and the waves were too choppy. So, we just bummed it around this island and bumped into a 9-hole par-3 sort of pitch and putt golf course. We rented the golf clubs and played. I just remember, in that 9-hole, connecting with a couple of shots and thinking, "Hm, that was quite a nice feeling. That was different. Certainly different than swimming." We returned to the mainland, and I said to my father, "You know, I quite liked that. I'd like to pick it up a little more seriously." And so, he bought me a set of golf clubs.

I was just starting to drive at the time, so I would go down to the driving range nearly every night. I would say probably from age 15 to 20, I probably hit anywhere from 150 to 200 golf balls a day. As a result, I got down to scratch in two years. My godfather played golf, and he was a good golfer, so I would play with him. And, eventually, I read every golf book I could get my hands on. I watched every video. This was the era of David Leadbetter and Nick Faldo, essentially the best teacher and golfer in the world.

I turned professional and started coaching my first tournament player at 19 years old. I continued growing my teaching business in London. And in 1994, I got headhunted by the Leadbetter organization and moved out to Orlando when I was 23.

Sometimes life can go full circle. I ended up working with David Leadbetter, my teaching hero at the time, and then six-time major champion Nick Faldo. Actually, Nick Faldo is a student of mine now. It's quite bizarre how one day you can be looking at someone who is your hero and your role model, and 25 years later, you can be actually coaching and mentoring and working with that person.

I worked with Leadbetter for three and a half years. I coached eight national amateur champions in that time. Then I moved back to London and started coaching tournament professionals. One of my students, who was actually an ex-Leadbetter student himself, won in 1998. It was nice to take a student that had worked with my mentor and actually get him better. Then, one of my students won the French Open in 2003.

Soon after, I published my first book *The 7 Laws of the Golf Swing* which went on to sell over 80,000 copies around the world. Now, you have to remember, this is a bestselling book from a kid who was told in school that he would pretty much amount to nothing. I wasn't very good at school. My attention span was very small. I found education boring the way it was presented to me because it was far less visual than it is today. Frankly, it didn't really stimulate me at all.

I moved back to the US in 2005. In 2006, I started working with Justin Rose who at the time was 125th in the world. I worked with him on improving his game, and my father was very pleased to see that in 20 months we were European #1 and World #5 in the official golf rankings. In 20 months, I experienced a complete transformation. My career was really in ascendancy. I was in every magazine, I had just released my second book, and I was really in a stage of momentum.

Then, on January 16, 2009, I landed into Wilmington, North Carolina and was on the way home when my brother called me and told me that my dad had passed on. He had died of unnatural causes. I didn't understand what that meant until my brother said that he had committed suicide. That was a devastating blow for me. As a result, probably about a year after that news, I started to wane in terms of my professional drive.

I began to let a lot of my clients go because my performance simply wasn't up to the task. I was suffering quite a bit with anxiety. It developed physically into heart palpitations. I would go to doctors, and they would say I was fine. But, I would have panic attacks quite regularly. I remember one time I was walking with my daughter, and she said to me, "Daddy, why is your hand shaking?" Basically, I was having an anxiety attack.

I just said to her, "Sweetheart, I'm just hungry. When I get home, I'll get some food in me."

At some point in your life, your adversity sort of instructs you. When I reached that point, I said to myself, "If my dad were still here or even if he wasn't, he'd want me to carry on." And at that point, I said the following to myself: "You know what? I give up. I submit. I'm letting go." It was very Alan Watts. I was not in this fight anymore. Within two or three days, I can honestly say, I was back to where I was before my dad's death from a physical standpoint. I wasn't waking up in the middle of the night. I wasn't shaking. The second I submitted, things turned around.

People ask if I was depressed, and I say it was more like PTSD. I'd wake up in the middle of the night with my heart racing and breathing very quickly. I would sit up in bed and ask myself, "Alright, what happened?" I'd have no memory of what got me to that point. That's a very typical malady, having no idea what got you to that point. I would shake uncontrollably, and it got so bad that I could actually feel my adrenal glands, which are located under the ribcage on the left-hand side, I could actually feel them firing. As I would uncontrollably shake, my heart would, in fear, get out of rhythm. I went to two or three heart specialists, and they looked at me and said, "Get out of here. You're just uptight and you have anxiety."

What really helped me was my studies about anxiety and PTSD. I learned that you have a small almond-shaped gland in the brain called the hypothalamus that controls the basics in your body which sustain your life. It coordinates the autonomic nervous system and is essential. As I studied the hypothalamus, I realized that what happens to people in very dramatic circumstances is rather like an apple being dropped from a tall building and then getting bruised. The hypothalamus goes through exactly the same process. You bruise it with an emotional event, and like any bruise, you just have to sit and wait it out. You can't smash a bruise through the hopper. In my path to healing, I did my fair share of waiting. I did my fair share of meditating.

And I found, the more you can understand the problem, the quicker it will dissipate. If you don't understand why you have a fear of flying, if you don't understand why you have a fear of asking a girl out, if you don't understand your fear, then you will never overcome that obstacle. But the old saying that fear is false evidence appearing real is actually quite correct at the end of the day.

Today, I've done my Ryder Cup consultancy, I've produced a world champion, I've now taken a player to Official World Golf Ranking #1 and #5. I'm just about to release my third book, and I'm a mentor to high-performing businessman and sportsmen.

I think a lot of teachers and mentors out there can rightly be accused of lecturing. I never wanted to lecture someone if I wasn't practicing the art of what I preached myself. And so it was a perfect challenge for me really, once I had that clarity again, after the walk with my daughter, to say to myself, "Okay, you are now going to train yourself to be back as one of the top golf teachers in the world."

And so I did, I sat down, and I thought about what I taught people about being emotionally intelligent when they were hitting a tee shot at the masters. I coached myself about how to meditate and strongly visualize using theta waves, which is also something I teach people. I started to mentor myself and to watch my internal language. Once I developed that clarity and that self-observation again, I was able to start to direct my thinking. I knew this stuff worked because I had circumstantial evidence that it had moved the best athletes in the world to the right areas and made them prolific winners. I had the proof of the pudding, but I had to be humble enough to apply this knowledge to myself and to take the risk that it might not work on me.

Fortunately, I did. And now, we are here. The story has turned around.

TWEETABLE

An emotional event is like any bruise, you just have to sit and wait it out. You can't smash a bruise through the hopper. I found, the more you understand the problem, the quicker it will dissipate.

Nick Bradley is one of the world's top golf coaches, working with the best players on the PGA & European Tour. The bestselling author of The 7 Laws of the Golf Swing, *Nick is a also a mentor to high-performing businessman and sportsmen as an international speaker and corporate trainer. His mission is to provide content that can be used immediately by his audiences to elevate their performance. To learn more visit https://www.nickbradleygolf.com/.*

RESILIENCE

GET CONNECTED

Access Resources From the Authors of this Book

Go to

KyleWilson.com/ResilienceBook

Additional Resources

Order in Quantity and SAVE

Mix and Match

Order online KyleWilson.com/Books

RESILIENCE

Turning Your **Setback**
into a **Comeback**

**Receive Special Bonuses When Buying
The *Resilience* Book**

To Receive, send an Email to
gifts@ResilienceBookLessons.com